English Literature to 1785

D0781207

HARPERCOLLINS COLLEGE OUTLINE

English Literature to 1785

Kathleen McCoy, Ph.D.
Seton Hall University

Judith A.V. Harlan

■ HarperPerennial
A Division of HarperCollins*Publishers*

This book is dedicated to Jack, Jimmy, and Maggie Nachlin
and to
Joellen Valley, Hugh, Tannis, and Rachel McCammon,
and to Lawrence H. Cooke

An American BookWorks Corporation Production

Editor: Thomas Quinn

LIBRARY OF CONGRESS CATALOG CARD NUMBER 91-55401

ISBN: 0-06-467114-3

92 93 94 95 96 ABW/RRD 10 9 8 7 6 5 4 3 2 1

Contents

Preface vii

1   Old English Literature (410 to 1100): Old English Period 1

2   Old English Literature (410 to 1100): *Beowulf*
    And Other Old English Secular Poems 9

3   Late Medieval English Literature (1066 to 1485):
    Late Medieval Period 16

4   Late Medieval Period (1066 to 1485): Chaucer 27

5   Late Medieval Period (1066 to 1485): Prose and
    Popular Literature 41

6   English Renaissance Literature (1485 to 1603):
    Renaissance Period 50

7   English Renaissance Literature (1485 to 1603):
    Poetry and the Development of the Sonnet 58

8   English Renaissance Literature (1485 to 1603):
    Development of the Drama 68

9   English Renaissance Literature (1485 to 1603): Shakespeare . . . 75

10   English Renaissance Literature (1485 to 1603):
    Development of Prose 88

11   Early Seventeenth-Century English Literature (1603 to 1660):
    Early Seventeenth Century 94

12   Early Seventeenth-Century English Literature (1603 to 1660):
    The Cavalier Poets 101

13   Early Seventeenth-Century English Literature (1603 to 1660):
      The Metaphysical Poets 113

14   Early Seventeenth-Century English Literature (1603 to 1660):
      The Christian Epic 124

15   Early Seventeenth-Century English Literature (1603 to 1660):
      Development of the Drama 134

16   Early Seventeenth-Century English Literature (1603 to 1660):
      Prose 141

17   Restoration Literature (1660 to 1700): Restoration Period . . . 149

18   Restoration Period (1660 to 1700): John Dryden 154

19   Restoration Period (1660 to 1700): Minor Poetry and
      Prose 160

20   Restoration Literature (1660 to 1700): Development
      of the Drama 170

21   Eighteenth-Century English Literature (1700 to 1785):
      Eighteenth Century 176

22   Eighteenth Century (1700 to 1785): Swift, Gay, Pope,
      Addison, and Steele 183

23   Eighteenth-Century English Literature (1700 to 1785):
      Johnson and Boswell 197

24   Eighteenth-Century English Literature (1700 to 1785):
      Lyric Poetry 203

25   Eighteenth Century (1700 to 1785): Drama and
      the Novel 209

26   Literary Names and Terms: Literary Forms 222

27   Literary Names and Terms: Glossary 225

28   Literary Names and Terms: People and Places 263

      Index 273

Preface

The HarperCollins College Outline text, *Introduction to English Literature to 1785* presents what great English men and women thought and felt, and then wrote down in good prose and beautiful poetry in the English language. In its broadest sense, English Literature is simply the written records of a people, including its history and sciences as well as its poems, plays, essays, and novels. As a written record of the human spirit, it both preserves the ideals of a developing civilization and is one of the most important and delightful subjects that can occupy the human mind.

The outline offers both the student and the general reader an historical and cultural context within which the authors and their works may be examined and appreciated in relationship to their different periods. The reader should find their understanding and appreciation enhanced by the detailed time lines and the introductions which precede each chapter as well as by the clear, concise text. Content Summaries and Selected References appear at the end of each chapter and emphasize both recent scholarship and classic studies. The glossary is an important and integral part of the book.

The book is designed to be useful to the student or reader as a ready reference whether as a review book in conjunction with any of the standard college anthologies, or as a textbook for initial study with individual selections. The amount of detail devoted to each form, author or writing is in proportion to the difficulty or complexity of the subject. We have not tried to give subtleties of interpretation or enter into any controversy, but it is not possible to describe a literary work without some implied interpretation. We have tried to be mainstream at the risk of stating the obvious.

It is a pleasure for us to acknowledge the scholarly contributions and constructive editorial assistance of those who have done so much to make this book possible. We thank each person.

Dr. Edward T. Brynes of Seton Hall reviewed in detail the manuscript and made recommendations that have improved the final book.

Mikos Grieco assisted with the research, while Tom Quinn, Susan McClosky and Tannis McCammon reviewed, edited, and proofread the manuscript with keen eyes and great skill. Each made useful suggestions, "good catches," and offered continuing encouragement to us. Our friend, Noreen Morin, prepared the endless drafts and the final manuscript but most importantly, she offered her constant support, encouragement, and enthusiasm throughout.

1

Old English Literature (410 to 1100): Old English Period

410	Roman legions leave Celtic Britain
428	Germanic tribes begin invasion of Britain
449	Bede's date for Germanic invasion of Britain by Hengist and Horsa; the Anglo-Saxon Conquest
563	St. Columba founds monastery on Scottish island of Iona; Celtic Christianity spreads from there
570–632	Mohammed
601	Augustine becomes first archbishop of Canterbury
663–664	Synod of Whitby resolves differences between Celtic and Latin Christianity
670	Caedmon, first English poet known by name, composes *Hymn*
670–725	Northumbrian Renaissance, the high point of Anglo-Saxon civilization
675–725	Runes on Ruthwell Cross show a portion of *A Dream of the Rood*
731	Bede, *Ecclesiastical History of the English People*
768–814	Reign of Charlemagne
787	First Viking (Danish) invasion of England
865	Danes establish large settlement in England
871–899	Reign of Alfred the Great, first king of all England

878   Peace of Wedmore recognizes Danish overlordship in part of England

c. 880   Translations from Latin to Old English; the unique *Anglo-Saxon Chronicle* probably begun

911   Normandy area of France recognized as an independent Norse duchy

937   Heroic poem *Battle of Brunanburh*

979–1016   Second period of Danish invasion of England

991   Heroic poem *Battle of Maldon*

c. 1000   Oldest extant manuscript of *Beowulf*

1016–1035   Canute rules over England, Denmark, and Norway

1066   Battle of Hastings, Norman conquest of England

1087–1100   Reign of William II

1088   English census, the *Domesday Book*

1096–1099   First Crusade

At the beginning of the fifth century of the Christian Era, the island of Britain was occupied in the south by Roman legions, defenders of the marginal outposts of a huge empire already in decline. In the north and west, roughly in the territories of modern Scotland and Wales, lived the Celtic people who had been displaced by these Romans. Both of these cultures were Christian, but they had little else in common. The Celts spoke their own language, of which little remains in modern English. The Romans spoke Latin; the influence of their occupation survives in place names. For example, the Latin word for camp is castra, *which still shows in place names such as Chester and Lancaster. The English language had not yet come into being.*

THE ANGLES, THE SAXONS, AND THE JUTES

By 410 the Roman legions had been recalled, but the Celts were not able to resettle their lost lands in the southern portion of the island. Instead, this desirable land was seized by invading bands of Anglo-Saxons, Germanic peoples from northern Europe of which there were three main tribal divisions: the Angles, the Saxons, and the Jutes. Rivals in conquest, these three groups were nevertheless similar in language and culture. They shared the same pagan religion and clannish social structure; they competed in establishing control over various sections of land, creating a shifting patchwork of rival kingdoms. Generally:

> the Angles ruled in Northumbria and Mercia (northern and central England);
>
> the Saxons held Wessex (the southwest);
>
> the Jutes controlled Kent (the southeast).

This arrangement was threatened in the ninth century by a new group of Germanic invaders, the Vikings from Denmark.

The Saxon King Alfred the Great unified the Anglo-Saxons to resist the Vikings, and together they succeeded not in expelling these Danes but in confining them to a limited area of the island, called the Danelagh (Dane law).

After the reign of Alfred, the Anglo-Saxons were not again united under a single king until the rule of Edward the Confessor in the eleventh century. Edward's reign ended with the defeat of the Anglo-Saxons at the battle of Hastings in 1066 by the Norman- French king, William the Conqueror.

CHRISTIANITY

Meanwhile, Roman Christianity had taken hold. Pope Gregory had sent his missionary Augustine to Kent in 597, and later missions followed to the other kingdoms. Once the Anglo-Saxon kings were converted, the earls (their chief nobles) also accepted Christianity.

Bede (c. 673–735)

At the beginning of the eighth century, a learned Benedictine monk, the Venerable Bede, described the growth of English Christianity in the *Ecclesiastical History of the English People* (731).

ECCLESIASTICAL HISTORY OF THE ENGLISH PEOPLE

This work was written in Latin, the scholarly clerical language. At the time of Alfred's rule (871–899) both Christian doctrine and Latin learning were well established.

Alfred (849–899)

Alfred made his court a center of literary activity. He promoted the reading and writing of Old English among the nobility as well as the clergy, and he sponsored the translation of Latin texts into the Old English language.

ANGLO-SAXON CHRONICLE

Alfred initiated the writing, in the vernacular, of the unique *Anglo-Saxon Chronicle*, an annual historical record of his people. He also preserved many of the remaining ancient texts. Alfred's Wessex dialect is the language in which the great epic poem *Beowulf* was recorded.

OLD ENGLISH LANGUAGE

The Old English (or Anglo-Saxon) language was, like its speakers, of basic German stock. It was heavily inflected, which means that the grammatical relationships of words within a sentence were indicated not by the order of words but by the word form. Changing the relationship of words, then, was accomplished by changing the word forms, such as by adding prefixes or endings or even by modifying the root syllable—for example, from *man* to *men*.

Most modern readers read works of Anglo-Saxon literature in translation. However, any good translation of an Old English poem, for example, should retain some of the stylistic qualities of Old English poetry as a whole:

> its repetition with variation;
>
> its lofty diction;
>
> its use of alliteration rather than rhyme.

Poetic Forms

A line of Old English poetry is divided into two half-lines, and each half-line contains two stressed syllables with a variable number and arrangement of unstressed syllables. The pattern of stresses is reinforced by alliteration. In alliteration, the two stressed syllables of the first half-line and the first stressed syllable of the second half-line all have the same initial sound. Two or more words are said to alliterate if they begin with the same sound. Usually these are consonant sounds, but in Old English poetry, any two initial vowels can be used to alliterate. The result is a somewhat heavy effect, slow and stately. Here is a line from *Beowulf*:

> Beowulf waes breme blaed wide sprang
>
> (Beowulf was famous, his renown widespread) 1. 18

The words beginning with *b* are also the stressed syllables; *sprang* is also stressed to make up the pattern of four. Notice that the idea of *breme* (fame) is repeated and elaborated in the phrase in the second half-line. When we remember that rather than reading the poem the original audiences listened to the tribal poet, the scop, recite it, the repetition and slow pace seem natural and necessary.

FORMULAIC POETRY

The scop had a memorized stock of half-lines that he could combine in new patterns and vary to suit the details of his narration. His composition was usually partly original, but the basic outlines of the events and the standard descriptive phrases were a part of the poetic heritage on which he drew. Such poetic composition is called formulaic, meaning that each stock descriptive phrase is a formula to be combined with others to create the poem.

The Old English scop used essentially two types of figurative language, the kenning and litotes.

Kenning. A kenning is a compound metaphorical term such as *whale-road*, meaning the sea, or *heaven's candle*, meaning the sun. A kenning may comprise a standard half-line.

Litotes. A litote is a negative understatement, a sometimes grimly humorous or ironic remark. For example, in *Beowulf*, when Grendel's mother makes a revenge attack and murders one of the king's men, the poet observes that it was "no good bargain that they had to pay" with the life of a friend. *Bargain* and *pay* are mild terms, considering the horror of what actually happened. The deliberate disparity between diction and reality creates the ironic tone. Such an attitude was compatible with the tough and gloomy Anglo-Saxon outlook on life.

ANGLO-SAXON SOCIETY

The society of the Anglo-Saxons consisted of many small units, each focused on the central figure of the king. The king was the leader during warfare, the legislator and guide in time of peace. He showed his approval and gratitude to his retainers by giving them rich gifts from his store of treasure or from the captured hoard of an enemy. His chief noblemen, his earls, were his blood relations—usually both his legitimate and illegitimate uncles, sons, nephews, and cousins. This body of men and their male relatives were his retainers, or thanes. The king's wife was likely to be the daughter of some neighboring king, their marriage being partly a treaty of friendship between the tribes.

The remainder of the tribe consisted of the churls, who were freemen, and slaves captured in battle. There was no middle class.

The one professional post in the tribe was that of the scop. The scop was the tribal poet or bard whose function it was to record and celebrate the deeds of the king and the earls. Attached to the king, the scop was also chief spokesman and interpreter of the values and ideals of the noble class.

VALUES IN ANGLO-SAXON SOCIETY

In a world fraught with danger, the individual Anglo-Saxon warrior or thane had only his courage and his weapons to depend on. Though loyalty to the king and to fellow members of the tribe was the ideal, it could not always be counted on. Men did desert, courage did fail, fate was sometimes fickle. Fate, or Weird, might be forestalled temporarily by unusual efforts or luck, but ultimately the hero was caught by the forces of his doom.

Old English epic poetry, therefore, celebrates the qualities of the hero that help him endure. The primary value was courage. The king and his thanes must be ready to risk their lives for each other against the common foe. But in addition, the hero must also know:

> how to behave honorably;
>
> how to speak skillfully and diplomatically before an assembled tribe;
>
> how to avoid unintended insult;
>
> how to boast properly of his own deeds;
>
> how to give and receive gifts in a spirit of trust;
>
> how to accept his fate when it comes.

In a society with such high ideals of personal conduct, not everyone could measure up. The king was chosen partly because of heredity but also because of his potential for fulfilling the ideal. The effectiveness of his reign depended on his ability to inspire personal loyalty and thus to keep the tribe unified. Feasts, ceremonial drinking, and the giving of gifts helped cement the unity of the tribe. To be excluded from the tribal society, therefore, was the most lamentable position for any retainer; isolation was little better than death. The dominant theme of Old English lyrics is not lost love but exile from the band of followers of a good king.

Poetry of Tribal Scops

The role of the epic poet, the tribal scop, was to reinforce cultural values and hold up examples of both ideal and faulty behavior. The scop was not expected to be original or fanciful; his materials were the legends and history of his people, which he would weave together by allusion and digression to extend and elaborate the central episodes of his hero's life. The scop's songs were the vehicle of renown for heroes, whose reputations during life and immortality after death found expression in them. Thus there existed a reciprocal relationship:

> the poet taught heroic behavior to the warrior;
>
> the warrior's heroism was celebrated by the poet.

Frequently, the scop implied that the heroes of the past were greater, that the contemporary moment was a point in the decline of values. He was nostalgic for more glorious times, he was a conservative.

ORAL COMPOSITION

The scop's compositions were always oral. He carried the narrative line and an arrangement of episodes in his head, along with a large stock of formulaic phrases, learned from a master scop, adapted to the alliterative line or half-line. At feasts of the tribe, the scop, accompanied by his harp, spun out the poetic story, varying the emphasis and details as the occasion demanded. He was a vital functionary of the court, a spokesman for the glory of the king and the thanes. Because of its oral beginnings, surviving epic literature in Old English tends to be fragmentary. It achieved written form only after a long period, perhaps even centuries, of oral transmission.

Lyric poetry of the Anglo-Saxons is similar in form to epic poetry. It is based on a four-stress line held by a pattern of alliteration. Shorter and more personal than an epic poem, the lyric poem usually focused on the situation of a given moment, often expressing melancholy complaints of loss or separation. The speaker often laments his or her present situation and evokes earlier, happier times.

Early Christian Poetry

While Latin was the official language of the Church, poetry addressed to the people was written in Anglo-Saxon. Early Anglo-Saxon Christian poetry is lyric in form with a four-stress line of alliteration. Usually the speaker tells of a spiritual experience, a vision or a dream based on Christian lore.

CAEDMON'S *HYMN*

Caedmon's *Hymn* was included in Venerable Bede's *Ecclesiastical History of the English People*. It purports to describe an incident in the life of a gifted monk, Caedmon, (d. 680). Caedmon, it was said, was a herdsman who had no talent for singing. One night after leaving a feast early to avoid being asked to sing, Caedmon was visited in a dream by an angel who commanded him to sing about the Creation. Caedmon tried and was startled to find himself singing an original hymn, which is recorded in Bede's *Ecclesiastical History of the English People.* After his reception into the abbey at Whitby some years later, Caedmon composed other songs on biblical themes. However, only his first hymn survives.

Composed about 670, the hymn is only nine lines long. Almost half of the eighteen half-lines are epithets naming God by His attributes as Creator, Father, Lord, and Guardian. The poem praises God's work as maker of heaven, middle-earth, and earth used by man. Bede recorded a Latin version of the poem, but some later manuscripts include the Old English version in alliterative verse.

A DREAM OF THE ROOD

Scholars believe that *A Dream of the Rood* was written in the late seventh or early eighth century. The poem was discovered in a late tenth-century manuscript along with a number of other Old English poems.

In this dream vision, the speaker reports seeing a lofty and bejeweled tree, the cross on which Christ died. As the dreamer gazes at it, the tree is transformed; it begins to bleed from a wound on the right side, just as Christ did. It becomes drenched with blood and then speaks. The tree tells the story of how it was cut down and carried away to make a cross on which to crucify a criminal. Instead, the tree is used to crucify Christ. It describes Christ's agony, and then His removal from the cross. The cross is then hewn down and buried, but is later retrieved and exalted as a symbol. It now speaks as a warning to humanity to be ready for judgment. After the speech of the tree/cross, the dreamer expresses hope and confidence in salvation, in eternal joy.

The theme of Anglo-Saxon lyric and epic poetry is the rigors of survival and the necessity of courage to endure. The stately form of Anglo-Saxon poetry gives dignity and power to the poet's images of a dangerous and difficult life. The simple Christian lyrics express the religious feeling of devout speakers spreading the tenets of their faith among a newly converted people.

Selected Readings

Alexander, Michael. *Old English Literature.* New York: Schocken Books, 1983.

Barber, Richard W. *King Arthur: Hero and Legend.* 3d ed. Ipswich: Boydell, 1986.

Greenfield, Stanley B. *The Interpretation of Old English Poems.* London: Routledge, 1972.

Pope, John C., ed. *Seven Old English Poems.* Indianapolis: Bobbs-Merrill, 1966.

Rau, B. C. *The Art and Background of Old English Poetry*, 1978.

Stevens, Martin and Jerome Mandel, eds. *Old Engish Literature: Twenty-two Analytical Essays.* Lincoln: University of Nebraska Press, 1968.

Thompson, A. Hamilton, ed. *Bede: His Life, Times and Writings: Essays in Commemoration of the Twelfth Centenary of His Death.* New York: Russell, 1966.

2

Old English Literature (410 to 1100): Beowulf And Other Old English Secular Poems

c. 110	Tacitus, *Germania*
428	Germanic tribes begin invasion of Britain
441–453	Attila the Hun invades the Roman Empire
449	Bede's date for Germanic invasion of Britain by Hengist and Horsa; the Anglo-Saxon Conquest
731	Bede, *Ecclesiastical History of the English People*
757–796	Some scholarly supposition that *Beowulf* was written for the court of Offa the Great, king of Mercia
768–814	Reign of Charlemagne
787	First Viking (Danish) invasion of England
865	Danes establish large settlement in England
871–899	Reign of Alfred the Great, first king of all England
878	Peace of Wedmore recognizes Danish overlordship in part of England
c. 880	Translations from Latin to Old English; the unique *Anglo- Saxon Chronicle* probably begun

911	Normandy area of France recognized as an independent Norse duchy
937	Heroic poem *Battle of Brunanburh*
975	Exeter Book names Cynewulf as poet of Northumbrian kings
979–1016	Second period of Danish invasion of England
991	Heroic poem *Battle of Maldon* celebrates battle of same name
c. 1000	Oldest extant manuscript of *Beowulf*
1016–1035	Canute rules over England, Denmark, and Norway
1731	*Beowulf* manuscript survives fire of the library and literary collection of Sir Robert Cotton

The nonreligious poetry of the Anglo-Saxon culture is mostly in epic form, telling of battles and the deeds of heroes. However, a few short and personal lyrics also have survived. There is no way to tell how much has been lost or whether the proportion of epic to lyric reflects the amounts created. Regardless, the complexity and richness of Beowulf seems to indicate that it must have been an important poem, one that survived because of its superior quality and wide fame.

BEOWULF

Beowulf is an epic poem that embodies the history, values, and ideals of the early medieval Germanic peoples who had migrated to England. Originally an oral composition, it describes events that were supposed to have taken place in pagan times. One of the effects of this late transmission was the introduction of Christian elements into a basically pre-Christian story of treachery, revenge, and fame.

Composition of the Epic

Of the many epic poems assumed to have been created by Anglo-Saxon scops, only one has come down to us complete and relatively intact. (The manuscript, damaged by fire in the eighteenth century, is now preserved in the British Museum.) *Beowulf* was composed sometime between the late seventh and the mid-ninth century. The surviving 3,183-line version was recorded in a manuscript about the year 1000.

The poem is assumed to be basically the work of a tribal scop who, drawing on traditional Germanic materials, described events that took place before the tribe migrated into Britain and before Christianization. However, the poet and his audience were Christians, so he used and expected they would understand his many allusions to Old Testament figures and events: the Creation, Cain's murder and damnation, the flood, and Hell. He made no mention of Christ, whose message of mercy and salvation was perhaps less compatible with the ethos of revenge so central to Anglo-Saxon culture.

Form of Beowulf

Written in rhymeless alliterative verse, the epic tells of the life and death of Beowulf, prince of the Geats, hero and king.

The two main episodes presented are:

> Beowulf's voyage to the realm of the Danish King Hrothgar, where Beowulf defeats the monster Grendel and Grendel's avenging mother;

> King Beowulf's death years later in a battle against a fire-breathing dragon.

The story of Beowulf's youthful adventure in a swimming contest is added into the first episode, so that we learn about the hero in three stages of his development:

> in youth;

> at the height of his powers;

> in his decline.

The poet also includes brief or extended allusions to other heroes and their exploits to create a context of parallels and contrasts for Beowulf's deeds.

THE GRENDEL EPISODE

Starting with the genealogy of King Hrothgar of the Danes, the poet describes the construction of Hrothgar's mead hall, Heorot, and its subsequent violation by the monster Grendel, a descendant of Cain, whose attacks have driven the Danish warriors out of their feasting place. Beowulf the Geat, hearing of this violation, sails to the Danish seacoast with a band of fourteen thanes. Hrothgar receives Beowulf with due dignity and hospitality, but the hero is verbally challenged by Unferth, one of Hrothgar's men, who taunts Beowulf, expressing doubt that the Geat can accomplish what none of the Danes has been able to do—drive out Grendel. Beowulf responds as he should, with a boast, an assertion of his own powers. He describes his swimming contest with Breca, during which he was attacked by sea monsters but emerged victorious. During the evening's feast, Beowulf is welcomed by Hrothgar's queen, Wealhtheow. Thus the poet has demonstrated Beowulf's skill in speech and the proper and improper ways to treat a stranger.

That night Beowulf and his Geatish band occupy the mead hall to wait for Grendel. Beowulf decides not to use his sword because he knows that Grendel uses no such weapon. (As it happens, Grendel is proof against swords, so Beowulf has made a lucky decision.) Grendel breaks into the mead hall and devours one of the sleeping Geats. Beowulf then grabs Grendel, and a fierce hand-to-claw battle ensues. The mead hall shakes with the violence of their combat. Beowulf manages to twist off one of Grendel's arms at the shoulder joint, and the monster retreats to his den to die.

The next day the joyous Geats and Danes celebrate. Grendel's arm and claw is hung as a trophy from the roof of the mead hall. The Danish scop then chants the tale of Sigemund, another monster- slayer. Congratulatory speeches are exchanged, and Beowulf receives from Hrothgar rich gifts of weapons and horses. The scop sings a tale of treachery and revenge at Finnsburg. Queen Wealhtheow thanks Beowulf and asks his friendship for her two sons.

But all this celebration has been premature, for Grendel's fierce mother, whose existence has been unsuspected, goes to the mead hall that night to seek revenge on the sleeping Danes and Geats. She snatches away a Danish warrior and retrieves her son's severed claw. Once more Beowulf volunteers to do battle. Equipped with a sword given to him by Unferth, he pursues Grendel's mother (dam) to her underwater cave. Confronting the she-monster, Beowulf finds this sword, as we might expect, ineffective. He grapples with the beast, protected only by his coat of mail. By chance Beowulf spots among the contents of the cave a giant sword, which he seizes and slays her with. He notices that her blood eats away the blade. Beowulf returns to the Danish mead hall once again, and is rewelcomed as hero and savior. Hrothgar delivers a lengthy speech praising Beowulf but also warning him of the dangers of pride. The next day, the king gives the hero more gifts and kisses him good-bye. The Geats return home laden with treasure and glory.

THE DRAGON EPISODE

The Dragon Episode explains that Beowulf has become king of his people. The final part of the epic describes King Beowulf's defense of the Geats against a fire-breathing dragon who is burning their dwellings in revenge for the theft of a rich plated cup from the hoard of treasure that he has hidden in a barrow, or mound of earth. Beowulf, now an old man and the veteran of many battles, leads a band of twelve retainers to the dragon's lair. The dragon attacks; Beowulf fights bravely but does not prevail. His frightened companions fail to support him, except for Wiglaf, who scolds the others for their weakness of heart and then fearlessly steps forward to assist his king. Beowulf strikes at the dragon again, and this time his sword breaks. Luckily Wiglaf is able to get in a crucial blow, and together they dispatch the dragon. Beowulf, however, has received fatal wounds. He makes a dying speech, calling on Wiglaf to show him the rich treasure they have liberated from the dragon. Beowulf then nominates Wiglaf as his successor. The poem ends with a description of the elaborate funeral of Beowulf. A great funeral pyre is adorned with costly weapons and other treasure and set ablaze. The poet- scop ends the poem by praising Beowulf's courage and his kindness to his people.

The conclusion of the poem reinforces the sense of doom that hangs over the heroes of Old English poetry. Fate or Weird cannot be evaded indefinitely. The world is full of danger and treachery; even loyal service and friendship are not infallible. Wiglaf's speech indicates that the days of heroism are in the past; the poem looks back to greater times, now gone.

ANGLO-SAXON IMAGE OF HEROISM

The great epic poem *Beowulf* preserves the image of the heroic life. Beowulf and his companions show how, despite the rigors of a difficult environment and the threat's of violence from monstrous enemies and betrayal by false friends, the courageous man can hope for help from the fates during his life and for the immortality of fame after death. Although the life depicted in this epic is distant in time, the heroic values of bravery, loyalty, endurance, and dignity in the face of defeat provide a set of standards by which later heroic figures can be measured.

The Battle of Maldon

A heroic poem, *The Battle of Maldon* is set in alliterative verse. This poem is not complete; that is, the opening and closing passages are missing, but the account of the battle is adequate to give an indication of the whole.

The poem recounts an actual historical confrontation that took place in 991 between a group of Anglo-Saxons led by Birthnot, the earl of Essex, and a band of Danish Viking raiders. It is told from the Anglo-Saxon point of view, even though it describes their defeat. Scholars believe it was composed not long after the actual battle.

THE BATTLE GROUND

At the opening of the fragment, the Anglo-Saxon warriors are moving forward into battle positions along the banks of the river Panta, near Maldon, northeast of present-day London. Birthnot rides his horse among his warriors to give orders and encouragement. One of the Vikings on the opposite bank calls out that they will retreat in peace if the Anglo-Saxons pay them a rich ransom. Birthnot rejects the offer scornfully. Then the Vikings complain that they cannot engage in combat from the opposite bank of the river. Birthnot decides to pull back his troops, allowing the Vikings to cross on a narrow causeway and thus to enter the battlefield.

THE FIGHT

The battle begins. Blow by blow and wound by wound, the epic poet describes how the courageous warriors fall, naming each hero. But some flee; Godric and his brothers choose to save themselves. Godric escapes on Birthnot's horse, thereby creating the impression that Birthnot himself is running away. But the remaining heroes fight on, encouraged by the exhortations of an old warrior, Birthwald, who cries out that as their might lessens, their courage shall grow.

The rest of the poem has been lost, but it seems clear that the Anglo-Saxons are losing the battle, as historical records indicate that they did. Their glory, therefore, lies not in the victory but in their determination and loyalty.

OLD ENGLISH LYRICS

At Exeter Cathedral in Devon, England, reposes a late tenth-century manuscript, an anthology of anonymous and untitled poems in alliterative verse.

Many of these poems are elegies, that is, laments in which the speaker expresses his longing for lost friends or homelands. The poems allude to historical and legendary Anglo-Saxons in similar situations. Scholars have determined from the poems' language that the poets were Christians. Their attitudes toward life and death are, however, essentially pagan, expressing stoical courage and an acceptance of fate.

The Wanderer

A seven-line introduction depicts a lonely rower on the open sea. The rest of this poem is an extended soliloquy or monologue in which the speaker laments that he has been separated from his kinfolk and from his lord and companions of the mead hall. He reflects on the fate of men, how they die in battle, how their wealth and splendor must end in ruin and death. Alone in the sea-storm, he repeats that all good things are fleeting. After the soliloquy, the poet concludes by suggesting the consolation of God's mercy.

Deor's Lament

This short lyric, unlike most other Old English poetry, is organized in stanzas of from two to six lines, separated by a refrain. Each stanza alludes to some disaster or grief suffered by a character from heroic lore. However terrible it was at the time, each sorrow came to an end. The allusions are brief; the speaker expects his audience to recognize the heroes referred to and to know their histories. In the last stanza, extended to fourteen lines, Deor introduces himself by name and tells how he was a successful scop for many years until he was supplanted in his lord's favor by a rival scop. This sorrow, too, he hopes, will come to an end.

Both the *Wanderer* and *Deor's Lament* express the sorrows of exile, the loss of an acknowledged and useful place in an organized social unit. They also suggest that such a meaningful way of life is passing out of existence, that the speaker is a victim of the social decay that marks the end of an era.

The Exeter Book also contains a few lyrics describing personal or domestic relationships. In *The Wife's Lament* and *The Husband's Message*, each speaker grieves because of separation from a beloved spouse. In *Wulf and Eadwacer*, a woman longs for her lover, a theme that looks forward to the major theme of the Renaissance lyric, sexual love.

These few lyrics and the epic fragment suggest the range of subjects of those Anglo-Saxon poems that did not survive. Their tone of sadness and sense of loss indicate the general themes of the literature of this era.

Early Anglo-Saxon poetry illustrates some formal language patterns, such as the four-stress line that remained in popular verse long after the Anglo-Saxons and the Old English language had passed into history. At the same time, the body of poetry of this period is an important historical resource, showing the social structure of tribal life, the ideals and anxieties of the Anglo-Saxons, and the birth of Christian ideas and ideals into this fatalistic culture. The courage, tact, and self-sacrifice of the hero Beowulf provide a standard of conduct against which to measure later, more refined heroes.

Selected Readings

Chambers, R. W. *Beowulf: An Introduction to the Study of the Poem with a Discussion of the Stories of Offa and Finn.* Cambridge, Eng.: Cambridge University Press, 1959.

Dunning, T. P. and A. J. Bliss, eds. *The Wanderer.* New York: Appleton, 1969.

Fry, Donald K., ed. *The Beowulf Poet: A Collection of Critical Essays.* Englewood Cliffs, NJ: Prentice-Hall, 1968.

Lawrence, William Witherle. *Beowulf and Epic Tradition.* Cambridge: Harvard University Press, 1928.

Mitchell, Bruce, ed. *The Battle of Maldon, and Other English Poems.* New York: St. Martin's, 1965.

Pope, John C., ed. *Seven Old English Poems.* Indianapolis: Bobbs-Merrill, 1966.

Sisam, Kenneth. *The Structure of Beowulf.* Oxford: Clarendon, 1965.

3

Late Medieval English Literature (1066 to 1485): Late Medieval Period

1000–1350 High Middle Ages

1066–1087 William the Conqueror, duke of Normandy, reigns as king of England

1100–1135 Henry I reigns as king of England

c. 1100 First recorded "miracle" or Saints play in England, the *Play of St. Catherine* at Dunstable; earliest Irish romantic work, *The Book of the Dun Cow*; the great period of French troubadour poetry begins with *Chanson de Roland*

c. 1100 Arabic numerals first used in Europe; paper manufactured in Constantinople; University of Paris founded

c. 1136 Geoffrey of Monmouth's *Historia Regum Brittaniae*, *History of the Kings of Britain* gives first detailed account of Arthurian court

1144 Beginning of Gothic style of architecture and art

1154 Last entry in the *Anglo-Saxon Chronicle*

1154–1189 Henry II begins Plantagenet line of English kings

1167 Oxford University founded

c. 1200 Prose version of Arthurian legend composed, reputedly by Walter Map; *The Sayings of Alfred* composed in English; Old English Charters *Bury St. Edmunds* translated into shire dialect of English

1202–1205	France takes Normandy, Anjou, Maine, and Brittany from England
1205	Layamon, *Brut*
1209	Cambridge University founded
1215	Signing of the Magna Carta
c. 1215	Ormin, *Ormulum*
1216–1272	Henry III reigns as king of England
1230	Guilliame de Loire, *Roman de la Rose*
1245–1272	Westminster Abbey built
1250	*Northumbrian Psalter*
1258	Provisions of Oxford essentially strip king of political independence
1265	Parliament includes for first time burgesses and knights as well as barons and prelates
1267–1268	Roger Bacon, *Opus Maius*
1267–1273	Thomas Aquinas, *Summa Theologica*
1271–1295	Marco Polo in Asia
c. 1280	*Owl and the Nightingale*, English language ballad
1307–1321	Dante, *Divine Comedy*
c. 1328	Chester cycle of plays composed
1337–1453	Hundred Years' War
1340	Richard Rolle of Hampole, *Pricke of Conscience*
1347–1351	Black Death sweeps Europe
1351	English Parliament passes beginning of Statutes of Labourers
1353	Boccaccio, *The Decameron*
1359	Chaucer in France with English army
1359–1400	*Sir Eglamour, Morte Darthur, Sir Gawain and the Green Knight* and other romances
c. 1362	Langland, *The Vision of Piers Plowman*; English language used to open Parliament
c. 1375	*Paternoster* and *Creed*, first morality plays
1377	Believed to be date of version B, *The Vision of Piers Plowman*
c. 1380	Wycliffe translates Bible into English
1381	Peasants' Revolt in England; phrases from "Piers Plowman" quoted in revolutionary context
c. 1382	Chaucer, *Troilus and Criseyde*

1385	English used in universities
1387	Chaucer writes the Prologue to *Canterbury Tales*; sets 1387 as the year in which action takes place
1399–1413	Henry IV establishes Lancaster line of kings
1399	Chaucer sends *Compleint to His Purse* to the king
c. 1415	York realist revises passion sequence of *York Play of the Crucifixion*
1415	Battle of Agincourt returns Normandy to England
c. 1425	*The Second Shepherd's Play*
1429–1431	Joan of Arc leads French to victory over English; Joan of Arc burned at the stake
1436–1438	Kemp, *The Book of Margery Kemp*
1455–1485	War of the Roses
1471	Caxton translates into English and prints *Recuyell of the Historyes of Troy* while in Cologne
1474	*The Game and Playe of the Chesse*, said to be the first book printed in England
c. 1475	Morality play *Mankind*
c. 1478	First Caxton edition of Chaucer's *Canterbury Tales*
1483	Richard III deposes boy king, Edward V
1485	Morality play *Everyman*
1485	Henry VII begins Tudor line of English monarchs

*T*he Anglo-Saxons who overran British territory in the fifth century were not the only successful Germanic raiders. The Norse Vikings, or Normans, had captured and settled in northern and western France, the area today called Normandy, and had gradually expanded their influence. They had adopted the French language and were ambitious to rule both in France and in England. Therefore, in 1066 when William the Conqueror, duke of Normandy, defeated the Anglo-Saxons, he was merely adding to his domains, which were still centered on the continent.

William consolidated his rule in his new English territories by establishing the highly organized Norman concept of feudalism. He confiscated and divided Anglo-Saxon lands into feudal estates owing dues and services to himself as monarch, and he put his barons in charge of the lands, displacing the Anglo-Saxon aristocracy. His most distinguished administrative achievement was the compiling of the Domesday Book, *a census of all his subjects and their possessions.*

With the attacks by barbaric forces ended and the people declared subjects of William and his heirs, stability returned to England. Gradually the population grew. Trade and towns expanded, travel increased, and the desire for knowledge reawakened. Although Latin remained the language of those who received a clerical education, the mass of the people were ignorant of it and spoke their own dialects of Anglo-Saxon. The religious revival of the eleventh century had a strong effect in Normandy. Both the knights and churchmen who came to England with William and during his son's reign founded abbeys, which, as centers of learning and work among the poor, maintained and spread culture. Thus the English citizens of London and the English poor peasants in the country received the new religious teaching from the foreign noble and the foreign monk. Nevertheless, all were drawn together through a common worship.

RELIGIOUS LITURGY

The main drama of the period was the religious liturgy. The Mass itself was a dramatic spectacle; the sanctuaries of first the Norman-Anglo Romanesque and then the Gothic cathedrals were the sacred stages. Dramatic elements of the religious rites of high holy days were explicitly developed. Indeed, sometimes the feasts served as the basis for little plays that appealed to the imagination and intensified the piety of the faithful. With these developments, there arose a desire for religious handbooks in the English tongue.

This coincided first with the revolt of the Norman-English barons, (appropriately so-called after some 150 years in England), which produced the Magna Carta, (Great Charter), and then with the reign of Henry III, the first wholly English king since before the conquest. Ormin's *Ormulum*, a religious handbook written about 1215, is composed entirely in English. Other religious books in English followed: the *Northumbrian Psalter* of 1250 is only one of the many devotional pieces written largely in English through 1300. Many English priests had studied in Paris and had come back to teach at Oxford or Cambridge in England. Able to talk to Norman noble, English student, or English peasant, they had the effect of uniting all these diverse segments of the English population. As a result, Normans as well as Englishmen soon began to write religious works in English. William of Shoreham translated the whole of the Psalter into English prose about 1327. In 1340 the *Remorse of Conscience*, translated from the French, exemplified how English prose was rising through religion. About the same year Richard Rolle of Hampole wrote in Latin, and then in Northumbrian English for the "unlearned," a poem called *Pricke of Conscience*. This poem was the last known religious poem of any importance until *The Vision of Piers Plowman*.

CHRONICLES

The Normans had always had a historical bent and had created a valuable historical literature written in Latin. The men who wrote it were called chroniclers. At first these were mere annalists, who recorded the events of each year, without attempting to bind the records together into a connected whole. But from the time of Henry I, another class of chroniclers arose. These men wrote at court rather than in monasteries scattered near and far. Living at the center of political life enabled and inspired them to write their histories in a philosophic spirit and to weave together into a unified whole their records of the growth of law, national life, and foreign affairs. A distinctly English feeling soon sprang up among these Norman historians.

ENGLISH STORY-TELLING

English patriotism was far from dead; *The Sayings of Alfred* were written in English by the English. These and some ballads and early English war songs were collected by the Norman historians. English story-telling grew out of this historical literature. Besides *The Romance of Sir Tristram*, many tales about Arthur's knights as well as other stories had originated in England. They had been translated into French, and then years later, at just about the time that King Edward I was making the Normans and the English into one people, they were translated back into English. By 1300 the number of French words appearing in otherwise English writings had increased, and the French romantic manner of telling stories had become more and more marked in English works. It had taken nearly a century for the French romantic style of poetry to become assimilated into English literature; it was assimiliated at about the same time that England as a nation had absorbed its French elements and become entirely English.

The most disastrous conflict of the period was the Hundred Years War, from 1337 to 1453, during which the Anglo-Norman kings tried to assert their power over all of France. The war matched Europe's two strongest monarchies, France and England, against each other in a struggle over England's continental possessions. This long struggle sapped the energies of the English for many generations; military conflict diverted attention and resources from cultural development. Only two years after the end of the Anglo-French conflict, which England lost, a struggle for the throne between the noble houses of Lancaster and York plunged England into civil war. This conflict, called the War of the Roses because each side used a rose as its symbol, ended in 1485 with the establishment of the Tudor monarchy, beginning with Henry VII of the Lancaster side.

THE PEASANTS' REVOLT

Another important event of the fourteenth century was the appearance in 1347 of the Black Death, a plague that swept Europe and parts of Asia and killed approximately three-quarters of the population before it subsided twenty years later. The consequences of the Black Death greatly affected feudal life. For the rural economy, it meant the end of the feudal farm system. Some peasants prospered when the loss of population resulted in more work for those who remained. However, when the government tried to limit wages and to levy excessive taxes, the result was the Peasants' Revolt of 1381. The revolt, however, failed to improve the conditions of the poor.

Originally, the coming together of the Normans and the English was due to the common worship and to the preaching of the priests in the thirteenth century and to the noble example they set of service to both the urban and peasant poor. When the priests, however, became rich, while pretending to be poor and impure of life, while pretending to be pure, the religious feeling they had stirred turned against them, and strong cries went out both on the Continent and in England for truth and purity in private life, in government, and in the Church.

MIDDLE ENGLISH LANGUAGE AND FORMS

Readers of modern English can soon learn to read Middle English (with the help of a glossary), especially if they are familiar with French or some other Romance language. Much of the vocabulary of Middle English is similar to that of modern English, but the similarities may be hidden by different spellings. For example, *rokkes* is "rocks," *daunce* is "dance," *sorwe* is "sorrow." Some Middle English words have become obsolete, such as: *eek* (even, also), *wight* (being, person), and *coude* (knew). Some words have changed meanings: *lust* meant "pleasure" and *clerk* meant "scholar, divinity student." Double negatives are common in Middle

English. The past participle is often indicated by an initial *y*, as in *yseen* (seen) and *yfalle* (fell, happened). Although most plurals of nouns are formed by adding *s*, some common words have irregular plurals, such as *yen* (eyes). Spelling and usage could vary within a single work, and especially among works in different regional dialects. Generally, however, the unfamiliar-looking page of Middle English poetry will become comprehensible with slow and attentive reading, reinforced, as it usually is in modern texts, by notes and glossaries.

Middle English Poetry

In trying to read the poetry of this era, the reader should practice pronouncing the words. The meter of Middle English poetry cannot be rendered accurately, however, unless two rules are observed: first, pronounce all the consonants, even those in consonant clusters, such as the *k* in *know* and *knight* (the *gh* is pronounced like *ch*). Second, pronounce the final *e* as a separate syllable wherever the meter of the poetic line requires it. Middle English poets used many complex meters, and experimented with stanzas of different lengths. In an imitation of French poetry, they used rhyme, although alliteration was still a favorite device of ornament and emphasis. (Some fourteenth-century poets tried to revive alliterative verse, but it did not catch on.) Rhyming words may appear in alternate lines or, as in Chaucer, in two sequential lines, forming a couplet. Lines in lyric poetry tend to be short, having only two or three stressed syllables, but are longer in narrative and dramatic poems. There are many variations and exceptions, however, because the Middle English poet seems to have felt free to combine and experiment.

THE NARRATIVE ROMANCE

The narrative poetry of adventure in Middle English was the romance. The form was used in imitation of the long narrative adventure poems of the Romance languages of the old Roman Empire, particularly of France. A romance has many qualities in common with an epic poem. But while it tells of the deeds of a central heroic figure, the spirit of a romance is less gloomy than that of the old Anglo-Saxon epics. The hero's courage is still crucial to the plot, but so is his chivalry, his code of courtesy, and his gallant behavior, especially to ladies. The romantic hero of Middle English not only slays monsters but also falls in love. Indeed, the hero's monster slaying may be a lesser triumph than his emotional self-control and generosity of spirit.

THE LAY OR LAIS

Some of the early English romances were in the form of lais, clever poetic stories written by Anglo-Normans in their own French language but derived from the legends and history of Britain. Those based on Celtic legend are called "Breton lais."

THE ARTHURIAN ROMANCE

Another important source for the subject matter of romantic poetry was the Latin *Historia Regum Britanniae*, written in the twelfth century by Geoffrey of Monmouth. This work laid the foundation for the legends surrounding King Arthur and his knights, a body of folk materials that passed through Geoffrey's *Historia* into the mainstream of European narrative materials.

The techniques and conventions of romance were developed in France and reinterpreted by Middle English poets in the fourteenth century, the outstanding example being *Sir Gawain and the Green Knight.* At the end of the medieval period, Sir Thomas Malory summed up the Arthurian romance in his prose version, *Morte Darthur.*

THE FABLIAU

A shorter and less lofty narrative in verse was the fabliau, a clever verse tale often dealing with humorous and frequently bawdy incidents from daily life. Many of Chaucer's pilgrims tell fabliaux. *The Miller's Tale* is an unusually complex and skillfully told fabliau. The pilgrim characters also tell beast fables, adaptations of lais, moral allegories, and brief romances.

THE SOURCE OF NARRATIVE FORMS

The rich variety of narrative forms in English literature of the late fourteenth century was a product of cross fertilization among French, Anglo-Norman, Latin, and Middle English literary materials. Originality was not a goal; poets borrowed, adapted, and embellished a common international stock of stories, characters, and incidents from three sources: the subject matter of Britain (Arthur and his knights), the subject matter of France (Charlemagne and his followers), and the subject matter of Rome (stories from classical antiquity, including those about the Trojan heroes and the founding of Rome).

Sir Gawain and the Green Knight

This poem, and the religious poems *Pearl*, *Patience*, and *Purity* were found in the same manuscript. All were written in the same dialect of Middle English, so all are assumed to be by the same unknown writer. The dialect is not of London; it is unlike Chaucer's, but from the provinces. The verse is alliterative, part of a revival of the Old English form, but it also employs rhyme in the five lines that end each stanza. The stanzas are not regular in length; they function as paragraphs in verse.

This poem is a moral romance, one of the finest romances in Middle English. It contains elements of folklore (the beheading of the knight; his green color, symbolic of fertility) and elements of the Arthurian legend (Gawain is King Arthur's nephew and a member of his court). The elements of magic and the rendering of similar events in series of three are typical of romantic literature, as is the testing of the hero's moral and physical courage. The lessons of Christianity emerge from Gawain's temptation and his ultimate fall into deceit, humiliation, and penance.

THE GREEN KNIGHT'S CHALLENGE AND SIR GAWAIN'S RESPONSE

Part One. The poem opens in King Arthur's castle, Camelot, on New Year's day. Arthur's court is described as the epitome of chivalry. Unexpectedly, the court is visited by a strange, and almost gigantic man dressed in green. The man's hair and skin are green also, as is his horse. This color associates the knight with figures from early fertility myths. The bizarre visitor proposes to allow a challenger to behead him with an ax if he may then cut likewise at his opponent one year later. Arthur's men are astonished; only young Sir Gawain volunteers. Gawain severs the Green Knight's head, but the headless one promptly picks it up by the hair and rides away, reminding Gawain to meet him in one year at the Green Chapel for the return blow.

Part Two. Exactly ten months later, on November 1, Gawain puts on his armor, including the mystical pentangle or five-pointed star (a symbol of truth that adorns his coat and shield), and sets out to find the Green Chapel. He arrives at Christmas at a great castle in a wood, where he is graciously received by the lord and his lady. Three days of feasting ensue. On December 27, Gawain tells of his quest and asks the location of the Green Chapel. Learning that it is nearby, Gawain decides to spend the next three days at the castle and ride out early on New Year's morning to keep his appointment. Meanwhile, he is invited to rest while his host goes out each day to hunt. Gawain and his host agree to exchange at evening whatever they have won during the day.

Part Three. Gawain has new problems. The lady of the castle begins to show him more attention and to make more demands than he can satisfy. She visits his bedchamber, where she flirts with him and kisses him. That evening, when the Lord returns with a deer he has killed, Gawain gives him the kiss in exchange. Thus Gawain has resisted the temptation to sin with the lady and honorably kept his bargain with the lord. The second day, the same pattern is repeated. The host returns from the hunt with a wild boar and receives from Gawain two kisses that the knight had been given by the lady. The third day, in addition to three kisses, the lady offers gifts. Gawain refuses them until she offers him a magic green girdle or belt that has the power to preserve the life of the wearer. Gawain yields and accepts the girdle, thinking to save himself from the ax of the Green Knight. That evening Gawain gives his host three kisses in exchange for a fox's pelt, but he keeps the magic belt, thus breaking his word. He has preserved his chastity but fallen instead into deceit.

Part Four. On New Year's day Gawain goes to the Green Chapel and finds that it is merely a rough mound. Gawain hears the sound of an ax being ground sharp. The Green Knight appears, ax in hand. Gawain bends for the blow but as it falls he flinches, shrinking back. The Green Knight reproves him and takes a second stroke, again missing. On his third try, he merely nicks Gawain's neck. Gawain then learns from the Green Knight that the two strokes that missed were for the bargains he kept in exchanging the kisses for the prizes of the hunt. The little cut he received on the third try represents his punishment for holding back the gift of the girdle. Although the Green Knight absolves Gawain of any further obligation, Gawain keeps and wears the green girdle as a reminder of his sin of pride. He returns to Arthur's court and tells of his adventure. All his fellow knights adopt the girdle also as a sign of their brotherhood and humility.

The Vision of Piers Plowman

This poem, probably written between 1362 and 1389, appears in various versions in many manuscripts, indicating that it was popular and widely read. The original, called Text A by scholars, is 2,400 lines long. Texts B and C, the two revisions, are expansions of this loosely structured work. In general, scholars agree that Text B has the greatest literary merit of the three.

The poet, William Langland, is totally obscure. It is not even known if he wrote all three versions. What can be inferred about him is that he lived in the Malvern Hills of western England, where the poem is set. What is certain is that the poem became so well known by 1381 that leaders of the Peasants' Revolt used phrases from it as rallying cries during the insurrection.

The Vision of Piers Plowman is a dream allegory, a form usually employed for poems about love, whose theme is the salvation of the soul and its progress from the world of the flesh to that of the spirit. The poet describes a series of dreams populated by allegorical figures representing Christian concepts and values. Figures representing vices and virtues, the Church, and biblical figures are presented in dialogue and in action. The lines are alliterative rather than rhymed. They are irregular in length, and there are no divisions into stanzas. The poem is not easy to read because of its abrupt shifts of scenes and characters. Certain passages of it are well known, however, especially the opening scene of the Prologue, the Fair Field of Folk, which presents a satiric view of society. The main character, Piers the Plowman, lies down by a brook to sleep and dreams of a field located between the tower of Truth and the dungeon of Wickedness. This field is full of a variety of people who represent the poet's society: workers and loiterers, rich and poor, clergy and layman, the proud and the foolish, many seeking their own profit and indulging in idle pleasures. Each brief description is emphasized by alliteration. Then emerges a king accompanied by knights, and the dreamer sees a vision of good government, as the king and community, or commons, unite for mutual benefits. This scene then dissolves into a cat and rat fable reflecting the then-current political rivalries. Thus the poem shifts focus throughout its long progress toward the ultimate moment when the dreamer awakens on Easter morning to the sound of church bells.

Both "Sir Gawain" and "Piers Plowman" describe the conflict between good and evil. In the Gawain adventure, however, the conflict is internal—Gawain yields to temptation. In *Piers Plowman* the forces of good and evil are allegorically represented as diverse figures in conflict with each other.

The clearest embodiment of medieval ideas about how life ought to be lived was the romance. Full of ideal figures, the medieval romance expresses the chivalric concept of right actions and refined manners. It is organized around a series of adventures undertaken by a knight to test and prove his courage and worthiness. The audience is not only entertained by the surprising adventures of the knight; they are also inspired by his example. By contrast, a religious poem such as Piers Plowman *shows what is wrong in the world, exposing bad actions and warning people against moral failure.*

Selected Readings

Barber, Richard. *King Arthur: Hero and Legend.* 3d ed. Ipswich: Boydell, 1986.

Dunn, Charles W. and Edward T. Byrnes. *Middle English Literature.* Rev. ed. New York and London: Garland, 1990.

Fox, Denton, comp. *Twentieth Century Interpretations of Sir Gawain and the Green Knight: A Collection of Critical Essays.* Englewood Cliffs, NJ: Prentice, 1968.

Salter, Elizabeth. *Piers Plowman: An Introduction.* Cambridge: Harvard University Press, 1962.

Spearing, A. C. *Criticism and Medieval Poetry.* New York: Barnes, 1972.

Vasta, Edward, comp. *Middle English Survey: Critical Essays.* Notre Dame, IN: University of Notre Dame, 1965.

Vasta, Edward, ed. *Interpretations of Piers Plowman.* Notre Dame, IN: University of Notre Dame, 1968.

Weston, Jessie L., ed. *The Chief Middle English Poets.* New York: Houghton, 1914.

4

Late Medieval Period (1066 to 1485): Chaucer

1154–1189	Henry II begins Plantagenet line of English kings
1167	Oxford University founded
1170	Thomas à Becket murdered in Canterbury Cathedral
1174	à Becket canonized
1202–1205	France takes Normandy, Anjou, Maine, and Brittany from England
1215	Signing of the Magna Carta
1230	Guilliame de Loire, *Roman de la Rose*
1307–1321	Dante, *Divine Comedy*
1327–1377	Reign of Edward III
1337–1453	Hundred Years' War
1353	Boccaccio, *The Decameron*
1359	Chaucer in France with English army; taken prisoner and ransomed the next year
1359–1400	*Sir Eglamour, Morte Darthur, Sir Gawain and the Green Knight*, and other romances
1369	Chaucer, *Dethe of Blaunche the Duchesse*
1372	Chaucer on first of three trips to Italy
1374–1386	Chaucer controller of the customs and subsidies on wool for the port of London; writes poems *Compleynt of Mars* and the *Parliament of Fowls*

1377–1399	Reign of Richard II
c. 1382	Chaucer, *Troilus and Criseyde*
1385	Chaucer writes Prologue to *Legend of Good Women*
1385–1386	Chaucer is member of Parliament for Kent
1387	Chaucer writes the Prologue to *Canterbury Tales*; sets 1387 as the year in which action takes place
1399	Chaucer sends *Compleint to His Purse* to the king
1399–1413	Henry IV establishes Lancaster line of kings
1400	Chaucer dies
1478	Caxton prints first of two editions of Chaucer's *Canterbury Tales*

The most productive and innovative poet of the late medieval period in England was Geoffrey Chaucer. He was able to create good works in all the major forms of poetry, except drama, that flourished during this period. Yet he is more than merely representative of the period; his individualistic style, subtle wit, and gentle irony, along with his keen eye for the details of human gesture and voice, identify Chaucer as an extraordinary talent. Chaucer created a gallery of characters that not only reflects the society of his time and place; they have also become types in the tradition of English poetry. Chaucer was widely influential during the century after his death. Only the shifts in the English language obscured his richness until modern scholars reexamined and translated Chaucer's poetry.

GEOFFREY CHAUCER (1343–1400)

Although the feudal social system did not recognize the existence of a middle class, as commerce and industry in England grew and towns developed for the management of trade, a middle class began to emerge from those families who had become rich and influential through commercial activities. Chaucer came from such a family; his father was a wine merchant in London. Young Chaucer was placed as a page in the noble houses of two sons of King Edward III, Lionel of Antwerp and later John of Gaunt, whose son became King Henry IV. From these positions Chaucer was able to observe and absorb the values and manners of the court. He enjoyed patronage and employment from these nobles and their successors for the rest of his life. During his lifetime Chaucer was a soldier, a diplomatic agent, a customs officer, a justice of the peace, a member of Parliament, a supervisor of royal public works, and a receiver of many gifts from royal sources until the very end of his life.

All during this time, Chaucer was also writing poetry. Just when he composed each individual poem is not known, but generally scholars believe that he began as a young man with translations, most notably of the French allegorical poem *Roman de la Rose*, and ended his career preoccupied with *The Canterbury Tales*, which remained incomplete at his death. Chaucer absorbed much from French and Italian literature but transformed it greatly by his subtle and often satiric treatment. He used a wide range of narrative and lyric forms so that his works serve almost as an encyclopedia of medieval poetic materials.

Canterbury Tales

Chaucer created a narrative device that served to justify the wide variety of tales he wished to tell. The device is that of a pilgrimage, a religious journey to a place of special holiness, that allegorically represents the journey of the Christian soul to a state of salvation. Chaucer's thirty pilgrims represent a broad range of medieval English society with a variety of attitudes toward religious duty. The starting place for the journey is London. The pilgrims meet at the Tabard Inn at Southwerk, a southern suburb of the city. The goal of the pilgrimage is Canterbury Cathedral, seat of the Catholic church in England and site of the martyrdom of Saint Thomas à Becket, murdered two centuries earlier for his assertion of Church authority over King Henry II. The pilgrims meet by chance but become a group when the host of the Tabard Inn, Harry Bailly, proposes that they travel together and that during the journey they hold a story-telling competition to pass the time. Each pilgrim is supposed to tell two tales on the way to Canterbury and two tales on the return, for a total of 120 tales. But Chaucer did not nearly complete the cycle of tales; only 22 were finished at the time of his death in 1400. The tales exist in ninety partially complete or fragmentary manuscripts so that even the exact order Chaucer intended is uncertain.

The device of the pilgrimage allows Chaucer to provide a teller for each tale, so that the relationship between the pilgrim and his or her story is dynamic. Each tale is appropriate to the teller's social station and personality. Sometimes the pilgrims come into conflict, so that the tales they tell or their manner of telling them imply a rebuttal to a previous story. Several tales, referred to as "the marriage group," reflect the various attitudes toward marriage of several pilgrims (the Wife of Bath, the Clerk, the Merchant, and the Franklin). Between the tales, Chaucer provides "head-links" of dialogue between the pilgrims. The host keeps order and moderates disputes.

THE FORM OF THE *CANTERBURY TALES*

All of the *Canterbury Tales* are written in basically the same metrical pattern, the decasyllabic couplet—that is, the poetic line has ten syllables, and every two lines rhyme. Sometimes an extra *e* is pronounced at the end of a line to make eleven syllables, but that *e* is never stressed. The stressed syllables alternate, so that Chaucer's writings demonstrate an early, irregular version of what will become iambic pentameter. Here is a typical Chaucer line:

A Knyght ther was and that a worthy man

(There was a knight and that a worthy man)

This line is very regular; the stresses fall on the second syllable (knyght) and alternate syllables after that, so that the final syllable is stressed, and it also rhymes with "bigan" at the end of the next line. The reader should not expect every line to fit this pattern exactly; if all lines were regular, the effect would become monotonous. The following example is less regular:

Curteis he was and lowely of servyse

(He was courteous and humble in service)

Here the first syllable is stressed, but not the second or third, and the line ends with an extra *e*, which is unstressed.

Such a poetic form is adaptable to the various needs of a lengthy narrative poem. More complex stanzas were used in lyric poems and ballads of the same era, and by Chaucer himself.

THE GENERAL PROLOGUE

Chaucer sets up the framework of his story in a general prologue and elaborates on it in the linking passages between tales. The Prologue, thus, sets the scene and introduces the pilgrims. The pilgrims, who are the tellers of the tales, include one pilgrim who represents Chaucer himself. This pilgrim describes the others, and tells how they met at the Tabard Inn and how they decided to travel as a group. This character, the narrator, can be referred to as Chaucer-the-pilgrim to distinguish him from Chaucer-the-author, the person who wrote the tales.

The Prologue opens with a famous passage of eighteen lines describing the time of year, April, when the pilgrimage begins. Many of the details describing the warming weather and its effect on both crops and animals (including people) are similar to descriptive details found in lyric poems of the same era. As the days grow longer, the fowls grow restless and so do the folk, who get the urge to travel. They feel like making pilgrimages, for example, to Canterbury. Then the narrator focuses on the particular group of pilgrims he met by chance at the Tabard Inn, describing them one by one. The order of these descriptions seems to be according to social rank, with the Knight first (there are no nobility as such on the trip), but no great consistency of order is observed. Each character sketch includes some or all of the following details:

the pilgrim's background and significant experiences

his or her physical appearance—age, dress, mannerisms

the kind of horse he or she rides

the pilgrim's attitude and manner of speech

a general evaluation of the "worthiness" of the pilgrim

The narrator often cites details that give the reader a more negative impression than Chaucer-the-pilgrim expresses. The narrator seems naive, and there is a persistent ironic contrast between the reader's critical perception and the narrator's more simple acceptance of the pilgrims, whom he takes, apparently, at face value. For example, the self-indulgent Monk is described as scorning to live according to the old-fashioned strict rules of his order. Chaucer-the-pilgrim agrees with him, easily convinced, but the reader sees that Chaucer-the-author is not so approving. Much of the humor of *The General Prologue* arises from the disparity between what the pilgrims pretend to be and what the details of their speech and appearance reveal about them.

The Knight and Squire. However, the first pilgrim, the Knight, is unambiguously an ideal figure. It is revealed that the Knight has fought in many battles in defense of worthwhile English and Christian causes. Though he is an able warrior, his manners are gentle and quiet. His rust-spotted garments show that he is just back from a campaign and that he has not bothered to put himself into fancy clothes for the trip to Canterbury. He is accompanied by his son, a young Squire, who provides a contrast to the Knight in many ways: youth vs. age, inexperience vs. experience, fancy dress vs. rusty garments, and preoccupation with love of ladies vs. love of God. The jolly Squire is good at dancing, singing, and writing love songs. At the age of twenty, he has been in a few battles, but he mostly fights to win ladies' admiration. He is a satiric version of the courtly lover who cannot sleep because he is lovesick. However, father and son are not in conflict; the Squire is respectful. These two pilgrims are accompanied by a yeoman, a free man acting as their servant and battle attendant. He is an expert archer and keeps his gear in fine condition.

Religious Personages. The narrator shifts his attention to a group of religious personages, a Prioress and her attendants, a Monk, and a Friar, none of them as ideal a figure as the Knight. The Prioress, the head of a convent, is an ambiguous figure. Her manners, though neat and modest, are tinged with a hint of courtliness, as if she might prefer a life of gallantry instead of a life of devotion to pious thoughts. Madame Eglantine, the Prioress, not only has a romantic name, but she also dresses fashionably and wears a gold brooch with the motto *Amor vincit omnia* (love conquers all). Her charity has as its objects not the poor folk she meets along the way but her little dogs, which she spoils with rich foods. As a woman of high status, the Prioress has a retinue of followers: a nun, who serves as her secretary, and three priests. As a primary female figure of the *Canterbury Tales*, the Prioress is often contrasted to the Wife of Bath.

The Monk and the Friar are two religious figures who seem not at all well suited to their vocations. The Monk appears preoccupied with riding and hunting, ignoring his monastery's ancient rules as too restrictive. He is fat, bold, and jolly and enjoys feasting and dressing well. The character of Friar Huberd is more complicated. He is a skillful fundraiser, allowing easy penances in exchange for donations, but he spends some of this money on women, buying them gifts and eventually paying the costs of marrying them off if they become pregnant. He appears to be a fun-loving man, singing and playing a fiddle, popular at weddings and feasts, avoiding the poor and the sick in favor of more jovial companions.

Professionals and Tradesmen. Chaucer next turns to a group of middle-class professionals and tradesmen, all with some pretensions to affluence and expert knowledge. As a group, they aspire to more status than society is perhaps willing to grant them. The Merchant likes to talk impressively about trade routes but keeps his debts a secret. The Sergeant of Law, a lawyer and local justice, is always talking about some legal rule or case and seems impressed with his own shrewdness. The Frankelain, or Franklin, a country gentleman, lives like a lord and keeps a bountiful open house. Chaucer gives a rich description of the luscious things the Franklin likes to eat and drink. Also traveling on the pilgrimage is a group of five guildsmen, members of a fraternal order. They are the Haberdasshere (a dealer in sewing supplies), the Carpenter, the Webbe (a weaver), the Dyere, and the Tapicer (a maker of tapestries). They are very well dressed for tradesmen, all in the uniform or livery of their guild. Chaucer-the-pilgrim finds them impressive and smart enough to be aldermen. Their upwardly mobile wives (who are not present) apparently insist on being addressed as "madame." These men bring their own cook, who is a skillful chef but a bit unsavory to look at (he has an ulcer on his skin) and likes to drink ale. The final professional figure is that of the Doctor of Physics, a man well schooled in theoretical knowledge, astrology, ancient medical texts, and the theory of humors, which was a widely accepted hypothesis that temperament and disease were based on the four elemental fluids of the body. He is not expert on the Bible, but rather on making money from his practice. He has a profitable arrangement with his druggist and has accumulated a fund of gold from the time of the plague.

Among this group of worldly and pretentious men are two who stand out by contrast—the Clerk of Oxford and the Shipman. The Clerk is unworldly; he loves to study. Lean and poorly dressed, he spends any money he gets on books. He speaks seldom, but when he does his remarks are brief and full of meaning. He teaches as gladly as he learns. At the other extreme is the Shipman, a rough and violent fellow, a heavy drinker, but still a skilled seaman familiar with many harbors. He has none of the glossy surface of the middle-class professionals.

The Wife of Bath. The Wife of Bath, who is the last of the middle-class group to be described, is one of the most complex and fully developed pilgrim characters, both in *The General Prologue* and in the lengthy prologue to her own tale. She is ridiculously overdressed, fat, and bold-faced in contrast to the Prioress, the only other female pilgrim described. The Wife, who lives in the town of Bath, is much traveled and many times married. She follows the cloth-making trade but is so sensitive about her social status that if she cannot be first at the collection box in church, she becomes angry. The Wife of Bath seems outgoing; it may be that she is looking for another husband on this pilgrimage. She reveals more of her history and attitudes in the prologue to her tale, but it is clear from the beginning that the Wife does not fulfill the courtly ideal of woman as chaste and modest.

The Poor Parson. The most ideal pilgrim, the one who seems wholly pure in his motives for making the pilgrimage, is the Poor Parson, a clergyman who takes his religious role seriously. Both learned and charitable, the Parson is presented as an example of Christian belief and dutiful service to the folk, forgiving of the sins of the weak but severe toward the obstinate, whether of high or low degree. He is accompanied on the pilgrimage by his brother, the Plowman, a simple and devout worker who gives his labor to the needy as a form of charity.

The Miller, the Manciple, and the Reeve. As part of the final group of pilgrims consists of a miller, a manciple, and a reeve, men who serve as agents and minor officials. The Miller grinds the grain produced by others. The Miller is a coarse fellow, brawny and fierce-looking. He likes to tell crude stories (although the story he tells is artfully constructed in order not to be offensive). However, it becomes known that the Miller is not entirely honest; he cheats in the measurement of grain at his mill. The Manciple is a steward or manager for a group of lawyers who, although more learned than the Manciple, are easily cheated by him. This pilgrim is a sharp dealer. The Reeve also exploits his employer; he manages a large farm in such a way as to benefit himself more than the lord who owns it. The Reeve has manipulated matters so that the lord has had to borrow from him out of the goods produced on the land. Perhaps because of his irritable disposition, the Reeve rides last in the procession of pilgrims.

The Summoner and the Pardoner. Near the end of the group ride two friends, the Summoner and the Pardoner, both low-level church functionaries and both corrupt. The Summoner, a church officer who calls sinners into ecclesiastical court, is a frightful-looking man of diseased complexion as well as a drunk. He pretends to be learned by repeating the few scraps of Latin that he has picked up in his work, but like a parrot, he does not know the meaning of the words he speaks. The Summoner is a lecher who allows other lechers to escape the court's summons in exchange for bribes. The Summoner and his friend the Pardoner ride in the procession together, singing love songs. The Pardoner, thin, pale, and fashionably dressed, is presented by Chaucer-the-author as the depth of corruption; a religious con man and a homosexual, clearly to be despised in Chaucer's scheme of values. The Pardoner claims to have just returned from the head church in Rome, bringing holy relics (all fakes) and a bag full of pardons to sell. He is a skillful salesman and an effective preacher, however, able to extort money from even the poorest folk.

Chaucer-the-Pilgrim. At the conclusion of *The General Prologue,* Chaucer-the-pilgrim turns his attention to himself and to his role as narrator. He asks the reader to excuse him for any vulgarities in the following stories; he claims that accuracy in reporting will require that he sometimes repeat vulgar words. He also apologizes for the confused order of his portraits of the pilgrims and generally pleads that his "wit is short," that he is a simple fellow. He then briefly tells how the Host of the Tabard Inn, Harry Bailly, a large and jovial man, proposes to go to Canterbury along with these pilgrims and further proposes the story-telling competition. Bailly will be the judge of the best tale, and the prize will be a free supper on the group's return to the Tabard Inn at the end of the pilgrimage (to be paid for by all the others). All agree; the Host is appointed their guide and governor. The next morning they set out together. They draw lots to see who should begin the tales; the Knight wins and willingly begins, telling a romance of noble lovers.

THE MILLER'S TALE

In response to the lofty tale told by the Knight, the drunken Miller insists on telling a lively fabliau of two lovers plotting against the woman's dull old husband, a carpenter. The young wife, Alison, and the boarder, a student named Nicholas, are conducting a secret affair. Meanwhile, Absolon, a young parish clerk, also woos the wife. Nicholas pretends to have discovered astrologic signs of a coming flood and advises John, the Carpenter, to prepare three large tubs for them and for Alison, the tubs to be hung from the roof and cut free when the flood rises. The foolish John prepares the tubs as instructed, and all three ascend into them, but Alison and Nicholas silently climb down again, and go to make love in the Carpenter's own bed. Near dawn, the amorous Absolon creeps up to their chamber window and, believing Alison is alone inside, begs a kiss. Scornful Alison in the dark puts out her backside to receive the kiss and mocks poor Absolon, who, instantly cured of desire, vows revenge. Absolon fetches from the blacksmith shop a hot iron and again begs a kiss at Alison's window, but this time it is Nicholas who puts out his bottom, only to have it branded by the iron. Nicholas cries out "water." At that the Carpenter believes the flood has come and promptly cuts the ropes holding his tub, fainting as it falls to the ground. General mayhem follows, and John's folly is exposed to public scorn. The Miller has skillfully woven together two jokes—the plot to deceive the husband, and the plot to take vengeance with a hot iron—into one complex but well-knit and funny story, a superb fabliau.

THE WIFE OF BATH'S PROLOGUE AND TALE

Experience is the opening word of the Wife's prologue, a rambling autobiography and apology for her rather free lifestyle. Her prologue is twice as long as her tale. After making the argument that chastity is an ideal but not an absolute commandment, the Wife describes all five of her marriages. Starting when she was thirteen, the Wife has married a series of three old but wealthy husbands whom she was able to control with her sharp tongue and by withholding or demanding sexual favors. She offers herself to other wives as an expert advisor in matters of marriage and gives an example of the type of harangue she used against each victim-spouse. She lists the standard accusations and complaints made against wives and then defends herself on each point, turning the accusations against the husband. By the fourth marriage, however, the Wife is no longer so young; she finds the tables turned when she learns that her husband has a mistress. She manages to arouse his jealousy; then he suddenly dies. Her fifth husband, Jankyn, was younger than she, and she loved him best. He was a scholar with whom the Wife had flirted even before the death of her fourth husband. She showered him with her accumulated wealth and her affection, but after their marriage, he began to upset her by reading each evening from a book that was a compilation of antifeminist literature, and he even quoted proverbs against women. One night when she couldn't take any more, the Wife in a rage tore out three pages of the book and hit Jankyn, knocking him down. He got up and knocked her down, where she lay still. Aghast, Jankyn bent over his wife and begged forgiveness. She hit him again, but eventually the couple made up, coming to a new understanding in which the wife ruled the roost. The insulting book was burned, and they lived happily for some time. But now the Wife is again a widow.

The Tale of the Wife of Bath is a fairy tale set in the days of King Arthur. It concerns a young knight who violates the rules of chivalry by raping a maiden. The knight is given over to the queen and her ladies for punishment;

they assign him a task. He has one year to find an acceptable answer to the question: what is it that women most desire? Sorrowfully, the knight travels around, finding many various answers, all partly true but none perfect. At the end of his allotted year, the knight wends his way back to the queen's court, still in doubt about his answer. He meets an old hag, a "loathly lady," who offers to give him the correct answer if he will promise to grant her a request. He agrees. The two appear before the queen, and the hag's answer is pronounced good—that what women desire most is "sovereynetee," that is, sovereignty, control over their husbands. Next, the hag appeals to the queen for her promised request from the knight. To his horror, she wants him for her husband. The marriage scene is skipped over, and we next find them in bed on the wedding night; the old hag wife complaining of her husband's coldness. He responds that she is too old, too ugly, and too low born. She explains to him that low birth is no shame, just as high birth is no assurance of gentilesse, or true nobility of conduct. Likewise, she says, poverty is no shame; even Christ was poor. As for the problem of her age and ugliness, she makes him an offer: she can use her power to make herself young, pretty, and the object of rival lovers, or she can stay ugly and always be faithful. The knight-husband is stymied by the dilemma; he leaves the choice to her, which of course is the right answer. Having sovereignty, she chooses to be both fair and faithful. This blissful conclusion parallels the Wife's own fifth, and happiest, marriage.

THE FRANKLIN'S TALE

The last tale of those usually included in the marriage group is a Breton lay. That is, it is a short romantic poem derived from the Breton or Celtic people who lived in the part of northern France called Brittany. It tells of the faithful love of Arveragus and his wife Dorigen. During her husband's absence, Dorigen is courted by the jolly squire Aurelius. She resists, vowing to return his love only after he has removed all the rocks that block the coast of Brittany, an apparently impossible task. Heartsick, Aurelius prays to Apollo for a miracle. Meanwhile, Arveragus happily returns to his wife. All is well with the couple, but Aurelius languishes in despair. Aurelius's brother seeks out a magician who can conjure up visions and who agrees, for 1,000 pounds, to create the illusion that the coast is free of rocks. This done, Aurelius claims the love of Dorigen. She is caught in a dilemma: if she denies Aurelius, she breaks her word; if she submits, she breaks her marriage vows to Arveragus. After much weeping and anguish, she confesses to her husband, who feels compelled to send her to Aurelius as a matter of honor. But when Aurelius sees his beloved's agony, he relents, pities her distress, and sends her home untouched. Because of the great act of gentilesse, the magician cancels his debt. At the end of his tale, the Franklin asks his audience which of the characters, the husband, the lover or the magician, was "most free"—most noble and generous. He leaves the question open.

THE PARDONER'S PROLOGUE AND TALE

In his prologue, the Pardoner gives his fellow pilgrims a sample of the performance he puts on in churches when he takes over the pulpit and sells his fake relics of holy people, claiming that they can cure all sorts of ills and bring about good harvests. He then admits to the group that he is a fraud, and he boasts of how profitable his trade has been, and of how skillful he is at persuasion and deception. Although greedy himself, he preaches mainly against the sin of avarice, or greed. He assures the group that he can get money from the poorest folk to satisfy his own need for pleasure.

The Pardoner's Tale is a skillfully constructed exemplum, a moral story, illustrating the destructive power of greed. Beginning with a rambling diatribe against drunkenness and other sins, the Pardoner opens his story in a town where three riotous fellows, on hearing the tolling of a funeral bell, swear to each other to seek out Death and to slay him. At the start of their search, they meet an old man who complains that he cannot get Death to take him. The rowdies demand to know where they can find Death. The old man directs them to a tree where, instead of their foe, they find a hoard of gold. They forget about finding Death and instead calculate how to protect this treasure until dark when they can safely carry it home. One fellow is sent for bread and wine while the other two stay on guard. In his absence the two plot to kill him in order to have more gold for themselves. Meanwhile, the fellow fetching the bread and wine buys some poison with which to eliminate the other two so that he can have all the gold for himself. Both plots work; the returning fellow is stabbed by his former friends, who then sit down and unknowingly drink the poisoned wine. They have, ironically, all indeed found Death.

At this point, the Pardoner breaks into a sermon against wickedness and solicits offerings for his fake pardons and relics, apparently forgetting that he has already admitted his hypocrisy to the pilgrims. He calls upon the Host to kiss the relics, but the Host responds angrily. The Knight steps in to keep the peace.

THE TALE OF SIR THOPAS

After a pious tale of martyrdom told by the Prioress, Chaucer-the-pilgrim is called upon by the Host to tell a tale. The Host's invitation includes a brief description of Chaucer-the-pilgrim as a small and quiet man, shy and gazing at the ground. Chaucer responds to the request for a "tale of mirth" by saying that he knows only one tale, a rhyme that he learned long ago. He begins at once.

The tale itself is written in jogging rhymed stanzas of six short lines. The style is that of a trite romance, lacking all the dignity and spirit of high romantic literature. The hero, Sir Thopas, is described in a rather mechanical, head-to-foot survey. We then learn that he is accomplished in archery and wrestling, two low-level sports. He is pictured as rather pointlessly spurring his horse so hard that the horse bleeds, then stopping for rest. Sir Thopas aspires to the love of an elfin queen. He enters Fairy Land, where he is immediately challenged as an intruder by the gigantic Sir Oliphaunt. Promising to meet the challenge on the next day, Sir Thopas rushes home to get his armor.

The last five stanzas of the first Fit (part I) consist of a tedious description of the knight's battle dress. The beginning of the second Fit alludes to other popular heroes, who are knights from other romances. Just as Chaucer-the-pilgrim seems to be drifting back toward the subject of his tale, the Host interrupts impatiently, calling the tale stupid doggerel and asking the pilgrim if he cannot tell in plain prose a simpler story in which there might be some "mirthe" (pleasure) or "doctrine" (meaning). Chaucer-the-pilgrim responds agreeably, promising to tell the Tale of Melibee, which turns out to be a moral allegory.

The Tale of Sir Thopas is a parody of the worst sort of trite romance, full of pointless catalogs of birds and plants. The stanzas are padded with formulaic phrases to accommodate the rhyme scheme or to fill up a stanza short on subject matter. For example, every few stanzas the phrase "I tell you in certain" or "as I you tell" or some variation fills up a half line and slows down the pace. Ironically, Chaucer is depicting himself as the least skillful storyteller of the group. This modest self-depiction corresponds to the image of Chaucer-the-pilgrim at the end of *The General Prologue*, where he apologizes for his lack of "wit." Of course the reader realizes that this is a role Chaucer chooses to create for himself within this great, richly diverse poem. His self-mockery is a joke shared with the reader and, at the same time, a mask behind which the real Geoffrey Chaucer could retreat.

THE NUN'S PRIEST'S TALE

This beast fable is loosely related to the marriage group of tales in that it depicts the domestic life of a husband, the cock Chauntecleer, and his wife, the hen Pertelote. Beast fables draw on folk material and exist in many versions. During the Middle Ages, beast fables were often also used as part of sermons. The fable the Priest tells, however, is mock-heroic in tone. The grandeur of Chauntecleer, the cock of the poor widow's yard, mirrors human pride. Gorgeous and learned, Chauntecleer is nevertheless troubled by a bad dream that he will die because of an ugly beast. Pertelote, the favorite of his seven wives, scolds him for cowardice in taking a dream seriously.

Practical and full of medical lore, she diagnoses that he is suffering from an imbalance of humors and prescribes a laxative for him. In response, Chauntecleer relates many instances where he has read that significant dreams were fatally ignored. His long lecture contains ancient examples and traditional wisdom. Chauntecleer then turns his attention to the beauty of Pertelote and forgets his dream.

Meanwhile, the fox has sneaked into the farmyard. At this point in the tale, the Priest digresses to question the pilgrims as to whether it is predestined that Chauntecleer will die; he also cites the evil counsel of women. The Priest then goes back to the tale. Chauntecleer is startled by a glimpse of the fox among the cabbages; his first impulse is to flee. Then the fox begins to flatter him about his superb singing voice. At the fox's request, Chauntecleer stretches his neck to sing. The fox quickly grabs him by the neck and runs off toward the woods. The Priest intones a lofty lament, calling on Venus and alluding to the tragedy of King Priam from the *Aeneid*. He tells the pilgrims that the hens shriek as the Roman matrons did when Nero burned the city. The poor widow, her daughters, and the dog all chase the fox, followed by the rest of the farmyard animals. Even the bees abandon their hive to join the chase. But Chauntecleer cleverly advises the fox to defy the pursuing crowd. When the fox opens his mouth to do so, Chauntecleer escapes into a tree. The fox tries to coax the cock to come down, but Chauntecleer is not to be fooled twice; this time he resists the flattery. The fox curses himself for not keeping his mouth shut, and the Priest draws his moral: resist flattery.

THE PARSON'S INTRODUCTION AND TALE

The Parson's tale is usually assumed to be the one Chaucer intended to conclude the collection. As the journey nears its end, the Host asks the Parson to tell the last tale. The Parson avers that he is no storyteller but that he will give them a sermon, a "meditation" without rhyme or alliteration but full of meaning. He follows his introduction with a long sermon in prose. It is a serious treatment of penitence, but includes a long digression describing the Seven Deadly Sins.

Chaucer's Retraction. At the end of the Parson's sermon, Chaucer-the-author adds a retraction, a statement of regret that he has written so much involving sin and "worldly vanities." He asks Christ's forgiveness for most of his poetry, including the *Canterbury Tales*. Feeling the nearness of death, Chaucer says that he intends to devote himself to penitence and confession, in hopes of salvation. Thus at the end of his life, Chaucer seems not to look back on his literary career as full of great accomplishments; rather he regrets and apologizes for using his talents in what he concludes were sinful ways.

Chaucer's Minor Poetry

As a courtier, Chaucer contributed light lyrics to the literature of complimentary poems and occasional verses (composed for special occasions) that marked the social world he moved in. The best known of his lyrics is the "Compleint to His Purse." A complaint is a conventional type of love poem in which the lover complains that his lady is cold to him. Chaucer humorously borrowed this form and applied it to his purse as if it were a creature whom he calls upon for help and comfort. More serious in tone are his poems *Gentilesse* and *Truth*. The first of these poems is a moving statement of a common medieval theme, that true nobility arises not from birth or social rank but from virtue and honor. *Truth* expresses another familiar medieval idea, that a retreat from the world leads to inner peace and to moral and philosophical truth. Both poems end with an envoy, an address to someone Chaucer knew and to whose life the poem would be pertinent.

Medieval England has as its spokesman a poet of suprisingly wide range. Chaucer established himself as the first in a long line of witty observers of the human scene, who captured the ideals of medieval life in the heroic deeds and courtly manners of the knight and also presented the racy realism of everyday life. He mocked and criticized the inadequate and corrupt members of the clergy without attacking Christian belief, believing that sinful individuals only prove the need for a guiding faith. When Dryden set out 300 years later to modernize some of Chaucer's tales he said of them, "Here is God's plenty."

Selected Readings

Bowden, Muriel. *A Commentary on the General Prologue to the Canterbury Tales*. New York: Macmillan, 1948.

Bowden, Muriel. *A Reader's Guide to Geoffrey Chaucer*. New York: Farrar, 1964.

Howard, Donald R. *The Idea of the Canterbury Tales*. Berkeley: University of California, 1976.

Hussey, Maurice, A. C. Spearing and James Winny. *An Introduction to Chaucer*. Cambridge, Eng.: Cambridge University Press, 1965.

5

Late Medieval Period (1066 to 1485): Prose and Popular Literature

c. 1215	Ormin, *Ormulum*
1230	Guilliame de Loire, *Roman de la Rose*
1245–1272	Westminster Abbey built
1250	*Northumbrian Psalter*
1267–1268	Roger Bacon, *Opus Maius*
1267–1273	Thomas Aquinas, *Summa Theologica*
1270–1280	Anonymous writings and translations into English of *Romance of Sir Tristam*, *Havelok the Dane, and King Horn*
1271–1295	Marco Polo in Asia
1272–1307	Reign of Edward I
c. 1280	*Owl and the Nightingale*, English ballad
1307–1321	Dante, *Divine Comedy*
c. 1328	Chester cycle of plays composed
1337–1453	Hundred Years' War
1347–1351	Black Death sweeps Europe
1359–1400	*Sir Eglamour, Morte Darthur, Sir Gawain and the Green Knight*, and other romances

c. 1362	Langland, *The Vision of Piers Plowman*
c. 1375	Beginning of morality plays with *Paternoster* and *Creed*
c. 1380	Wycliffe translates Bible into English
1381	The Peasants' Revolt
1387	Chaucer writes the "Prologue" to *Canterbury Tales*; sets 1387 as year in which action takes place
1399–1413	Henry IV establishes Lancaster line of kings
1400–1450	Wakefield Master cycle of plays
c. 1413–1415	Margery Kemp vows chastity and begins pilgrimage to Jerusalem
1415	York Realist revises passion sequence of *York Play of the Crucifixion*; Battle of Agincourt returns Normandy to England
c. 1425	*The Second Shepherd's Play*
1429–1431	Joan of Arc leads French to victory over English; Joan of Arc burned at the stake
1436–1438	Kemp, *The Book of Margery Kemp*
1450	Gutenberg Press
1455–1485	War of the Roses
1456	The Gutenberg Bible
1469–1470	Malory, *Morte Darthur*
c. 1475	Morality play *Mankind*
1485	Morality play *Everyman*
1485	Caxton prints Malory's *Morte Darthur*
1485	Henry VII begins Tudor line of English monarchs
1515–1516	Skelton, *Magnificence*
1765	Percy, *Reliques of Ancient English Poetry*
1882	Child, *The English and Scottish Popular Ballads*

While Chaucer dominates poetry of the late Middle Ages, popular poetry, drama, and prose were also developing. Beyond the influence of the court and the literature of the Continent, ordinary folk in towns and villages created songs, told stories, and watched simple plays performed by their neighbors. Spring songs, love songs, hymns, and ballads developed through oral transmission, acquiring a set of formal conventions and traditional images. This noncourtly literature was permeated by Christian concepts, but it also retained the texture of the countryside. Even a play based on biblical lore, such as The Second Shepherd's Play, *clearly took its setting and characters from rural*

England, not from Bethlehem. Finally, Malory wrote in prose the last great romance of the era, Morte Darthur, *looking forward to the age of the printing press and the wider dissemination of reading.*

MARGERY KEMP (1373–1438)

One unusual example of Middle English prose comes from Margery Kemp, an illiterate housewife and mother who nevertheless left a dynamic record of her own life. After the difficult birth of her first child, Kemp, the daughter of a mayor and the wife of a prosperous townsman in York, began to experience visions in which she carried on conversations with Christ. As if one of Chaucer's pilgrims come to life, Kemp, driven by a deep spiritual need, traveled to Jerusalem, to Rome, and then back to York. Her autobiography was dictated to followers, one a priest.

The Book of Margery Kemp   This early spiritual autobiography, composed between 1436 and 1438, contains many of the formal characteristics of similar works written in the seventeenth and eighteenth centuries. It details Kemp's initial spiritual suffering, her visions of evil, her fall into the sin of pride, and her subsequent impulse toward self-destruction. These dark periods are relieved by healing visions of Christ. Gradually, Margery becomes immersed in a life of holiness. She separates from her husband and devotes her life to spiritual experience, which often takes the form of uncontrollable crying. Ultimately, Kemp is able to defend herself against charges of heresy before the archbishop of York.

MIDDLE ENGLISH LYRICS AND BALLADS

The surviving songs of the Middle Ages are assumed to represent only a small fraction of the many songs generated by the people. Some popular songs have come down to us in several versions, but since these compositions were neither courtly nor of the Church, they were not preserved in manuscripts, except by chance.

Secular Lyrics   Lyrics are relatively brief poetic outbursts of emotion, usually about love. One important exception in the Middle English repertoire of lyric poetry is the "simple pleasures of spring" song. "The Cuckoo Song," for example, is a spontaneous outpouring of joyous energy. Like other creatures, the poet-singer experiences the invigorating effects of spring; his song imitates the birds' songs. Observations of springtime's effects on the animal world are also contained in love lyrics of the era. In the first stanza of "Alison," for example, the poet-singer recapitulates spring's effects on plants and birds and then on his own state. He also is aroused by spring, but as his beloved has gone away, he is left with a feeling of bittersweet grief. Likewise, the songs "Fowls in the Frith" and "Now Springs the Spray" combine the topics of spring and lost love. An extremely candid song of this type is "Western Wind," in which the poet gives a short (four lines), anguished cry for his lover and his bed. Unlike this last poem, however, most love lyrics incorporate subtle, courtly notions of separation and longing and of praise for the lady's beauty.

Religious Lyrics

Religious lyrics of the late Middle Ages also praise a lady's beauty, but this time the lady is Mary, the mother of Christ. To the author of "I Sing of a Maiden," for example, Mary is "matchless." Other religious lyrics of the time are holiday caroles or meditations on events in the life of Christ or of other religious figures. Both religious and secular lyrics use the same type of short line stanzas of two, three or four feet with a rhyme pattern called ballad measure. The final line or refrain is a poignant emotional climax.

Ballads

Like lyrics, ballads of the Middle English period arose as popular, orally transmitted forms. Unlike lyrics, however, ballads tell stories. A ballad, therefore, is a narrative with characters, a situation, and action. The ballad narrative may, however, be somewhat vaguely told, with some details merely suggested or hinted at. Because such songs were orally transmitted, the most vivid and sensational parts are the ones most likely to be remembered. Thus the complexities of plot and motivation were often omitted.

The stories ballads tell come from folklore or from folk perceptions of historical figures and events. Most were created during the thirteenth through sixteenth centuries, but ballads continued to be developed and variations introduced even into the eighteenth century, when antiquarians recorded and collected them in print. One of the first great collections was *Reliques of Ancient English Poetry*, published by Thomas Percy in 1765. However, Percy was not always accurate; he "revised" some ballads to "improve" them. The most comprehensive and authoritative collection is F. J. Child's *The English and Scottish Popular Ballads* of 1882, which also contains variants of most ballads.

A typical ballad uses ballad measure, a four-line stanza with a rhyme pattern of a b a b. The lines are short; a four-beat line alternates with a three-beat line. Where the line is longer, as in "Lord Randall," the number of unstressed syllables is expanded. In any case, the stanza fits into a tune, so that unstressed syllables are run together, or elided, as necessary. Many ballads contain a refrain, sometimes of nonsense syllables or words, such as the "down, derry, derry, derry, down, down" of "The Three Ravens." The refrain reinforces a dark and sinister tone. Another common device is incremental or gradual repetitions, such as in "Edward," where the repeated questions of the mother are met with answers that vary only slightly from one stanza to the next. Some suggestive phrases occur in many ballads. Variants of "make my bed soon," for instance, indicate the speaker's sense of imminent death, as in "Lord Randall" and "Barbara Allen." Many ballads obscurely or eerily describe some tragic event. In "The Wife of Usher's Well," for example, a widow's three absent sons return as ghosts, having drowned at sea. Their ghostliness is hinted at rather than stated in such a way that the listener realizes that the men are dead while the mother appears not to. The effect can be quite dramatic, especially when the dialogue moves the story to its climax. The wide appeal of these ballads accounts for their survival over centuries of oral transmission.

MEDIEVAL DRAMA

Drama was popular in the medieval period: that is, it was created for people at large rather than for a courtly audience. The local priests and the people of the towns created, supported, and performed early plays as part of their religious life. As the drama matured, it became separated from religious ceremony, but its broad popular appeal remained essential.

Mystery Plays

One of the first mystery plays was the Easter play, in which four priests represented an angel and the three Marys who came to Christ's tomb on Easter morning. This dramatization took place before the altar of the church. When the Angel asks the Marys whom they are seeking, they respond that they seek the body of Christ. The Angel replies in Latin, "He is risen," at which point that joyous refrain resounds through the church. From these simple beginnings, the play was expanded to show more details, and plays about the rest of Christ's life were developed. Later the major events of the Old Testament were dramatized.

Eventually, the plays became so popular and so extensively detailed that their entertainment value began to predominate over their religious lessons. The plays were moved out of the church and into a public place. Certain prosperous towns gave yearly performances on the Feast of Corpus Christi. Each of the craft guilds of the town undertook to present one play, with guild members refining the script, making the costumes, and performing the roles. In a fully developed cycle of plays, the townsfolk and neighboring peasants could watch dramatizations of all the major events in the history of Christianity, from Adam and Eve in the Garden of Eden through the Resurrection of Christ, on a series of mobile platforms or wagons, called pageants, that were stationed about the town. These were called mystery plays because they showed the religious mystery of God's influence in the world. The biblical characters were represented as being similar to the folk of the English town; no attempt was made for historical accuracy. It became conventional to depict some characters humorously; for example, the wife of Noah in the ark was portrayed as a comically disagreeable, nagging scold.

The written scripts for these plays were produced largely by the local clergy. Some of their authors, whose names are not known, were obviously very talented writers. Working with traditional scripts, they often created subtle characters and rich plots that both entertained and taught a moral lesson to the faithful.

The plays were composed in complex verse form, usually with rhymed stanzas. The lines of each stanza varied from four to three feet in length, with some short or "bob" lines of a single foot. Frequent alliteration provided emphasis and perhaps also helped the amateur actors remember their lines.

THE SECOND SHEPHERD'S PLAY

This play comes from the manuscript of a cycle of plays by the Wakefield Master, who wrote for the town of Wakefield about 1400–1450. The play depicts the biblical event of the announcement of Christ's birth to the shepherds in the fields as being surrounded by amusing incidents based on folk life. The shepherds complain of their difficult work, the hard times they are living in, and their exploitation by landlords. Their problems, of course, reflect medieval social conditions, not those at the time of Christ's birth. The character Mak is reminiscent of the tricksters in some of Chaucer's tales, while the comic action develops surprising parallels to the biblical event. For example, Mak, the thief, announces a birth to the shepherds, but it is a fake. Mak and his complaining wife, Gill, attempt to hide a sheep they have stolen by pretending it is their newborn child. At first the searching shepherds are fooled, but their charitable impulse to give the child a gift brings them back into the house and enables them to discover their missing sheep. After making a number of jokes to the effect that Mak's "child" resembles him, the shepherds again act charitably by not giving Mak up to the law but executing their own mild justice by tossing him up in a blanket. These worthy shepherds then receive the divine message of the birth of Christ and go forth to seek Him. The final scene with Mary and the infant changes the tone from farcical to reverent, but the play is unified by the parallels of the actions of searching, discovering, and giving gifts.

THE YORK *PLAY OF THE CRUCIFIXION*

In the prosperous town of York during the fifteenth century, a playwright called the York Realist, whose identity is not known, developed a cycle of mystery plays with unusual emphasis on the suffering of Christ. In the *Play of the Crucifixion*, he presents the Roman soldiers as they nail Christ to the cross. They are callous men, preoccupied with getting a difficult job done, concerned about wedging the cross upright, and scornful of Jesus. Their attitudes contrast with the mildness of Jesus' brief speech of forgiveness, thus emphasizing the merciful message of the Crucifixion as well as the physical harshness of the act itself.

Morality Plays

At about the same time that mystery plays were being developed into elaborate and lengthy cycles, another form of play emerged. Not much is known about the authorship or the actual production of morality plays. Toward the end of the fifteenth century, these plays may have had some semiprofessional production, but at first they must have been put on by the guilds or the clergy because there were no other kinds of actors during the medieval period. A morality play differs from a mystery play in that rather than depicting events from the Bible it portrays virtues and vices in competition for the soul. In a morality play, each abstract quality considered an obstacle or an aid to salvation, such as idleness or penance, is personified. These characters are set in motion in a plot that depicts the vices' devious and sometimes comic struggles to win control of the individual's soul. The religious teaching dominates and leads to a happy conclusion—salvation rather than damnation.

EVERYMAN

The anonymous play *Everyman* was written about 1485 and printed early the next century. It is composed of rather loosely written couplets with many irregularities of rhyme and meter. The central character, Everyman, who stands for every Christian person, is confronted with Death, who comes to Everyman in the midst of his idleness and ignorance. Everyman pleads for time to prepare to die. Frightened, he first asks his usual supporters, Fellowship, Kindred and Cousin, and Goods (wealth) to go with him, but they all refuse. Then, in a self-searching soliloquy, Everyman concludes that he needs better helpers to cope with Death. Everyman then turns to Knowledge and Good Deeds. Knowledge takes him to confession and shows him the usefulness of his own qualities: Discretion, Strength, Five-Wits, and Beauty, all of whom appear as characters. At the ultimate moment of death, however, Everyman is accompanied to salvation only by Good Deeds.

The play aims to warn and to teach. It has repeated metaphors of account books, reckoning, and payment, indicating to the Christian audience the need to build up a stock of virtues to balance against sins at the final judgment.

These plays, with their realistic dialogue, rich characterizations, and sensational action, laid the foundation for the great flowering of drama in the following era; they are the artistic ancestors of Shakespeare and his contemporaries. The mixture of the comic and the serious, the use of soliloquies, and the vigorous action are all enduring traits of English drama.

SIR THOMAS MALORY (1408–1471)

Like most medieval authors, Sir Thomas Malory left little information about himself, but legal records of the time show that he was imprisoned for various crimes during most of the last two decades of his life. During that time, the era of the War of the Roses, Malory devoted himself to retelling, largely from French sources, the stories of King Arthur and his Knights of the Round Table.

Malory and the End of Chivalry

Like the legends, Malory's book *Morte Darthur* is long and loosely arranged, with many minor characters. But the book serves to sum up the end of the era, the age of chivalry and romance. Malory's book was among the first printed in England. Its printer, William Caxton, prepared an edition in 1485, in which he included a somewhat skeptical preface pointing out the dubious historical status of Arthur and his knights.

MORTE DARTHUR

Although the title means "the death of Arthur," Malory covers all the legendary adventures of Arthur, from his drawing out the sword Excalibur from a stone, thus identifying himself as the true king, through the various trials and adventures of his knights. Arthur's death provides the tragic climax and conclusion of the work. The romance is written in prose, unlike other romantic literature before 1420. Malory's style is simple and natural; he creates realistic dialogue between the characters, making his book seem very modern. The poignant dialogue between Lancelot and Guinevere, for example, recreates the timeless situation of distressed lovers who see that separation is inevitable. The concluding passages of the book show how the adulterous love of these two resulted in the breakup of the Round Table, the pitting of knight against knight, and the final confrontation between Arthur and his son Sir Mordred, in which the king is fatally wounded. Sir Bedivere, whom Arthur calls upon for help, acts in bad faith by trying to keep the jeweled sword Excalibur for himself. Finally Bedivere helps Arthur into the barge that carries the king to death and to paradise, Avilion. Guinevere and Lancelot, oppressed by their sins, languish and die. Thus Camelot, the ideal representing the old order, is gone.

Caxton's printing of Malory's book marks a point of transition from medieval to Renaissance culture.

Malory was correct when he depicted in Morte Darthur the passing of a glorious age. The English would have to wait until the second half of the sixteenth century for new great poets to arise. But meanwhile, the rich and varied popular tradition continued to develop. The drama gradually became professionalized, and songs and ballads were embellished and handed down. Although Renaissance literature would borrow refinements from Italy and France, these would be grafted onto the strong stock of the native English tradition.

Selected Readings

Barber, Richard. *King Arthur: Hero and Legend.* 3rd ed. Ipswich: Boydell, 1986.

Cawley, A. C., ed. *Everyman, and Medieval Miracle Plays.* New York: Dutton, 1956.

Dillon, Bert. *A Malory Handbook.* Boston: G. K. Hall, 1978.

Dunn, Charles W. and Edward T. Byrnes. *Middle English Literature. Rev. ed.* New York and London: Garland, 1990.

Spearing, A. C. *Criticism and Medieval Poetry.* New York: Barnes, 1972.

Vasta, Edward, comp. *Middle English Survey: Critical Essays.* Notre Dame, IN: University of Notre Dame, 1965.

Weston, Jessie L., ed. *The Chief Middle English Poets.* New York: Houghton, 1914.

6

English Renaissance Literature (1485 to 1603): Renaissance Period

1482–1509	Reign of Henry VII
1485	Caxton publishes Malory's *Morte Darthur*
1485–1500	Morality play *Everyman*
1485–1603	Henry VII begins Tudor line of English monarchs
1490–1520	Humanist education established at English universities: classical scholarship, biblical and literary criticism
1492	Columbus reaches America, claims the New World for Spain
1497	John Cabot claims North America for England
1498	Da Vinci completes fresco *The Last Supper*
1501	First collection of polyphonic music printed
1508–1512	Michelangelo paints frescoes in Sistine Chapel
1509	Erasmus visits England
1509–1547	Reign of Henry VIII
c. 1511	Erasmus, *In Praise of Folly*
1516	More, *Utopia*
1517	Luther posts his "Ninety-five Theses" in Wittenberg; Protestant Reformation begins

1517–1518	More, *History of Richard III*
1519	Cortez conquers Mexico
1519–1522	Ferdinand Magellan's fleet circumnavigates the globe
1520	Pope Leo X excommunicates Luther
c. 1520	Skelton's poetical satire: personal, political, and ecclesiastical
1525	Tyndale, *New Testament*: first printed English translation of any part of the Bible; influenced later phrasing
1529	First use of the term *Protestant*
1529–1532	Thomas More, Lord Chancellor of England
1532	Machiavelli's *The Prince* published; Calvin, *Institutes of the Christian Religion*
c. 1533	Rabelais writes first books of *Gargantua and Pantagruel*
1534	Act of Supremacy formalizes Henry VIII's break with Rome; Henry VIII head of Church of England; Cartier explores St. Lawrence River for France
1535	Henry VIII begins confiscation of monastic properties; old manuscripts lost or destroyed
1535	Coverdale's first complete English Bible
1540	"The Great Bible," in English, installed in churches
1543	Copernicus, *On the Revolution of the Spheres*
1545	Reign of Edward VI
c. 1545	Laws passed making traveling actors subject to arrest as vagabonds
1548–1552	*Book of Common Prayer* published
c. 1552	Udall, *Ralph Roister Doister*, first real English comedy
1553–1558	Reign of Mary Tudor
c. 1555	Roper, *Life of Sir Thomas More*; Cavendish, *Life of Cardinal Wolsey*
1557	*Tottel's Miscellany*, (Songs and Sonnets); Stationers' Company incorporated
1558	Knox, *First Blast of the Trumpet against the Monstrous Regiment of Women*
1558–1603	Reign of Elizabeth I
1561	Hoby's translation of Castiglione's *Il Cortegiano (The Courtier)*
1563	Sackville's "Induction" to portion of *Mirror for Magistrates*
1564	Papacy publishes *Index of Prohibited Books*
1567	Golding publishes translation of Ovid, *Metamorphoses*
1570	Ascham, *Schoolmaster*
1576	The Theatre built, London's first permanent structure for the presentation of plays

1579   Publication of Spenser's *The Shepheardes Calender*

1582   Sidney, *The Defense of Poesy*

1584–1585   Raleigh's first of three voyages to North America; Raleigh fails in effort to colonize Virginia

c. 1587   Marlowe, *Tamburlaine*

1587   Monteverdi; first book of madrigals

1588   War between England and Spain; defeat of Spanish Armada

c. 1590   Shakespeare begins career as playwright

1590   Spenser, *The Faerie Queene*, Books 1–3

c. 1590–1625   High point of English secular song and instrumental music

1591   Sidney, *Astrophel and Stella*, sonnet cycle

1592–1593   Marlowe, *Dr. Faustus*

1593   Shakespeare, *Venus and Adonis*

1594   Nashe, *The Unfortunate Traveler*

1595   Sidney's *The Defense of Poesy* published

1596   Spenser, *The Faerie Queene*, Books 4–6

1597   Shakespeare, play *Henry IV*

1597   Bacon, first edition of *Essays*

1598   Ben Jonson begins career as playwright

1599   The Globe Theatre built; occupied by the Chamberlain Men, the company of actors with which Shakespeare was associated

1602   Shakespeare's *Hamlet* published

1603–1625   Reign of James I, first Stuart monarch

Under the rule of the great Tudor monarchs Henry VII, Henry VIII, and Elizabeth I, the English nation grew and prospered, emerging in the seventeenth century as a major European power, the economic and military rival of both France and Spain.

During the 120 years of Tudor rule, England gradually changed from a feudal society to one focused on manufacture and trade. Woolen goods were the chief product. Henry VII put English shipping under government protection and arranged commercial agreements with other nations. Exploration by sea brought new wealth.

More people could read; printing made books more available; and as more people lived in towns, fewer were deprived of cultural stimulation. The literature of the Tudor era tended to be conservative. Although new literary forms developed, the world depicted in poetry and drama was still the old feudal world of the court and country folk. A middle class had not yet emerged. Theater was an urban phenomenon, but on stage the audience saw the castle or the battlefield more than the city street.

RELIGION AND NATIONALISM

During the reign of Henry VIII, the Roman Catholic church was displaced as the national religion in favor of the newly established Church of England or Anglican church, with the monarch as the head. This "national" church reinforced the patriotic identity of the English against the Roman Catholic powers of Europe. Later, the figure of Queen Elizabeth I came to symbolize the glory and independence of England. Nevertheless, religious teaching remained an important subject of literature, along with the celebration of English history and culture. When European literary forms, such as the sonnet, were imported into England, they were quickly adapted to the English language and English attitudes. During this same period, London became not only the center of government and commerce but also a place of thriving theaters and a focal point of literary innovations. The great aristocratic families of England had sufficient leisure and wealth to patronize poets and to dabble in writing poetry themselves.

EDUCATION AND THE RENAISSANCE MAN

One of the central ideas explored in Renaissance literature is the education of the prince; that is, how the young man of high birth should be trained—intellectually, physically, and spiritually—so that he conforms as closely as possible to the ideals of his aristocratic culture and class. The ideal of the times was the "Renaissance man," who was able to perform equally well on horseback in battles, when singing a love song, and when dancing at a ball. The Renaissance man was learned, temperate, and generous. He had a well-cultivated sense of honor and truth and behaved like a Christian warrior. He respected ladies and even rescued them when necessary.

This ideal of the Renaissance man was a product of the courtly medieval tradition, but it also reflected the ideas of the new humanism, the intellectual movement that began in Europe with the revival of the study of ancient Greek and Roman texts.

HUMANISM

Unlike medieval church teachings, which depicted this world as merely a trial in preparation for the next, classical literature stressed living in the present and cultivating and enjoying the pleasures and satisfactions of the here and now.

The goal of humanism was the study of human institutions and political behavior for their own sakes, and possibly for their improvement. Men began to attend Oxford and Cambridge not to become clergymen, but to become fluent in ancient languages and to attain a kind of polish and worldly wisdom. Education became important not only because it improved the individual but because it improved society.

PATRONAGE

Poets of this time still depended largely on patronage, that is, on the gifts and support of wealthy persons. Therefore, most literature was written for a courtly or aristocratic audience. Poems were still circulated in manuscript copies. Not all poetry was written for patronage; some wealthy talented individuals wrote poetry *and* practiced their other accomplishments. Even Queen Elizabeth wrote a few poems.

THE THEATER AUDIENCE

The greatest exception to the patronage system was the theater, where acting companies earned money by performing plays and could pay a playwright, a member of the company, to create them. The theatrical business in London did very well during the reign of Elizabeth I, though even then some Puritans were opposed to the theater. Actors were sometimes requested to give performances at court or in the homes of wealthy aristocrats. But popular support for the theater was widespread, and it was this support that gave Elizabethan drama its racy flavor. Intended to appeal to people with a wide range of tastes and levels of education, Elizabethan drama, unlike that of France, for example, had sensational scenes of violence, and scenes of earthy comedy were found in even the most tragic plays. In addition, some of the more powerful elements of the medieval mystery and morality plays persisted in refined form in the new drama of the Renaissance.

FORMS

Partly because of their study of classical literature, writers became more aware of the different conventions of the various types of poetry and drama.

Prose was not yet an important literary medium, although the study of Latin rhetoric stimulated some experiments in the writing of formal prose.

The medieval romance still influenced the narrative form. Additionally, renewed awareness of classical epics meant that stories were still told in verse, either the lofty poetry of the romantic epic or the more humble poetry of the pastoral romance.

Pastoral Poems

Pastoral poetry deals with the rustic life of shepherds, with their loves and complaints, and with the plain life of the country, far away from courtly ambition and urban strife. The pastoral poem tends to simplify life and to idealize the rustic setting. Its characters are unsophisticated but not vulgar.

Lyrics

The pastoral form is also seen in lyric poetry, in songs and elegies that celebrate a life of simple and rustic peacefulness. Many of these poems revolve around conflicts such as spurned love and a singing competition among shepherds.

Sonnets

Not all medieval lyrics are pastoral. Some imitate complex forms imported from Italy and France.

The most widely imitated form was the Italian sonnet, which very quickly was made more "English" by a generation of poets in the second half of the sixteenth century. The sonnet remains a popular form of English poetry to this day.

The fully developed Elizabethan sonnet cycle is a series of love sonnets written by one poet about his courtship of and devotion to a single woman. Sonnets were circulated privately in manuscript; besides, printers began to collect and publish anthologies of sonnets, helping spread the popularity of this type of poetry.

TOTTEL'S MISCELLANY

The full title of *Tottel's Miscellany* was *Songs and Sonnets Written by the Right Honorable Lord Henry Howard Late Earl of Surrey and Others*. This book, published in 1557 by the printer Richard Tottel, was one of the most popular and influential anthologies of lyrics. Of its 271 poems, about 40 are by Surrey; the rest represent several other poets. The authorship of about one-third of the poems is unknown. The many models of distinct lyric forms that the book contains were imitated by people of poetic inclination, including nobles, gentlemen, and ladies. This flowering of lyric creativity culminated in the great sonnet cycles of the 1590s.

Dramatic Forms

Dramatic forms were also increasing in variety and complexity. Despite medieval drama's evolution from church plays rather than from classical literature, by the sixteenth century, scholars at the universities were reading ancient Latin and Greek plays and studying the dramatic theory of Aristotle. These influences became part of the English dramatic material, although the popular theater continued to depend on the dramatic tradition of the morality play while borrowing some stock characters and complex plots from classical literature.

Renaissance playwrights wrote comedies and tragedies and also created tragic-comedies, history plays, and various mixed forms. They ignored the classical idea that plays should have unity of action, putting comic scenes into tragic plays and allowing some comedies to skirt the tragic only by a narrow margin. Elizabethan audiences not only tolerated such complex, mixed forms, they also thrived on the sensational scenes of violence and very sophisticated word play.

After 1576 theaters in the suburbs of London attracted an audience of mixed social classes; plays were also performed privately in the houses of wealthy patrons and even at court.

One very specialized aristocratic entertainment was the masque, which used music and allegorical figures to create a highly artificial performance.

At the other extreme, the city comedies, set in London shops and streets, had realistic characters of the middle and lower classes. One of the first and best of these was Thomas Dekker's *The Shoemaker's Holiday*. Plays were written in verse or prose or in a combination of the two. In the latter the upper-class characters, the royalty and nobility, spoke in verse while the soldiers or servants uttered prose.

The coming together of national and international influences made the Renaissance a rich period in the history of English literature. After the wars of the previous century, England had relative domestic peace under the Tudors. A new sense of national identity and national glory was celebrated by poets and playwrights. At the same time, English poets experimented with new ideas of the humanist thinkers and new literary forms from Italy and France. This encounter with other ideas and forms invigorated English literature and resulted in more elaborate and complicated literary forms. The spirit of the Renaissance was to strive for the ideal.

Selected Readings

Hooper, Walter, comp. *Studies in Medieval and Renaissance Literature.* Cambridge, Eng.: Cambridge University Press, 1966.

Lewis, C. S. *The Discarded Image: An Introduction to Medieval and Renaissance Literature.* Cambridge, Eng.: Cambridge University Press, 1964.

Rivers, Isabel. *Classical and Christian Ideas in English Renaissance Poets: A Student's Guide.* Boston: Allen, 1979.

7

English Renaissance Literature (1485 to 1603): Poetry and the Development of the Sonnet

1490–1520	High Renaissance in Italy
1504	Petrarch eclogues printed
1509–1547	Reign of Henry VIII
c. 1520	Skelton's poetical satire: personal, political, and ecclesiastical
1525	Tyndale, *New Testament*; translation influenced later biblical phrasing
1526–1527	Wyatt travels to France and Italy, where he develops interest in Petrarchan sonnets
c. 1537–1540	*The Court of Venus* miscellany contains a few poems of Wyatt
1554	Surrey's translation in blank verse of Virgil's *Aeneid*, Book 4
1557	*Tottel's Miscellany*, (Songs and Sonnets) included many of Wyatt and Surrey's lyrics and sonnets
1558–1603	Reign of Elizabeth I
1561	Hoby's translation of Castiglione's *Il Cortegiano (The Courtier)*
1572	Massacre of St. Bartholomew's Day in Paris
1579	Spenser's *The Shepheardes Calender* published

1590   Spenser, *The Faerie Queene*, Books 1–3

1591   Sidney, *Astrophel and Stella*, sonnet cycle published posthumously

1592   Daniel, *Delia* sonnet cycle

1593   Shakespeare, *Venus and Adonis*; Constable's and Lodge's sonnet cycles

1594   Shakespeare, *The Rape of Lucrece*; Drayton, *Idea* sonnet cycle

1595   Spenser, *Amoretti* and *Epithalamion*; Sidney's *The Defense of Poesy*

1596   Spenser, *The Faerie Queene*, Books 4–6

1599–1600   Marlowe's *The Passionate Shepherd to His Love* and Raleigh's *Answer to Marlowe* published

1602   Campion, *Observations in the Art of English Poesie*

1609   Shakespeare's sonnets published

1621   Publication of Wroth's *Urania* includes sonnet cycle *Pamphilia to Amphilanthus*

During the Renaissance poetry flourished in many lyric forms and in the narrative and epic forms as well. Poets' striving to express their delight in sensual pleasures and at the same time to realize their humanistic ideals gave the poetry of this era great beauty and force. The greatest and most accomplished poet of the time was Spenser, who wrote in many forms, including the epic, considered the highest form of all. But the playwrights Marlowe and Shakespeare also wrote important poems, and many other poets enriched the poetic scene, showing that the English language was capable of refined poetic expression. Individual poets found that they could link their private feelings to the developing body of the poetic images.

THE SONNET FORM

The sonnet is a poem having fourteen lines. It was used in Italy by Dante and especially by Petrarch (1304–1374), who wrote a series of sonnets, or a sonnet cycle, to his beloved Laura. The sonnet's complexity made it unlike any of the native English lyric forms of poetry. A very highly structured statement is compressed into its fourteen lines. It relies on an alert reader to notice and appreciate subtle variations of rather narrowly restricted subjects and images. It was a challenge to the English sonneteers.

THE ITALIAN SONNET

Italian sonnets have a two-part structure. The fourteen lines are divided into an octave (eight lines) and a sestet (six lines), each part having a separate set of rhymes. Petrarch also established certain conventions or rules about the attitudes and feelings that the sonnet-writing poet/lover could express:

> he praises the beauty of his beloved lady and finds her ideal;
>
> he suffers from her coldness or from her rejection of his love;
>
> he mopes and loses sleep and neglects himself and his own interests;
>
> sometimes he feels hope when she smiles at him;
>
> ultimately his love is unfulfilled and he must resign himself.

The poet's consolation is that his beloved has inspired him to create the poems; the very sonnets that give the history of his love will also make that love immortal. These experiences and feelings are expressed in many elaborated metaphors called conceits.

EARLY ENGLISH SONNETS

Although Chaucer had used some continental sonnet forms in his lyrics of the late medieval period, his innovations did not find immediate followers. In the mid-sixteenth century, however, Sir Thomas Wyatt went back to Italian models and rediscovered the sonnet.

Sir Thomas Wyatt the Elder (1503–1543)

When Wyatt began to write sonnets in the Petrarchan form, he followed many of the conventions the Italian poet Petrarch had established. Wyatt's results, however, were not always smooth. He used the iambic pentameter line and retained Petrarch's division of the fourteen lines into octave and sestet, but he began to rhyme the last two lines, forming a final couplet that soon became the hallmark of the English sonnet. Wyatt also wrote lyrics in other forms.

Henry Howard, earl of Surrey (1517–1547)

Another courtier-poet of the time was Henry Howard, the earl of Surrey, who, influenced by his friend Wyatt, took up the sonnet form and developed it into a smoother, more musical poem. Surrey also went back to the source, Petrarch, and translated some of his sonnets.

Instead of dividing the sonnet into octave and sestet, Surrey used three four-line units (quatrains) and a concluding couplet—the same form of sonnet later adopted by Shakespeare. The sonnet form was soon taken up by other poets and was further advanced by the publication of the anthology *Tottel's Miscellany* in 1557.

Besides revolutionizing the sonnet, Surrey was also the first English poet to develop blank verse, that is, iambic pentameter written with no rhyme. The playwright Marlowe later adapted blank verse to the drama.

SONNET CYCLES

None of these early sonneteers, however, composed cycles of sonnets to tell the story of an entire courtship. The first important sonnet cycle was written by Sir Philip Sidney, whose *Astrophel and Stella*, published in 1591, aroused new interest in the form.

The 1590s became the decade of sonnet cycles. In 1592 Samuel Daniel wrote the cycle *Delia*. Sonnet cycles by Henry Constable and Thomas Lodge, among others, appeared the next year. Michael Drayton first published his sonnet sequence *Idea* in 1594, but he revised and republished it several times during the next ten years. In *Amoretti*, finished in 1595, Edmund Spenser varied the Petrarchan sonnet pattern by allowing the lover and his lady to marry. He also used a smoother interlocking rhyme scheme of his own invention.

The most famous sonnet cycle written during the 1590s was Shakespeare's, although it was not published until 1609. The Shakespearian cycle represents a departure from Petrarchan conventions: some of the sonnets are addressed not to a lady but to a young male friend whom Shakespeare urges to marry; some are angry or satiric; many meditate on the passage of time.

LATER ENGLISH SONNETEERS

Early in the next century, Lady Mary Wrothe wrote an unusual sonnet cycle—unusual in that the speaker of the poems, the lover, is a woman. The cycle was titled *Pamphilia and Amphilanthus*. These names mean "all loving" and "he who loves two," indicating that the beloved is unfaithful. Shakespeare seems to have liberated the sonnet form from its Petrarchan model, and later poets such as John Donne, John Milton, and William Wordsworth used it to write about many subjects other than love.

Sir Philip Sidney (1554–1586)

Born into a powerful and aristocratic family, Philip Sidney was considered by some contemporaries to embody the ideal qualities of the courtier and the Renaissance man. After studying at Oxford, Sidney took a grand tour of Europe, where he witnessed the massacre of Protestants in France. While Sidney was a courtier and diplomat for Queen Elizabeth I, he was also a patron of other poets. He wrote his essay *The Defense of Poesy* as an argument for the importance of literature and the role of the poet.

Sidney's sister, Mary Herbert, was the countess of Pembroke; she shared his poetic interests, and it was for her that he wrote the prose romance *Arcadia*.

Sidney died a heroic death. At the age of thirty-two, he received a fatal wound in a battle against the Spanish in Holland. It is told that after he was wounded he called for a drink of water, but when it was brought, he saw a common soldier, also wounded, being carried past him. He gave the soldier the water, saying, "Thy necessity is yet greater than mine."

ASTROPHEL AND STELLA

This cycle of sonnets by Sidney, published posthumously in 1591 but written during the previous decade, consists of 108 sonnets and eleven songs in other forms. It follows the conventions of the Italian sonneteer Petrarch, loosely telling the story of an unfulfilled love between the poet/lover Astrophel, whose name means star-lover, and the lady Stella, whose name means star. The real woman in question, Penelope Devereux, married another suitor, Lord Robert Rich, and Sidney makes puns on the name Rich in some of the sonnets; for example, in Sonnet 37.

As in most sonnet cycles, in *Astrophel and Stella* Sidney presents a series of poems covering the various mood swings of the lover, from admiration to conflict and from hope to despair to resignation. In the opening sonnet of the cycle, Sidney describes the difficulty of writing about his feelings; he feels helpless until his Muse tells him to "look in thy heart."

Sonnet 39 is one of the most famous of this cycle. In it the lover calls on Sleep to release him from his restless longings. He promises Sleep that he will see Stella in his dreams. As in many sonnets, the name of the lady in the final line stands as a sort of answer to or compensation for the anquish that the poem has described.

THE DEFENSE OF POESY

Sidney wrote this essay in 1582, partly in response to an attack on literature by the Puritan critic Stephen Gosson. Sidney was well acquainted, however, with the traditional defenses of poetry found in classical literature. He disagreed with Plato's conclusion that poets' fictions are merely lies. Sidney claimed that poets do not pretend to tell the same sort of truths that historians tell, since these are confined to facts, or that philosophers tell, since these seek abstract and general truths. Sidney held that the poet can invent new worlds that are better, more ideal than the real world. Sidney also surveyed contemporary English poetry and found that it lacked both polish and energy. He ends his "defense" with a scornful denunciation of men with "earth-creeping" minds who cannot enjoy poetry.

Edmund Spenser (1552–1599)

Unlike Sidney, his aristocratic patron, Edmund Spenser went to Cambridge University as an impoverished student. He spent most of his life as the assistant to and the dependent of men of wealth and power. Although he had strong Puritan beliefs, he was also very much interested in the technical problems of writing English verse, and he experimented both with forms and with the effects of various meters and lengths of stanza. He often used old-fashioned spellings to give his poetic language an antique quality.

While Spenser was employed as a secretary to the earl of Leicester, he became acquainted with the earl's nephew, Philip Sidney. Sidney, who was also interested in the technical aspects of English poetry and who became Spenser's patron, did not approve of Spenser's quaint spellings.

In 1580 Spenser became secretary to Lord Grey of Wilton, who was then the queen's deputy in Ireland; thereafter, Spenser spent the rest of his life, except for brief visits to London, in Ireland. There he worked on his huge epic poem, *The Faerie Queene*, which he did not live to finish.

THE SHEPHEARDES CALENDER

In this early work, published in 1579, Spenser experimented with many different kinds of meter. The Calender consists of twelve poems, one for each month. This type of poem is called an eclogue, which is a form of pastoral poem in which shepherds conduct a dialogue in alternating stanzas or one shepherd sings to another. The purpose of this form is to create a rich and beautiful effect.

Spenser's eclogues are ornamented with references to pagan gods and goddesses, the sun, the moon, and the maiden queen. The eclogue for April is in praise of Queen Elizabeth I. The August eclogue presents a singing contest between shepherds. In the October eclogue Spenser complains of the neglect of poetry and poets.

THE FAERIE QUEENE

Like Chaucer's *Canterbury Tales*, Spenser's *The Faerie Queene* is a long, unfinished work. The new verse form developed by Spenser for this complex poem is called the Spenserian stanza. It consists of eight lines of iambic pentameter with a rhyme scheme of a b a b b c b c, plus one more line of six rather than five feet, rhyming with the *c* sound.

The nine-line stanza serves as a paragraph in verse. It is long enough to contain a description, an extended metaphor or a unit of the narration, any of which can be climaxed or summed up in the long last line. Or the long last line can be a transitional link to the next stanza.

The Spenserian stanza is flexible enough to sustain the various moods and strategies of an imaginatively told, highly ornamented narration.

In his introductory Letter, Spenser explains the poem's plan. Set in the time of King Arthur, each of the twelve books of the romantic epic was to introduce a knight who would represent one of the twelve virtues of a prince. Spenser finished only the first six books:

	Virtue	Champion
Book I	Holiness	Redcrosse
Book II	Temperance	Sir Guyon
Book III	Chastity	Britomart (a female knight)
Book IV	Friendship	Cambel and Triamond
Book V	Justice	Sir Artegal
Book VI	Courtesy	Calidore

In another of the books of *The Faerie Queene* Spenser also wrote some cantos or stanzas on the subject of mutability or change. All the virtues were to be combined in Magnificence or Prince Arthur, who appears in several books.

Besides giving examples of courtesy or correct behavior, the poem unites romantic adventures with a moral allegory. The Queene of the title is Gloriana, who represents Queen Elizabeth I.

A Letter of the Authors. In the preface called "A Letter of the Authors," Redcrosse presents himself at the Queene's court during a feast and begs to be assigned some heroic task that will prove his strength. When a lady comes in seeking the rescue of her parents, Redcrosse insists on undertaking the challenge.

Book I. The first book consists of twelve parts called cantos (Italian for songs). Redcrosse rides out to save the parents of Lady Una; his horse is a gift of Gloriana. Una, whose name stands for the one true church, the Church of England, rides behind on a white ass. They are followed by a Dwarfe, carrying her bag. Redcrosse is as yet untried; he still must prove himself. To avoid a rainstorm, Redcrosse leads Una into the wandering wood, to the den of the monster Errour. Redcrosse fights this ugly, stinking creature, defeating her at the third blow. This first victory, however, has come easily, because Errour is easily recognized as monstrous. As he moves on, Redcrosse is trapped by more subtle enemies, such as Archimago, the magician disguised as a holy hermit; and Duessa, the false, or Roman Catholic, church, who disguises herself as Fidessa, a maiden in distress. Through her Redcrosse is temporarily separated from Una and for a time becomes involved in combat with Duessa's three champions, Sansfoy (without faith), Sansloy (lawless), and Sansjoy (joyless). Redcrosse and Duessa visit the palace of Lucifera (pride) and witness a spectacular procession of the Seven Deadly Sins. Meanwhile, Una wanders amid perils until she is found by Prince Arthur. Una then brings Prince Arthur to the rescue of Redcrosse, who has been imprisoned in a dungeon by the Gyant. Arthur slays the Gyant and frees Redcrosse, who is finally reunited with Una. They go off together to seek and destroy the Dragon who has confined Una's parents, the king and queene. Redcrosse is victorious in his battle against this Dragon, and at the conclusion of Book I he is betrothed to Una.

Each book of *The Faerie Queene* is similarly full of fanciful adventures, sinister foes, and monsters to be slain, all allegorically representing the moral and evil forces of the world. Spenser embellishes each story with many allusions to biblical, historical, and classical events and characters. Exemplary stories are added, and characters whom the reader at first takes at face value turn out to be much more complex and sinister.

Spenser's Puritan beliefs dictate the underlying doctrines of the narration, but he is neither puritanical nor narrow-minded in his use of rich and sensuous descriptive passages.

AMORETTI

Amoretti means "little loves." Unlike most sonnet cycles, this cycle ends not in the despair or resignation of the lover but with his marriage, celebrated in another poem as the wedding song *Epithalamion.* Both were published in 1595.

In *Amoretti,* Spenser also uses the unusually difficult rhyme scheme a b a b   b c b c   c d c d   e e, which allows for only five different rhyme sounds in the fourteen lines.

Although Spenser employs some of the conventional Petrarchan themes in examining the progress of his love, he is more concerned with presenting the "true fair," or spiritual beauty, of which the physical beauty of his beloved is merely a reflection. (In this Spenser adopts ideas about love presented by Castiglione in *The Courtier.*)

The sonnets in *Amoretti* praise Elizabeth Boyle, Spenser's second wife. In Sonnet 79, he says that her "gentle wit" and "virtuous mind" are derived from the "fayre Spirit" or God, the source of all perfect beauty.

EPITHALAMION

This marriage song, based on Greek and Latin models, is Spenser's personal statement of joy on his marriage.

The poet/bridegroom calls his lady to awake on the morning of their wedding day. He richly describes her beauty, her procession to the church, the ceremony, his taking home of his bride, the celebration of church bells, the bridegroom's impatience for night to come, and the final "sweet pleasures" from which the new generation will be born.

Underlying its simple events, the poem's complex structure alludes to the passage of time, the seasons, and the hours of the day. These allusions, along with many references to classical gods and goddesses, tend to make the poem universal, so that it refers not only to this particular marriage but to all marriages and even to the ideal of marriage.

SHAKESPEARIAN SONNETS

The climax of the development of the English sonnet was the cycle of sonnets written by William Shakespeare during the 1590s. Shakespeare did not address his sonnets to a beloved lady but to a friend whom he calls "Master W. H." The exact identity of this person is a mystery that has fascinated scholars to this day. The opening sonnets of the cycle are spoken to a fair young friend who is urged by the poet to marry and to have children so as to perpetuate copies of himself for the future. The cycle then moves on to other topics. Some sonnets are addressed to a lady, and there is an implication, most explicitly stated in Sonnet 144, that the poet, the friend, and the lady may form a love triangle. The poet goes on to consider his own mortality as he observes himself growing old.

The tone of Shakespeare's sonnets varies from mocking satire, as in Sonnet 130, to righteous anger, as in Sonnet 129. If there is one overriding theme, it is time and the effects of the passage of time on human lives.

OTHER ELIZABETHAN LYRICS

The second half of the sixteenth century saw a great flowering of lyric poetry, of which the sonnet was only one important part. It was an aspect of a courtier's role to write lyric poems, and even members of royalty wrote songs or sonnets, often blending the fashionable Italian or French forms with the native materials of the popular lyric.

Queen Elizabeth I herself wrote occasional poems dealing with the emotional conflicts of her position as both woman and ruler. Another learned woman, Mary Herbert, countess of Pembroke, wrote some influential verse paraphrases of the Psalms. She was encouraged in this work by her brother, Sir Philip Sidney; she shared his interest in various metrical patterns, and it was he who initiated the project of rewriting the Psalms as English lyrics.

Other lyricists were interested in making verses for musical settings.

Sir Walter Raleigh (1552–1618)

A soldier and explorer as well as a writer, Raleigh organized colonizing expeditions to America, eventually arriving in Virginia. Raleigh's contemporaries knew him as a colorful and energetic courtier, one of Queen Elizabeth's favorites. After her death, however, King James I confined Raleigh to the Tower of London as a traitor. Raleigh was eventually beheaded.

Raleigh's friend the playwright Christopher Marlowe had written a very popular poem, *The Passionate Shepherd to His Love*, which presented the sweet ideal of pastoral love.

THE NYMPH'S REPLY TO THE SHEPHERD

Raleigh's poem is a parody written in response to Marlowe. In it Raleigh questions the possibility of ideal and simple love among the fields and flocks. His description of the coming of winter and of old age gives a cynical, or at least a realistic, answer to the pastoral.

Thomas Campion (1567–1620)

Campion was a composer, a musician, and a poet. He published a series of songbooks, of which *The Book of Ayres*, published in 1601, was the first. Campion was an advocate of quantitative verse, which is a meter characterized by alternating long and short syllables rather than stressed and unstressed syllables. Although he did not succeed in converting other poets to the use of quantitative verse, his songs were very popular.

THERE IS A GARDEN IN HER FACE

In this poem, perhaps one of his best known, Campion draws together a series of conventional similes—lips are cherries, teeth are pearls, skin combines roses and lilies. The poem sums up the conventions used to praise female beauty.

*T*he poetic richness of the Renaissance was a source of inspiration to later poets. It marks a high point of creativity, variety, and experimentation in sweet lyric poetry and imaginative narrative poetry. Enthusiastic about their roles as national poets of England, Spenser and his contemporaries created a wealth of poetic materials that constituted the heritage of the English poets of later centuries.

Selected Readings

Buxton, John. *Sir Philip Sidney and the English Renaissance*. New York: St. Martin's, 1954.

Harrison, G. B., ed. *Major Plays and Sonnets/Shakespeare*. New York: Harcourt, 1948.

Horton, Ronald Arthur. *The Unity of the Faerie Queene*. Athens: University of Georgia, 1978.

Muir, Kenneth. *Shakespeare's Sonnets*. Boston: Allen, 1979.

Nelson, William. *The Poets of Edmund Spenser: A Study*. New York: Columbia University Press, 1963.

8

English Renaissance Literature (1485 to 1603): Development of the Drama

1490–1520	Humanist education established at English universities: classical scholarship, biblical and literary criticism
1510	Oxford and Cambridge allow acting of Roman comic plays by Terence
1520	Original and translations of Latin plays acted in grammar schools
c. 1533	Rebalais writes first books of *Gargantua and Pantagruel*
c. 1545	Laws passed making traveling actors subject to arrest as vagabonds
1557	*Tottel's Miscellany*, (Songs and Sonnets); Stationers' Company incorporated
1558–1603	Reign of Elizabeth I
1561	Norton and Sackville's blank verse tragic play performed at Inns of Court
1576	The Theatre built, London's first permanent structure for presenting plays
c. 1587	Marlowe's *Tamburlaine* introduces "blank verse" to stage
c. 1588	Marlowe, *The Tragical History of the Life and Death of Doctor Faustus*
c. 1589	Marlowe, *The Jew of Malta*
c. 1593	Marlowe's lesser works *Massacre at Paris* and, in collaboration with Nashe, *Dido, Queen of Carthage*; Marlowe dies
1598	Marlowe's poem *Hero and Leander* completed by George Chapman

1599 Marlowe's poem *Come Live with Me and Be My Love* published in *The Passionate Pilgrim*

The high point of drama in England came during the Renaissance, the era of Shakespeare. Shakespeare flourished at a time when conditions were favorable for the theater, and he was not the only great playwright of his time. Popular drama had developed in the fifteenth century in the form of mystery and morality plays. These plays, presented to audiences not acquainted with the drama of ancient Greece and Rome, were based on situations and characters familiar to the English public. With the rise of humanism in the Renaissance, scholars began to read ancient plays, and schoolboys began to perform them as part of their studies. Later, English writers began to create original plays modeled on these by-now familiar tragedies and comedies. The vitality of popular drama in the form of mystery and morality plays also contributed to what became "the typical" English drama, plays of complex and varied action with intense contrasts and violent sensationalism.

CLASSICAL INFLUENCE

The models for English Renaissance comedy were the Latin playwrights Plautus and Terence. The greatest influence on tragedy was the Latin playwright Seneca, whose plays focused on the hero's fall from high station and great power. From these writers and from the study of Aristotle's *Poetics*, English playwrights derived the idea of different kinds of drama having distinct formal characteristics and effects.

The English playwrights learned to divide the action into acts and scenes; the five-act structure became standard. They also learned to exploit farcical characters and to intensify tragedy with lofty formal speeches. However, English playwrights did not confine themselves to the classic models; the English developed such forms as the historical play and the tragic-comedy.

ACTORS

While the actors of the late fifteenth century had been amateurs, guildsmen or the servants of noble houses, early in the sixteenth century acting began to become a profession, or at least a trade. Skillful actors, possibly servants, would take their performances to other noblemen's houses or to public places, such as inns or courtyards to earn money.

However, as theatrical professionalism grew, so did the opposition from Puritan factions who saw play-acting as the work of the devil. In 1545 Parliament passed laws making traveling actors subject to arrest as vagabonds. Therefore, it was useful for acting companies, even as they became more financially independent and self-supporting, to retain their nominal status as "servants" of some powerful lord.

Companies of boy actors were attached to the Chapel Royal and to St. Paul's Cathedral in London, much as musical choirs were sponsored by religious institutions.

THEATERS

As London grew, it was able to provide a large enough audience to support permanent acting companies. These groups erected their own buildings in which to present their plays.

In 1576 the first such structure, called The Theatre, was built just outside central London; others were built later—also outside London, because of the Puritan influence.

The plan of these early theaters was based on the courtyard, where, until then, plays had usually been performed. The theaters were oval or round structures that were open at the top for light. Plays were put on in the daytime. Three levels of seating rose along the inside walls; these were the seats for upper-class patrons. At ground level, lower-class patrons—servants, apprentices or poor artisans—stood to watch the play. They were called "groundlings."

The stage projected out from one side as a platform for the action. It was equipped with trap doors and curtains in front of a small inner stage at the end near the wall, but essentially it was a bare space, flexible enough to be a throne room in one scene and a street or a battlefield in the next.

In the absence of scenery, actors wore elaborate costumes for visual effect. They spoke vigorously and rapidly; the audience became adept at following complicated and imaginative language. The convention of the aside, a brief speech to the audience by an actor who has turned aside from the other characters on the stage, indicates how close the spectators were to the performance.

THE MASQUE

Sometimes plays were presented by invitation at court or in the large private houses of the aristocracy. In those cases, the play was put on indoors by artificial light, and the audience was small but select.

A theatrical entertainment called a masque was developed specifically for private performance. Masques combined scenery, costumes, music, and dance with very stylized acting to create a fantasy spectacle. Rather than being realistic, the characters represented abstractions, mythical figures or ancient deities.

The masque was an allegory with moral and sometimes political significance. It frequently ended with a tribute to Queen Elizabeth I or to the sponsoring nobleman.

ACTING COMPANIES

By the end of the sixteenth century, the London acting companies were well organized and prosperous. They occupied their own theaters. The major players owned shares in the company and determined what plays would be put on and who would take the various roles. An actor-playwright, such as Shakespeare, might write plays for the company, in which case the important roles would be written with a particular actor's talents in mind. The companies also trained apprentices to act. No women were allowed to join these companies. Therefore, there are few major roles for women in Elizabethan drama. Boy apprentices played the female parts. Plots involving young girls who disguise themselves as boys are common in Renaissance drama; of course, boys were acting the roles of girls who pretended to be boys. Apparently the audience was not confused.

PLAYWRIGHTS

Christopher Marlowe (1564–1593)

A shoemaker's son and a scholarship student at Cambridge University, Marlowe began writing plays while he was still a student. At the same time he was apparently also engaged in some secret service for Queen Elizabeth I; his activities were considered suspicious by college authorities, who wanted to withhold his M.A. degree. The Queen's Privy Council intervened on his behalf.

Marlowe's life was short but intense. His first play, *Tamburlaine*, written in 1587, introduces the main theme of all his tragedies: personal ambition swelled to overwhelming and ultimately tragic proportions. In the six years between his first play and his death, he wrote five more plays.

Marlowe is credited with introducing blank verse—iambic pentameter with no rhyme—as a dramatic line. Ben Jonson later termed it "Marlowe's mighty line." Shakespeare also used it in his plays, and it became the standard for drama.

Marlowe was repeatedly in trouble: he took part in a brawl in which a man was killed; he was accused of being a traitor and an atheist. His death came as the result of a stab wound in an argument over a bill at an inn. He was only twenty-nine years old.

THE TRAGICAL HISTORY OF THE LIFE AND DEATH OF DOCTOR FAUSTUS

The date of the composition of *The Tragical History of the Life and Death of Doctor Faustus* is not known. The play was first published in 1604 and published again in 1616, both times in very imperfect editions. No complete manuscript seems to survive from Marlowe's lifetime. An additional complication arises because some parts of the play were written by an unknown collaborator, who probably wrote most or all of the comic scenes. The very powerful opening scenes and the scene of Faustus's final damnation are clearly by Marlowe; they are the essence of the tragedy. The Faustus character is based on the German folkloric figure of a scholar/magician who sells his soul to the devil.

Act I. In act I Faustus is shown as an accomplished scholar who has mastered all the recognized and legitimate fields of human knowledge. In his opening soliloquy, he recapitulates his achievements in logic, medicine, law, and theology, but he acknowledges that none of this satisfies his intellectual ambition. Faustus's sin is rooted in pride; he wants to go beyond the limits of human learning. He therefore determines to take up the study of magic, which he sees as a means of acquiring godlike powers.

Act II. In act II, consulting magic books, Faustus conjures up Mephistophilis, the first lieutenant of Lucifer, the archdemon. Mephistophilis's calmness and manipulativeness contrast with Faustus's restless curiosity. Faustus himself proposes the fatal bargain. He offers his soul to Lucifer, the chief of all devils, in exchange for twenty-four years of magical powers and self-indulgence. Part of his pleasure, thinks Faustus, will be having Mephistophilis as his servant. In the second scene of act II, Mephistophilis has returned from hell to ratify their agreement with a deed, to be written in Faustus's own blood. Although his blood congeals and his Good Angel warns him against this action, Faustus signs the deed. But as soon as he begins to ask Lucifer to fulfill his promises, the drawbacks of dealing with devils become evident to him. For example, Faustus wants a wife, but since marriage is a church sacrament, Mephistophilis can provide only a whore. When Faustus asks questions about creation, the work of God, Mephistophilis becomes annoyed and conjures up a procession of the Seven Deadly Sins, the spectacular allegorical figures, to distract Faustus from his questions. Faustus is from time to time bothered by impulses toward repentance, but each time the impulses pass by unheeded.

The serious scenes between Faustus and Mephistophilis are mocked by parallel comic scenes with the clown, Robin, and his subordinate companion, Dick. They have stolen one of Faustus's books on magic, which they use to carry out petty theft. These scenes underscore the trivial nature of what magic can provide for humanity.

Acts III and IV. In acts III and IV Faustus goes abroad to Rome, where he plays silly tricks on the Pope, which appealed to the anti-Catholic sentiments of Marlowe's Protestant English audience. In act IV, Faustus has returned to the court of Emperor Charles in Germany. Faustus again shows off his magic powers but still accomplishes only trivial tricks and illusions. Robin and Dick are joined by other "fools" who challenge Faustus and lose. These comic scenes are theatrically good, as when Faustus has a leg pulled off and grows another, but they do little to advance the central discussion of Faustus's soul, except to show that what little he received in his bargain with Lucifer was not worth anything.

Act V. Act V focuses again on the main issue—damnation. After twenty-four years, Faustus faces the end. Having said farewell to his fellow scholars, Faustus locks himself up alone, rejecting the pleading of a mysterious old man that he give up magic and repent. Instead, Faustus conjures up a spirit in the shape of the beautiful Helen of Troy and makes a passionate love speech to it. Now in physical intimacy with an evil spirit, Faustus has sealed his damnation. Still, at the eleventh hour, Faustus begins a powerfully moving final soliloquy in which he curses himself and longs for nonexistence, begging the elements to swallow him up. At the ultimate moment, as midnight strikes, Faustus sees hell gaping before him. In his last line, when it is too late, he cries hysterically, "I'll burn my books." The devils surround him and carry him off, leaving the chorus to speak the moral of the play. Any audience who only half-believed in the presence of devils on earth would be shattered by the final moments of Doctor Faustus.

Marlowe was not the only writer active in the London theater of the 1590s. His contemporaries included Thomas Kyd, John Lyly, Robert Greene, George Peele, and Thomas Dekker, all of whom produced successful plays of various kinds before the end of the century. Ben Jonson's early comedies of humors belong to this era, as do the early plays of Shakespeare. The London theatergoer could choose among revenge tragedies, chronicle history plays, comedies of London life, and romantic comedies. This was the most creative period in the history of English theater.

Selected Readings

Rowse, A. L. *Christopher Marlowe: His Life and Work*. New York: Harper, 1964.

Schelling, Felix E. and Matthew W. Black, eds. *Typical Elizabethan Plays*. New York: Harper, 1949.

9

English Renaissance Literature (1485 to 1603): Shakespeare

1485	Caxton publishes Malory's *Morte Darthur*
1485–1500	Morality play *Everyman*
1490–1520	Humanist education established at English universities
1510	Oxford and Cambridge allow acting of Roman comic plays by Terence
1520	Original and translations of Latin plays acted in grammar schools
c. 1520	Skelton's poetical satire: personal, political, and ecclesiastical
c. 1545	Laws passed making traveling actors subject to arrest as vagabonds
1557	*Tottel's Miscellany*, (Songs and Sonnets); Stationers' Company incorporated
1561	Hoby's translation of Castiglione's *Il Cortegiano (The Courtier)*; Norton and Sackville blank verse tragic play performed at Inns of Court
1576	The Theatre built, London's first permanent structure for the presentation of plays
1582	Shakespeare marries Anne Hathaway
c. 1587	Marlowe's *Tamburlaine* introduces "blank verse" to stage
c. 1590	Shakespeare begins career as playwright
1590	Spenser, *The Faerie Queene*, Books 1–3
c. 1590–1625	High point of English secular song and instrumental music

1592–1593	Drama critic Greene makes disparaging reference to Shakespeare, apparently a well-established actor
1593	Shakespeare, *Venus and Adonis*
1594	Shakespeare, *The Rape of Lucrece*; theaters reopen after plague; Shakespeare a member of Lord Chamberlain's Men players
1595	Sidney's *The Defense of Poesy* published; Shakespeare, *Richard III*
1596	Spenser, *The Faerie Queene*, Books 4–6; Shakespeare, *Romeo and Juliet*, *Midsummer Night's Dream*
1597	Shakespeare, *Henry IV*, Part 1 and Part 2; *Henry V*, *Merry Wives of Windsor*
1597	Bacon, first edition of *Essays*; Shakespeare, *Merchant of Venice*
1598	Shakespeare, *Julius Caesar*; Ben Jonson begins career as playwright
1599	The Globe Theatre built and occupied by the Lord Chamberlain's Men, the company of actors with which Shakespeare was associated; Shakespearian comedies *Much Ado about Nothing*, *As You Like It*, *Twelfth Night*
1602	Shakespeare's *Hamlet* published
1602–1603	Shakespeare, *Troilus and Cressida*, *All's Well that Ends Well*, *Measure for Measure*
1603–1625	Reign of James I, first Stuart monarch
1604	Shakespeare, *Othello*; Marlowe's *The Tragical History of the Life and Death of Doctor Faustus* published
1606	Shakespeare, *Macbeth*, *King Lear*; Jonson, *Volpone*
1607	Shakespeare, *Antony and Cleopatra*
1609	Shakespeare, *Sonnets*
1610	Shakespeare retires to Stratford-on-Avon; writes *Tempest*, *Winter's Tale*, and *Cymbeline*
1611	King James Version of *The Holy Bible* published
1614	Webster, *The Duchess of Malfi*
1616	Shakespeare dies
1623	Heminges and Condell, *First Folio*, first collection of Shakespeare's plays, includes Jonson's poem *In Homage to William Shakespeare*

While the London theatrical scene in the late sixteenth and early seventeenth centuries produced many skilled and worthy playwrights, none was so prolific and versatile as Shakespeare. He wrote more plays and more different kinds of plays than anyone else, and he wrote them better. His contemporaries recognized his stature; either as rivals or as admirers they expressed their awareness of Shakespeare's unique powers. Yet the man himself is elusive. Shakespeare's own personality is hidden behind the many great characters he created.

WILLIAM SHAKESPEARE (1564–1616)

Most scholars consider Shakespeare to be the greatest dramatist of the English language. The son of a businessman, he was born in the provincial town of Stratford-on-Avon. Shakespeare's father is listed in town records as a "glover," or one who sells gloves, but records also show that he engaged in a variety of other enterprises. Although Shakespeare's formal education ended at the local school, his plays show that he was extremely learned and widely read. At eighteen he married Anne Hathaway. The couple had a daughter the next year and twins two years later. Shakespeare did not remain in Stratford; records from 1592 show that he was at that time active in the theatrical world of London. About 1593, when theaters were temporarily closed in London on account of the plague, Shakespeare composed and published the narrative poems *Venus and Adonis* and *The Rape of Lucrece*, both of which he dedicated to his patron, the earl of Southampton. When the theaters reopened in 1594, Shakespeare became a member of the theatrical company called Lord Chamberlain's Men. He worked with this company as an actor, playwright, and stockholder for the rest of his career, and he wrote his best plays, including the great tragedies, for its actors. Shakespeare retired in 1610 and went back to Stratford, where he bought a substantial house and wrote *The Tempest*, his final play. He died in April 1616, probably on his fifty-second birthday.

Myths about Shakespeare

There are two widely circulated myths about Shakespeare. One is that he was an "untutored genius"; that is, that he was not formally educated but had a natural and spontaneous insight, a sort of wild creative inspiration. However, it is obvious from Shakespeare's many allusions to characters and situations of classical literature, the Bible, and history that in fact he had an extensive store of knowledge at his command. He knew the literary conventions of the various types of poetry and drama of his time, although he did not always follow them religiously in his own works.

The second myth is that someone other than Shakespeare wrote the plays attributed to him. This myth, tends to ignore the many town documents, entries of the acting company, and contemporaries' comments revolving around his life and activities as a dramatist. The myth also rests on the conclusion that a person of little education would not be able to write such great plays. Both of these myths, then, seem to arise from a prejudice about the necessary relationship between a university education and solid intellectual or artistic achievement.

THE PLAYS OF SHAKESPEARE

Shakespeare wrote a total of thirty-six or thirty-seven plays; scholars think that one late play may be a collaboration. These plays represent a wide range of types.

As a young man during the early 1590s, Shakespeare wrote mostly light comedies, such as *The Comedy of Errors*, *The Taming of the Shrew*, and *A Midsummer Night's Dream*, and the historical plays. Only one important tragedy belongs to this period—*Romeo and Juliet*, the romantic tragedy of young lovers undone by family feuds. Most of Shakespeare's sonnets also belong to this period.

Between 1595 and 1601 Shakespeare wrote more mature comedies, such as *The Merchant of Venice* and *Twelfth Night*, which take up the issues of mercy and justice, and the satiric comedy *As You Like It*. He continued to write history plays as well, including the two plays about Henry IV.

The period of Shakespeare's great tragedies is 1602 to 1608, when he produced *Hamlet*, *Othello*, *King Lear*, and *Macbeth* as well as the dark comedy *Measure for Measure*.

After his retirement from London, Shakespeare wrote some theatrical romances, among them *The Tempest*, a play that suggests his farewell to the theater.

Shakespeare intended his plays to be performed; he did not concern himself about publication. During his lifetime, a few of his plays were published in imperfect versions as separate quartos or small books. After his death, two former members of Shakespeare's company, John Heminges and Henry Condell, collected all the plays except *Pericles* and published them in 1623 in a large book edition called the *First Folio*. (Quarto and folio refer to the size of the page.) This is the most authoritative edition of Shakespeare's plays. The folio included a complimentary poem by Ben Jonson, a tribute to Shakespeare as the greatest playwright of all time.

Henry IV, Part I

This is the most popular of Shakespeare's historical plays. As with some of the others, parts of it were loosely based on Raphael Holinshed's account of English civil conflict in his *Chronicles of England, Scotland and Ireland* (1577). The play's popularity, however, is largely because of the character of John Falstaff, a complex clown and rogue. Despite its title, this is one of a series of plays that actually explores the career of Henry IV's son, Prince

Hal, later King Henry V. In this play Hal is still an untried youth, wasting his time in taverns where he loiters and jokes with Falstaff and other drifters and fools. During the play, Hal will leave this self-indulgent life and surprise both his father and his enemies by turning into an effective warrior.

ACT I

In act I, King Henry IV has proposed to go on a crusade but decides instead to stay at home to deal with the growing rebellion. Conspiring to overthrow him are the earl of Northumberland, his brother the earl of Worcester, and Northumberland's son Henry Percy, called Hotspur, a rough but valiant soldier. They will be joined by the Welshman Glendower, a mystic, and the Scotsman Douglas, who has been creating troubles on the northern borders. Meanwhile, to the king's bitter disappointment, his son Prince Hal is wasting his time in a tavern where Falstaff and his companions are planning a highway robbery. As a joke, Prince Hal agrees to go along, but in the meantime he conspires with a fellow named Poins to desert the robbers and then rob them of what they have taken from the travelers—a counterconspiracy. Thus Shakespeare has set up two parallel actions involving plots of conspiracy and betrayal, one comic and one serious. In an important soliloquy at the end of act I, Prince Hal reveals to the audience that he is not really as idle as he seems; he is merely awaiting the right moment to "reform" and to take on his responsibilities.

ACT II

Act II moves the parallel plots forward. The king's enemies shape their plans, Hotspur displaying his fiery temper and impatient scorn of the king, whom he sees as a usurper of power, an illegal monarch. His character is further developed in a brief scene with his wife. Uninterested in any fond farewells, he mocks her as she tries to find out where he intends to fight. Meanwhile, Prince Hal's plan to rob Falstaff and trap him in lies works well. When Falstaff brags about having fought off an ever-increasing number of attackers, Prince Hal exposes his cowardice by telling the simple truth that Falstaff ran away at the first hint of danger. Then Hal and Falstaff indulge in a new form of fooling; they take turns playing the roles of king and prince, impersonating others and puffing up themselves. This tomfoolery is interrupted when the sheriff arrives, seeking the thieves. Hal protects Falstaff from discovery. One sees that Hal enjoys Falstaff for his wit and his cleverness at inventing verbal games, but he cannot admire Falstaff as a man of honor.

ACT III

Act III opens with a scene that would have been shocking to the Renaissance audience; Hotspur calls for a map of England and with the other conspirators begins to divide up its territories, squabbling with Glendower over one particularly fertile valley. Glendower, the host, is already annoyed because Hotspur shows his contempt for Glendower's mystical powers. Though the breach between Hotspur and Glendower is patched up, it foreshadows the eventual breakup of the conspiracy. By contrast, Prince Hal has a scene of sincere reconciliation with his father, King Henry. Hal then settles the matter of Falstaff's robbery by paying the money back to the victims. He then dispatches Falstaff and his cronies on missions that will of prepare them for battle in defense of the king.

ACT IV

In act IV the forces on each side gather for battle. As the decisive battle draws near, some of the conspirators' forces are delayed, sending various excuses. Falstaff, in the meantime, has used his powers of persuasion to extract bribes from able-bodied men to be substituted with a bunch of ragged and weak "scarecrows." The play shows that self-interest on both sides leads to failure to meet obligations.

ACT V

In act V all the major figures of the play find themselves at Shrewsbury, where the decisive battle will take place. In a last-minute attempt to prevent massive bloodshed, Hal offers to meet Hotspur in single combat to decide the issue, but he is scornfully turned down. During the battle, these two do combat each other. Prince Hal emerges victorious but pauses to make a speech in praise of Hotspur's spirit and bravery.

Those loyal to the king win the battle. Falstaff, who has played dead to avoid fighting, rises to make a soliloquy denying the reality of honor, saying that "the better part of valor is discretion," that is, it is better to know when to lie low and save yourself. The final scene looks forward to the next play, *King Henry IV, Part II*, with the king sending his sons and supporters out to confront those conspirators who had not been present at this battle.

Both parts of *Henry IV* show Shakespeare's interest in character development. Each of the major warriors presents a specific type:

> King Henry is calculating and somewhat tyrannical;
>
> his son Hal is clever and manipulative but still brave
> when necessary;
>
> Glendower, full of mystical knowledge and self-importance,
> is contrasted to
>
> Hotspur, the egotistical and crude warrior, who loves to fight.

In the background are a number of lesser characters, mostly agents and negotiators, who cope with the shifting rivalries of the main players. Ultimately, the conspiracy fails because those involved put their own interests before the needs of comrades. In his historical plays Shakespeare is not recreating history—indeed, he somewhat alters it—but he is writing about the politics of his own time and the need for honor and loyalty.

Hamlet, Prince of Denmark

This play, the first of the major tragedies, was written about the turn of the century; a quarto edition was printed in 1603. It was a successful play from the start, largely because of the character of the hero. We seem to be more intimate with the thoughts of Hamlet than with those of most dramatic heroes because he reveals himself in a series of meditative or anguished soliloquies. Yet ambiguities remain. To what extent is his madness an act? Does he slip into madness under stress? What causes his hesitation to take revenge? Is there some truth in his self-accusation of cowardice? How can we reconcile the charming, playful, and witty side of his personality with his rash and apparently callous acts toward others? What accounts for his rages against his mother and Ophelia? Even those who do not feel they have the answers to all these questions still enjoy the play and feel the authenticity of its main character.

HISTORICAL SOURCE OF HAMLET

The historical source of Hamlet was a legendary figure of Danish lore. He was mentioned in the *Historica Danica* of the late twelfth century. Shakespeare possibly picked up the story from a French source, Belleforest's *Histoires Tragiques*, published in 1570. There also seems to have been an earlier English play based on Hamlet, but it has not survived. The general type of play, the revenge tragedy, was known from the Latin playwright Seneca and was popular in England at the time of Shakespeare.

ACT I

Act I opens "in the middle of things." Hamlet's father, old King Hamlet, has died after being secretly poisoned by his brother, Claudius. Hamlet was away from Elsinore at the time, studying at the University of Wittenberg, so Claudius easily took over the throne and married the old king's widow, Gertrude, Hamlet's mother. On his arrival home Hamlet is disgusted to discover his mother's hasty remarriage to a man he deems much less worthy than his father. As act I opens, soldiers guarding the ramparts request that Hamlet's friend Horatio watch with them at midnight; they have seen a ghostly figure resembling old King Hamlet. The ghost reappears but will not speak to Horatio, so he and the soldiers decide to tell Hamlet what they have seen.

The second scene depicts a formal meeting of the new king and his court. Claudius delivers a brazen speech, asserting his authority and daring anyone to object to his questionable marriage. Turning to matters of state, he sends off ambassadors to Norway to forestall an attack against Danish borders. Then he behaves graciously to young Laertes, giving him permission to return to Paris. Lastly, Claudius addresses Hamlet, pretending similar kindness, but Hamlet rebuffs his attempts at cordiality. When Claudius asks Hamlet not to go back to the university, it takes the urging of his mother also to make Hamlet agree. Then the whole group of courtly persons withdraws, leaving Hamlet alone to make the first in his series of soliloquies. Hamlet expresses his grief that his mother has lowered herself to marry Claudius, and he suggests for the first time his wish to die. He is aroused from these thoughts by the entrance of Horatio and the soldiers, who report their sighting of the ghost. Hamlet agrees to meet them that night to see it for himself. In a brief scene Laertes says good-bye to his father, Polonius, and to his sister, Ophelia. Laertes warns Ophelia not to take Hamlet seriously as a suitor. This warning is reinforced by Polonius, who forbids her to speak with Hamlet, saying that the prince is not to be trusted. Act I ends with a scene in which Hamlet, on the ramparts of the castle, encounters the ghost of his father, who reveals to Hamlet his death at Claudius's hands and asks Hamlet to take revenge. Hamlet swears to do so, and he makes the others swear that they will keep this meeting a secret. He hints that he might act as if mad and that they are not to give away his act.

ACT II

Early in act II, Hamlet is apparently carrying out his plan to act as if he is mad, because Ophelia runs to her father with a story of how crazy and distracted Hamlet seemed when he came to visit her. She is frightened, and Polonius is sure that Hamlet is lovesick. In the next scene he reports this conclusion to King Claudius and Queen Gertrude, producing a love letter from Hamlet as proof that love has driven him mad. The king and queen, however, have doubts about Polonius's theory. When Hamlet enters, Polonius talks to him as one who humors a sick person; Hamlet makes a fool of him by mocking him in pretended madness. Two old friends of Hamlet, Rosencrantz and Guildenstern, arrive. He greets them warmly but also lets them know that he suspects they were summoned by Claudius to spy on him, which they admit. They also announce to Hamlet that a group of traveling players is approaching the castle. These actors soon enter; Hamlet greets them with great pleasure and asks the first player to arrange a special performance of a play about a murder. When all have left, Hamlet speaks his second soliloquy, cursing himself for delaying his revenge, but also revealing his plan to trap King Claudius by provoking a guilty reaction to a scene in the play resembling the murder of old Hamlet.

ACT III

The third act begins with the king and queen consulting their advisers and spies about Hamlet's condition. They set out Ophelia as bait to test Hamlet, but when he enters, he does not see her at first. At this time Hamlet speaks his famous third soliloquy, "To be or not to be . . .," in which he explores his thoughts about suicide. Hamlet concludes that only cowardice keeps him from killing himself. When he notices Ophelia, he is at first courteous to her, but he becomes rude and insulting as he begins to suspect that she is being used as a trap set by King Claudius and her father. As he speaks more and more wildly, she becomes convinced that he has lost his mind. The king, however, is less sure and decides to get rid of Hamlet by sending him to England.

The central scene of act III depicts the gathering in the hall of the castle to see the play. Everyone is present. Hamlet sits next to Ophelia so he can better watch Claudius for signs of guilt, but he also flirts with Ophelia as if there had been no trouble between them. When the play begins, Hamlet turns his attention to Claudius, pointing out to him those parts of the action that parallel the poisoning of old King Hamlet. Eventually Claudius reacts guiltily, calling for lights and rushing away. Hamlet is now absolutely sure that Claudius murdered the old king; Horatio confirms it. Then Hamlet's mother summons him to her chamber. On his way there, Hamlet passes Claudius kneeling in prayer. Hamlet decides that this is not the best moment for revenge; he assumes that Claudius is confessing his crime and would go straight to heaven if he died at that moment. Actually, Claudius is lamenting that he cannot pray because he is not willing to give up the fruits of his crime—the throne and the queen.

In the queen's chamber, Hamlet responds to his mother's scolding by scolding her in return. He tells her that he finds her marriage disgusting and even suggests that she was aware of the murder of her first husband. As Hamlet's anger grows, Polonius, who has hidden behind a curtain in the room, cries out in alarm. Hamlet, supposing it might be Claudius in hiding, stabs through the curtain and kills him. Hamlet feels little remorse; he concludes that Polonius got what he deserved for meddling. Hamlet pursues his argument with his mother. He becomes so angry that the ghost of his father reappears, telling Hamlet to concentrate on taking revenge against Claudius and not to distress his mother. Hamlet finally awakens her sense of shame and confides to her that he is only pretending to be mad. She promises to keep his secret and asks him what she should do. He asks her to behave with more reserve toward her husband. He then leaves, dragging out the body of Polonius.

ACT IV

Act IV is full of plots and rapid changes. Using the excuse that Hamlet has, in his madness, killed Polonius, Claudius hurries him off to England, with Rosencrantz and Guildenstern as escorts. They are carrying secret orders to the English king to execute Hamlet on his arrival. On his way, Hamlet encounters the officers of Fortinbras, a Norwegian prince who, unlike Hamlet, loves war. This leads to Hamlet's fourth soliloquy, in which he compares himself unfavorably with men of action like Fortinbras and vows henceforth to think of nothing but revenge.

Meanwhile, back at the castle, Ophelia has gone mad from the combined stresses of Hamlet's apparent madness and her father's violent death. In a pitiful scene, Ophelia gives out flowers and sings old songs about lost love. Her brother, Laertes, returning to avenge the death of his father, sees the wretched state of his sister and joins in a plot with Claudius against Hamlet, who is returning to Elsinore after discovering the plot against him and killing Rosencrantz and Guildenstern. They plan to lure him into a sporting duel and to dip one of their weapons in poison. At the end of act IV the queen announces and then describes the drowning of poor, mad Ophelia.

ACT V

Act V opens at the churchyard where gravediggers are preparing a grave for Ophelia. These characters give comic relief as they debate, in mock logic and riddles, whether Ophelia's death was suicide. Hamlet, passing by on his way home, stops to talk with them about graves and corpses. He discovers the skull of his father's jester, Yorick, and speaks to it: "Alas, poor Yorick. . . ." But when the funeral procession arrives and Hamlet realizes that it is Ophelia who has died, he is stricken with remorse and offended by the noisy grief of Laertes. Hamlet leaps forward, interrupting the ceremony and grappling with Laertes at the edge of the grave. Thus Laertes' vengeful intentions toward Hamlet are reinforced. But in the next scene calm is restored. Hamlet quietly talks with Horatio, explaining the manner of his escape and return, expressing regret for offending Laertes and stating that he now feels fully ready to carry out his revenge against Claudius, regardless of the risk.

Hamlet and Horatio are interrupted by a courtier, who announces the dueling competition. Hamlet feels prepared; all the court assembles to watch. King Claudius makes a hypocritical speech of confidence in Hamlet, throwing a rich pearl (containing poison) into the cup of wine that Hamlet will drink from during the fencing match. But every plan goes awry; when Laertes wounds Hamlet, Hamlet realizes that the swords are not blunted as for sport. In turn, he wounds Laertes, who confesses that the sword with which he wounded Hamlet is poisoned. Meanwhile, Queen Gertrude tries to show her support for her son by drinking to his success; she, however, drinks from the cup containing the poisoned pearl. Hamlet realizes all the traps laid for him, and in a rage he stabs the king. The stage is now strewn with the dying. Hamlet begs Horatio not to die and to explain the truth of what has happened. Hamlet dies; Fortinbras arrives to restore order, and the play ends.

Hamlet is an unusually long and complex play, even for Shakespeare. It is full of parallels and contrasts:

the revenge of Hamlet and the revenge of Laertes;

the false madness and the true madness;

soliloquies about death and jokes about death;

true friends and false friends;

the play and the play within the play.

The entangled action makes each role important and all the parts interdependent. Hamlet represents the situation of the individual caught by moral obligations in a corrupt world that he wishes he did not have to set right. The universality of its themes has made the character of Hamlet one of the most sought-after roles in the history of drama.

The Tempest

When he was in his middle forties, Shakespeare left London and returned to his home town, Stratford-on-Avon. He was no longer acting, but he did continue to write plays. The plays of this period are not tragic, but neither are they as light-hearted as his earlier comedies. Instead, the plays verge on tragic-comedies. They are also referred to as romances, and that term best fits *The Tempest*, written about 1610 or 1611.

Set on a remote sea island, the play involves young lovers, supernatural beings, lost royalty, and low-comedy drunks, all presided over by the powerful and wise Prospero. The air is full of music and strange sounds. The character of Prospero is thought by many to represent Shakespeare himself as the master enchanter, using his skill with wisdom and justice. The fantastic elements of the play suggest a masque, the type of entertainment being developed in the court of King James I. But it also reflects interest in the ongoing exploration of the New World and especially in a shipwreck that had occurred in the Bermudas about 1609. Shakespeare, however, places Prospero's island in the Mediterranean Sea, not in the Atlantic Ocean.

ACT I

Act I opens during a storm at sea. A ship containing Alonzo, King of Naples; Sebastian, brother of the king; Ferdinand, the king's son; Antonio, the current Duke of Milan; and their counselor, Gonzalo, wrecks on an island. On the island, Prospero, the deposed Duke of Milan, explains to his daughter, Miranda, how twelve years earlier he and Miranda had been cast out of Milan by his ambitious brother, Antonio, and set adrift to perish. However, Prospero and Miranda had reached the island and had lived there since, subduing the rude native, Caliban. Now, fortune and Prospero's magic have caused the whole royal party to be shipwrecked, thus putting them into Prospero's power. Miranda then sleeps while Prospero receives the report of his servant, the spirit-being Ariel. Ariel has frightened the mariners and now is dispatched to enchant Prince Ferdinand, to bring him to Prospero and to let Miranda see him. Prospero's plan requires that his daughter and the prince should fall in love; they do so at first sight.

ACT II

The second act opens with the survivors of the shipwreck, King Alonzo and his party, complaining and lamenting the supposed drowning of Prince Ferdinand. Ariel puts them all to sleep, except for Sebastian and Antonio, who, pretending to guard the king, conspire to murder him so that the throne will fall to Sebastian. Just at the crucial moment however, Ariel returns and wakens the king and his counselor Gonzalo. Caliban meets two surviving sailors, Trinculo and the drunken Stephano, who offer Caliban a drink of wine. Intoxicated, Caliban calls these fellows his new masters, his gods, and offers to show them the best of the island. He plans to leave the service of Prospero. Thus there is mutiny planned in both high and low circles.

ACT III

In act III, Prince Ferdinand willingly hauls logs for Prospero, because the prince is in love with Miranda. She visits him and offers him her help; then the two exchange vows of love. Meanwhile, Caliban conspires with his new master, Stephano, who supplies him with wine, to murder Prospero and to establish Stephano as king of the island, with Miranda as his queen. Ariel overhears this plotting. Elsewhere on the island, King Alonzo and his party, now weary of searching for Prince Ferdinand, pause to rest. Prospero has his servant-spirit Ariel set a feast before them, but just as they begin to eat, Ariel, in the form of a harpy (a she-monster with the body of a bird of prey), addresses them, reminding them of their past crimes against Prospero and promising them further misery, including the loss of Ferdinand.

ACT IV

At the opening of act IV, Prospero gives his blessing to the betrothal of Miranda and Ferdinand, warning them to preserve their chastity until they have exchanged sacred vows. He amuses them with a brief masque, featuring Ceres, goddess of fertility, and Juno, queen of gods, but not Venus, the goddess of love and passion. Then, remembering Caliban's plot to kill him, Prospero abruptly ends the masque, giving the famous speech, "Our revels now are ended . . . ," which has been interpreted by some as Shakespeare's farewell to the stage. Prospero calls Ariel, who has been leading Caliban, Stephano, and Trinculo on a wild goose chase ending at a rotten pond. By Prospero's order, Ariel sets out some gaudy garments to catch their eyes. While they are preoccupied with stealing this stuff, Ariel and Prospero drive them away, using a pack of spirit-dogs to frighten them.

ACT V

In act V Prospero begins by promising to release Ariel and lay aside his magic as soon as the present business is untangled. He has the party of the king brought in, all in states of enchantment. Prospero reveals his identity as the lost duke of Milan, causing repentance in those who deposed him. He then reveals Miranda and Ferdinand, playing a game of chess. The king rejoices at regaining his son and accepts Miranda as his future daughter-in-law, thus ending the play with reconciliation and joy. Ariel is free, and Caliban rejects his false god, Stephano. Everyone returns to his rightful place and condition, while the marriage of the young lovers promises an heir for both Naples and Milan.

Beneath the surface enchantments of *The Tempest*—the flitting spirit beings, the music and dance, the magical appearances and vanishings—lies a discourse about political power and the dangers of corruption. Shakespeare shows how those who usurp power are vulnerable to further usurpations. Freedom, on the other hand, is the constant theme of Ariel, the good servant who earns liberation.

Shakespeare's accomplishments in poetry and drama make him the most influential writer of all time. His treatment of human emotions and rivalries are so apt and enduring that his lines are quoted even by those who rarely see or read his plays. Concerned about the issues of his time, about political power and tyranny, about fidelity to the leader, and about loyalty in love, Shakespeare nevertheless set these issues in historical or even fantastical times and places, thereby giving them universal application. He was a master of the lofty speech, the anguished soliloquy, the bawdy joke, and the delicate speech of love. Everyone who enjoys Shakespeare feels that the playwright is speaking to her or him alone.

Selected Readings

Chapman, Gerald W., ed. *Essays on Shakespeare*. Princeton: Princeton University Press, 1965.

Fox, Levi, ed. *The Shakespeare Handbook*. New York: G. K. Hall, 1987.

Harrison, G. B., ed. *Major Plays and Sonnets/Shakespeare*. New York: Harcourt, 1948.

Hubler, Edward. *The Sense of Shakespeare's Sonnets*. Princeton: Princeton University Press, 1952.

Morgan, A. E. *Some Problems of Shakespeare's Henry the Fourth*. Folcraft, PA: Folcraft, 1974.

Muir, Kenneth. *Shakespeare's Sonnets*. Boston: Allen, 1979.

Palmer, C. *Shakespeare's Mystery Play: A Study of The Tempest*. St. Clair Shores, MI: Scholarly, 1972.

Wilson, John Dover. *What Happens in Hamlet*. Cambridge, Eng.: Cambridge University Press, 1959.

10

English Renaissance Literature (1485 to 1603): Development of Prose

1490–1520	Humanist education established at English universities: classical scholarship, biblical and literary criticism
1509	Erasmus visits England
1509–1547	Reign of Henry VIII
c. 1511	Erasmus, *In Praise of Folly*
1516	More, *Utopia*
1517	Luther posts his "Ninety-five Theses" in Wittenberg; Protestant Reformation begins
1520	Pope Leo X excommunicates Luther
1525	Tyndale, *New Testament*: first printed English translation of any part of the Bible
1529	First use of the term *Protestant*
1529–1532	Thomas More, Lord Chancellor of England
1532	Machiavelli's *The Prince* published; Calvin, *Institutes of the Christian Religion*; More resigns as chancellor over Henry VIII's claim as temporal ruler to be supreme head of church
1534	Act of Supremacy formalizes Henry VIII's break with Rome; Henry VIII head of Church of England

1535   Henry VIII begins confiscation of monastic properties; old manuscripts lost or destroyed

1535   More executed by order of Henry VIII

1540   "The Great Bible," in English, installed in churches

1545   Ascham, *Toxophilus*

1553–1558   Reign of Mary Tudor

c. 1555   Roper, *Life of Sir Thomas More*; Cavendish, *Life of Cardinal Wolsey*

1557   Posthumous publication of More's *Dialogue of Comfort*, *Treatise on the Passion*, and *History of Richard III*

1561   Hoby's translation of Castiglione's *Il Cortegiano (The Courtier)*

1567   Golding publishes translation of Ovid's *Metamorphoses*

1570   Ascham, *Schoolmaster*

1578   Lyly, *Euphues: The Anatomy of Wit*

1580   Lyly, *Euphues and His England*

1597   Bacon, first edition of *Essays*

*T*he development of prose writing during the Renaissance rose to satisfy the need of the early humanists for a medium other than Latin writing in which to express political, social, and moral thought. Humanism was less a secular movement than it was a rejection of what seemed narrow, pedantic, and rigid in medieval scholastic thought. The English studied the great literature of Greece and Rome in search of wisdom that would help them live well and "correctly." Translations of classical texts and of the Bible not only made these works more accessible to English readers, but they also showed that English was a worthy language for serious discourse.

Noblemen, who were often sent to Europe on diplomatic missions, learned Italian as the vehicle of new ideas, but they also wished to promote their own language as intellectually useful. Thus, after Thomas More's Utopia was published in Latin, an English version followed in 1551. In about 1510 More himself translated into English the Life of Pico, and he wrote his History of King Richard III in both Latin and English.

One common subject of the writings of More and others is education in behalf of excellence and liberal thought. Young men needed not only to be familiar with the basic texts of Western learning, they also needed to be able to think freely and to use their minds to explore, to understand, and to act.

SIR THOMAS MORE (1478–1535)

The major English contributor to the great Renaissance movement called humanism was Thomas More. Son of a lawyer, More had also studied law. He was interested in public affairs, but he also was attracted by the quiet life of scholarship and could not choose between the two for many years. He was a friend of Desiderius Erasmus, the great Dutch humanist philosopher. More was also noticed by King Henry VIII, who gave him a series of increasingly important public offices. The king named More his lord chancellor in 1529. This post was the highest possible government position; More was the king's closest adviser. When, however, King Henry broke with the Roman Catholic church and declared himself head of the Church of England, More would not go along with him and was dismissed. Persisting in his loyalty to the Church of Rome, Thomas More was arrested, tried, and beheaded for treason in 1535. The Roman Catholic church has declared him a saint.

Utopia

This prose work was written in Latin in 1516 while More was in Europe on diplomatic missions. Latin was still the language of international learning and of humanism. *Utopia*, published first in Holland, was translated into English thirty-five years later. It consists of two parts; the second section, the description of Utopia, was written before the first, which was added as an introduction.

BOOK I

The introduction realistically describes More as he passes time in Antwerp during a delay in diplomatic negotiations. He happens to meet an old friend, Peter Giles, who introduces More to a curious fellow, an old traveler named Raphael Hythloday. Hythloday had been a member of the expeditions of Amerigo Vespucci to the New World and thus had visited many unknown lands. Impressed by Raphael's experiences, Giles advises him to seek employment as an adviser to a king, but Raphael declines because, he says, kings are more interested in waging war than in governing well, and courts are places of envy and flattery, where new ideas are not welcome.

BOOK II

In the second book, Raphael gives a detailed account of an island nation he visited called Utopia. In Utopia property is all held in common, as a way to thwart the human tendency toward greed. No one is rich or poor. Raphael describes how gold and jewels are used for infants' toys and also as the chains and fetters of slaves and criminals. This republic, based partly on the *Republic* of Plato, is ruled by a democratic assembly. All inhabitants participate in basic agricultural labor, each citizen working two years on the farm. Raphael describes the Utopian laws and religion as well as farm practices and marriage customs, contrasting them with and at the same time satirizing the laws and customs of European nations. Though Utopia (which means *no where*) appears to be an ideal community, at the end More ironically comments that the social and economic arrangements of this strange place are absurd because they do not allow for "magnificence" or "splendor."

Thomas More's book was an attempt to criticize of the contemporary English social and economic system by showing how much it departed from the ideals of a Christian community.

SIR THOMAS HOBY (1530–1566)

A staunch Protestant, Hoby was educated at Cambridge University and traveled widely in Germany, France, and especially in Italy, where he encountered the courtesy book *Il Cortegiano*, or *The Courtier*.

Il Cortegiano This book, written by Count Baldasarre Castiglione, was a widely read and influential expression of the ideal of a noble gentleman. It takes the form of a dialogue between certain members of the Italian aristocracy that extends over four evenings. The topics of the four discussions are these:

> Book I covers the noble birth and education of the courtier and his training to be witty, brave, strong, and graceful;
>
> Book II discusses the behavior of the courtier, his social and artistic accomplishments, his skill and truth in speech;
>
> Book III focuses on the ideal qualities of a gentlewoman;
>
> Book IV takes up the question of love in a discussion that sets the terms for real-life discussions of love for the rest of the century.

Castiglione takes the idea of perfect beauty, derived from Plato, and unites it to the idea of love. Above the merely sensual level of love that is characteristic in young men exist the love of reasonable choice and the love of spiritual understanding. The best, most mature lover comes to love the ideal of beauty as traced in the face and mind of his beloved.

The Courtier During the 1550s Hoby did a vigorous English translation of *Il Cortegiano* but it was not published until 1561. In his translation, *The Courtier*, Hoby tried to use simple and direct English words rather than borrowing terms from Latin and Italian. His translation was reprinted three more times during the reign of Queen Elizabeth I. It was the essential courtesy book; its treatment of love provides the background for an understanding of the concepts of love as expressed by Spenser, Shakespeare, and Donne, among others.

ROGER ASCHAM (1515–1568)

The educator Ascham was a scholar of Latin and Greek at Cambridge, but he insisted that studying the great writers in these languages was only a way to gain clarity and eloquence in English.

Toxophilus

In *Toxophilus*, a treatise on archery written in 1545, Ascham included an argument in favor of cultivating the English language. Ascham became a tutor to Princess Elizabeth, and he returned to help her in the study of ancient authors even after she became queen.

The School-master

In his major work, *The Schoolmaster*, which was published after his death, Ascham argues for a humane and gentle style of teaching, believing that the teacher can gain more willing study from kindness and reasoning than from beating and frightening his pupils. He describes how translations from Latin to English and back to Latin, rather than memorization of grammatical rules, can be used to demonstrate clear expression to a child. Ascham shows that a teacher should link learning with pleasure so that a love of learning will remain in the students after school days are over.

JOHN LYLY (1554–1606)

Lyly was a student at Oxford University in the early 1570s, when the study of rhetoric was reaching a superrefined state. After taking an M.A., Lyly went to London in search of patronage.

Euphues: The Anatomy of Wit

His fiction *Euphues: The Anatomy of Wit*, written in 1578, was instantly popular and made him famous as the inventor of euphuism, a highly elaborate and artificial prose style that used balanced phrases of equal length and similar structure, with alliteration of major terms. This example of euphuism comes from the introduction of the main character:

"This young gallant, of more wit than wealth, and yet of more wealth than wisdom, seeing himself inferior to none in pleasant conceits, thought himself superior uo all in honest conditions. . . ."

Notice the alliteration of words starting with *w: wit, wealth, wealth, wisdom*. In the second part of the sentence, "pleasant conceits" is balanced against "honest conditions" with the emphasis of "inferior" and "superior" to mark a contrast. This is typical of euphuism. The style also incorporates proverbial sayings, literary and historical allusions, analogies to natural history, and extended similes.

The story of Euphues is a rather weak framework for a series of discussions between the main characters and his friends about questions of correct conduct. The popularity of this book led to a sequel, *Euphues and His England*, written in 1580. Women in particular were enthusiastic to speak "euphuistically." But the vogue was short. Lyly did not get the post at court that he wanted, although he did become a master at the St. Paul's Cathedral school for choir boys in London. For them he wrote witty comedies to be performed at court.

The Renaissance saw advancement and productivity in English literature. The English language became more modern and was enriched by many borrowings from continental languages. Poets and playwrights experimented with new forms and adapted existing forms from classical and contemporary European works. Translations served to spread sophisticated ideas about the ideal courtier and about love. With the patronage and encouragement of the court and the aristocracy, writers developed a richly varied and imaginative national literature that celebrated English history and values and the glory of the English monarchy. The printing of books meant that more people had access to new ideas and new literary forms.

Selected Readings

Chambers, R. W. *The Place of St. Thomas More in English Literature and History.* New York: Haskell House, 1964.

Martz, Louis L. *Thomas More: The Search for the Inner Man.* New Haven: Yale University Press, 1990.

Sargent, Daniel. *Thomas More.* New York: Sheed and Ward, 1933.

11

Early Seventeenth-Century English Literature (1603 to 1660): Early Seventeenth Century

1603 Florio, *Translation of the Essays of Montaigne*

1603–1625 Reign of James I, first Stuart monarch

1604 Shakespeare, *Othello*; Marlowe's *The Tragical History of the Life and Death of Doctor Faustus* published

1605 Bacon, *Advancement of Learning*; Gunpowder Plot by Roman Catholic extremists to blow up Parliament fails, but plot deepens anticatholic feelings; Cervantes, *Don Quixote*, Part I

1606 Shakespeare, *Macbeth*; Jonson, *Volpone*

1607 Captain John Smith and 105 cavaliers land on Virginia coast; start first permanent English settlement in the New World at Jamestown

1609 Shakespeare, *Sonnets*; Kepler, German astronomer, publishes first two laws of planetary motion

1611 King James Version of the *Holy Bible* is published

1614 Webster, *The Dutchess of Malfi*; Raleigh, *History of the World*; Coke, chief justice of King's Bench

1614–1620 Napier of Scotland, Burgi of Switzerland propose system of logarithms; Biggs of England modifies method by proposing ten as base

1616 Donne chaplain to King James I; Shakespeare dies

1618 Thirty Years' War begins in Europe

1619–1622 Inigo Jones, architect, Banquet Hall, Whitehall Palace

1620 Bacon, *Novum Organum*; Puritan separatists from Church of England land at Plymouth, beginning the Massachusetts Colony

1621 Burton, *Anatomy of Melancholy*

1622 First English newspaper, *The Weekly News*, published; Donne, *Sermon on Judges*

1623 Heminges and Condell, *First Folio*, first collection of Shakespeare's plays, includes Jonson's poem, *In Homage to William Shakespeare*

1625 Bacon, *Essays*

1625–1640 Reign of Charles I

1626 Peter Minuit buys Manhattan Island from Indians

1629 Milton, *Ode on the Morning of Christ's Nativity*; Bernini, architect of St. Peters basilica, Rome

1629–1640 Charles I reigns without Parliament

1632 Rembrandt, *Dr. Tulp's Anatomy Lesson*

1633 Donne, *Poems*; Herbert, *The Temple*; Milton, *L'Allegro* and *Il Penseroso*

1636 Harvard College founded in Massachusetts Colony; first public opera house opens in Venice; Rubens, *The Judgment of Paris*

1637 Descartes, *Discourse on Method*; Corneille, *Le Cid*

1640 Walton, *Life of Donne*; first book, *Bay Psalm Book*, printed in Massachusetts Colony

1642 Civil War begins; Royalists known as Cavaliers support king; opponents of king, many Puritans among them, called Roundheads, were led by Oliver Cromwell

1644 Milton, *Areopagitica*

1646 Vaughan, *Poems*

1646–1649 Charles I captured, imprisoned, then executed

1649 Lovelace, *Lucasta*

1649–1653 The Commonwealth, an experiment in republican government, tried, with political power in a one-house parliament; Council of State led by Cromwell conducts government operations; theaters closed

1651   Hobbes, *Leviathan*; Milton, *Defense of the English People*

1653   Cromwell assumes title of lord protector; Walton, *The Compleat Angler*

1658–1660   Cromwell dies, succeeded by son who later resigns and is replaced by General Monk, who restores Stuarts

1660   Restoration of the monarchy

Because of the political skills of Queen Elizabeth I, during the late sixteenth century the English people had joined together into one powerful and prosperous nation. Various interest groups and religious factions ignored their differences because most people felt at least some protection under the queen's toleration. Elizabeth squelched an attempted coup in the 1590s and strengthened her own power. Nevertheless, deep divisions existed within English society. Within the Protestant church, Puritan reformers who wanted to "purify" the Church of England struggled with the more conservative, authoritarian establishment of bishops. In secular society, the aristocracy defended their privileges against the newly rich and against the rural gentry. These conflicts and the increasingly sharp rivalry between the court and the Parliament caused the apparent unity of the Elizabethan era to crumble.

JAMES I

When Queen Elizabeth I died in 1603, she was peacefully succeeded by her cousin, King James IV of Scotland, a Stuart, who became King James I of England. James I was not as skillful a leader as Elizabeth; he was more dogmatic and much less tolerant. Furthermore, James's court was much less important as a center for the arts than Elizabeth's had been, although he did commission a number of masques. His greatest contribution was to commission an English translation of the *Holy Bible*. The resulting King James Version became a rich and timeless source of phrases and vocabulary.

During the reign of James I, religious factions became more extreme. In 1605, Roman Catholics fearful of persecution by Parliament tried to blow it up. This revolutionary act, however, only succeeded in solidifying the anti-Catholic fears of the Protestant majority. At the other extreme, some Puritans despaired of ever reforming what to them seemed the wicked and idolatrous practices of the established Anglican church. Many of those Puritans chose to emigrate, first to the Netherlands, a center of Protestantism, and ultimately to the Americas.

CHARLES I

In 1625 King James I died and was succeeded by his son Charles. Again the transfer of power was peaceful, but King Charles I was even less conciliatory than his father. His enemies were concentrated in both the House of Lords and the House of Commons in the Parliament. Both Houses sought to control him by refusing to advance him money. Parliament claimed that taxes demanded by Charles were illegitimate taxes and a threat to private property. Charles I asserted his declared taxes legal and that he ruled by "divine right," that is, by the "authority of God," and that he was responsible only to God for his actions and policies. Thus, Charles considered himself above the law and the Parliament and asserted that he could not be judged or controlled by his subjects. Charles I refused to call Parliament into session for long periods of time, thus causing the troublesome religious and political issues to unite.

CIVIL WAR

Civil war broke out in 1642 after King Charles I attempted to arrest five Parliamentary leaders. At first the "Cavaliers" or royalist forces, which supported the king, seemed to prevail. However, under the leadership of Oliver Cromwell, a country gentleman and a committed religious Puritan, the disciplined Parliamentary forces, or "Roundheads," defeated the king in a series of battles in 1644 and 1645. King Charles I was arrested, imprisoned, tried, and finally executed in 1649. The Puritans who had not originally intended to depose the king but only to curtail his powers, protested his execution. Furthermore, there was no alternative form of government ready to spring into action. By default, England became a republic, called a Commonwealth, with Cromwell as its head. Since Parliamentary government had broken down, the affairs of government were conducted by the council of state with Cromwell as the protector. When he died in 1658, his son was proclaimed protector. Richard Cromwell, however, lacked both kingly authority and the power of a military conqueror; he resigned because of his failure to govern effectively. The army took over and moved to restore the monarchy. Finally, by consensus, the various factions in England agreed to restore the monarchy by recalling from exile Charles Stuart, the son of King Charles I. In 1660 he was restored to the monarchy as King Charles II.

THE LITERARY SCENE

In any society, energy devoted to the arts tends to decline during times of intense factional dispute and civil warfare. During the early seventeenth century courtly patronage of literature declined. To members of the middle class, cultivation of literary interests seemed a decadent luxury; some religious Puritans even thought it ungodly. In 1642 an act of Parliament closed the public theaters, thus cutting off the development of dramatic literature for a whole generation. The printing presses of London produced primarily political tracts and papers on theological disputes. The career of John Milton epitomizes the era. A lyric poet in his youth, Milton largely suspended his poetic activity during the Commonwealth decades, while he was active in government service. It was not until after the Restoration of Charles II that Milton resumed writing, going on to create his great epic works.

LITERARY FORMS

Just as the second half of the sixteenth century is called the Elizabethan age after Queen Elizabeth I, so the early decades of the seventeenth century are referred to as the Jacobean and Caroline periods, Jacobus and Carolus being the Latin forms of the names of King James I and King Charles I. During the first four decades of the new century, the exuberant creative energies of the Renaissance began to decline, giving way to a more somber, dark, and melancholy mood. Lyric forms such as the sonnet and the song persisted, but the lyric became more complex, less sweetly charming, and more cynical or abstract. Satire in verse was developed, following the models of the great Roman satirists Juvenal and Horace.

Poetry began to separate itself into various schools or contrasting types, based on the differing purposes and loyalties of the poets. Some poets consciously rejected the poetic conventions of the previous generation and set out to create new effects. Others put poetry at the service of morality in a more clearly instructive or didactic mode.

The theater, the glory of Elizabeth's era, lost its broad, popular appeal. The great questions of state, of power and usurpation, began to be replaced by more domestic, nonheroic plots involving jealousy, infidelity, and intrigue. Though good playwrights abounded, they were unable or unwilling to articulate ideals of honor and virtue.

A vigorous new prose, meanwhile, was developing in the service of the need to express philosophical ideas and to cope with the public issues of an increasingly divided society where old truths had begun to be questioned on the basis of new discoveries and new experiences.

EARLY SEVENTEENTH-CENTURY LYRIC POETRY

The lyric poetry of this era is usually divided into the Cavalier and the metaphysical schools. Although most poets tended to write one kind of poetry or the other, some of the major poets could write in either school and thus are not easy to classify. Generally, however, one can distinguish the smooth, polished, and melodious lyrics of the cavalier from the rougher, more abrupt, and wittier lyrics of the metaphysical poets.

Cavalier School

The Cavaliers were poets of aristocratic heritage and taste. The term *cavalier* refers to their royalist sympathies; they were gentlemen—horsemen in the king's service. As a group they looked back to the great poets of the Renaissance, to Sidney and Spenser, for their models. These poets were not interested in originality; they tried instead to perfect the techniques of the love lyric or song. One of their favorite themes was *carpe diem*, a phrase that translates from Latin as "seize the day." Poems based on this theme encourage the reader to take the pleasures of the present moment rather than wait for the uncertain satisfactions of the future. The most outstanding of the Cavalier poets was Ben Jonson; his followers called themselves "Sons of Ben."

Metaphysical School

The metaphysical school of poetry arose as a reaction against the conventional and pretty smoothness of traditional lyrics. The metaphysical poets tried to see the world in new and surprising ways. They invented metaphors based on contemporary science and exploration. Instead of perfection of form, they valued wit; their poems made demands upon the readers' intellect. The chief poet of this school was John Donne. Donne never used the term *metaphysical* to describe his works. The word was first applied to the poetry of Donne and his followers by Samuel Johnson, who wrote almost a hundred years later in the mid-eighteenth century. Johnson criticized this poetry for being too difficult and too far-fetched in its metaphors. But the metaphysical poets were not concerned with being easy. They deliberately tried to create a new poetic situation for which the reader had not been prepared by the poetry of the classical or English past. They deliberately tried to surprise and to shock.

The first half of the seventeenth century can be seen as the end of the Renaissance or as a period of transition leading to the English Enlightenment. Along with much of Europe, England was moving from a rich and exuberant era newly liberated by humanism into a more restrained era concerned with examining the world and the individual's place in it. Political disruption called into question old assumptions about hierarchy and divine order; at the same time personal doubt and religious factionalism made assumptions about God's presence in the world harder to accept without examination. For many writers of the early seventeenth century, change was not celebrated as freshness but feared as decay. The discovery of a new world across the ocean, where European institutions were unknown, raised questions about the essential nature of human beings.

Selected Readings

Bush, Douglas. *English Literature in the Earlier Seventeenth Century: 1600–1660.* 2d ed. New York: Oxford University Press, 1962.

Grierson, Herbert J. *Crosscurrents in Seventeenth-Century English Literature.* Gloucester, MA: Peter Smith, 1965.

Wedgewood, C. V. *Seventeenth-Century English Literature.* London: Oxford University Press, 1950.

12

Early Seventeenth-Century English Literature (1603 to 1660): The Cavalier Poets

1596–1598	Jonson, *Every Man in His Humor*
1601	Jonson, *Cynthia's Revels*
1603–1625	Reign of James I, first Stuart monarch
1604	Shakespeare, *Othello*; Marlowe's *The Tragical History of the Life and Death of Doctor Faustus* published
1605	Cervantes, *Don Quixote*, Part I; Gunpowder Plot by Roman Catholics
1606	Shakespeare, *Macbeth*; Jonson, *Volpone*
1608	Jonson, *The Masque of Beauty*
1609	Shakespeare, *Sonnets*; Jonson, *The Masque of Queens*
1610	Jonson, *The Alchemist*
1614	Jonson, *Bartholomew Fair*; Webster, *The Duchess of Malfi*
1616	Jonson appointed poet laureate; Jonson, *Works*; Shakespeare dies
1618	Jonson, masque *Pleasure Reconciled to Virtue*; Thirty Years' War begins in Europe

1623   Heminges and Condell, *First Folio*, first collection of Shakespeare's plays, includes Jonson's poem *In Homage to William Shakespeare*

1629   Milton, *Ode on the Morning of Christ's Nativity*; Herrick moves to Devonshire as country clergyman

1629–1640   Charles I reigns without Parliament

1640   Posthumous publication of Jonson's *The Underwood*; Walton, *Life of Donne*

1642   The Civil War begins; Royalists known as Cavaliers support king

1646–1649   Charles I captured, imprisoned, then executed

1648   Herrick, secular poems, *Hesperides* and religious poems, *Noble Numbers* published

1649   Lovelace, *Lucasta*

1649–1653   The Commonwealth, an experiment in republican government, tried; Council of State led by Cromwell

1651   Hobbes, *Leviathan*; Milton, *Defense of the English People*

1653   Cromwell assumes title of lord protector

1657   Marvell becomes assistant to the blind Milton

1658–1660   Cromwell dies, succeeded by son, who later resigns and is replaced by General Monk, who restores the monarchy

1660   Marvell becomes member of Parliament and uses position to "protect" Milton

1681   Marvell, *Miscellaneous*

*L*iterally, a cavalier is a horseman. During the English Civil War, the followers of Charles I were called Cavaliers, at first in mockery by their opponents, the Parliamentarians, who thought them superficial and not to be taken seriously. However, the Royalists adapted the term to describe themselves, giving it heroic and idealistic connotations. The Cavalier poets were courtly, not only in their military actions but also in their attitudes toward women and love.

BEN JONSON (1572–1637)

By the strength of his intellect, scholarship, and wit Ben Jonson rose from humble beginnings (his stepfather was a master bricklayer) to become the preeminent man of letters of his generation. He went to Westminster School and became deeply interested in classical literature, which served as models and inspiration for his own poetry. But Jonson also lived an active life. He was a soldier, fighting against the Spanish in Flanders, where he killed an opponent in single combat. He worked as an actor and wrote plays, mostly comedies, for the Chamberlain's Men, formerly Shakespeare's company. He was jailed for a short time for killing an actor. After James I became king, Jonson became a court favorite and was employed to write a series of twenty-eight masques. These were elaborate courtly entertainments, usually concluding with compliments to royalty. Jonson continued to write for the theater. He produced a series of brilliant satiric comedies that while following the formal characteristics of classical Roman comedy were enriched with scenes and situations of contemporary London life. Meanwhile, Jonson became the center of a group of younger poets, who called themselves "Sons of Ben." In 1616 King James I made Jonson poet laureate, the official poet of the court, and assigned him an annual pension. During that same year, Jonson published all the poetry he had thus far written in a collection called *Works*. This was an unusual move for a writer, and it signaled his sense of professionalism and his confidence in the lasting quality of his writing.

Much of Jonson's poetry was occasional; that is, composed for special occasions such as celebrations and commemorations. Many of his poems are dedicated to a particular person; these poems are tributes to the living or elegies to the dead. Most of his songs were written for his masques or plays. Thus much of Jonson's poetry arose in response to an external event or a need rather than spontaneously. That he could produce such excellent poetry on demand indicates Jonson's rich imagination and the store of learning he had at his command. It also shows the public role he adopted as poet.

On My First Son

This short, unusually personal elegy is a cry of grief on the death of his son on the boy's seventh birthday. Jonson translates the meaning of the boy's name, Benjamin, as "child of my right hand" and calls the boy his "best piece of poetry," that is, his best creation. Jonson consoles himself with the traditional thought that at least the boy has missed much of the evil in the world by dying young. He also warns himself against loving anyone else so much.

Inviting a Friend to Supper

This poem has precedent in the work of the classical Roman poet, Horace. It is complimentary to the friend and mildly self-mocking. It lists an extensive supper menu containing both mutton and rabbit along with many types of fowl. The entertainment Jonson promises is his servant, "my man," reading aloud from one of Jonson's favorite Latin authors, followed by a discussion. Jonson promises not to read his own poetry. There will be sweet wine, but no one will overindulge or say anything that he will regret the next morning. Altogether, Jonson describes an ideal occasion of simple but abundant food and of good masculine companionship.

To Penshurst

This is a topographical poem, that is, a poem that describes and praises a place. This particular place, Penshurst, is the country estate in Kent, southern England, of the Sidney family. As Jonson mentions, the Renaissance poet Sir Phillip Sidney was born there. The poem begins by comparing Penshurst to other, more showy homes. Penshurst is not fancy and rich but old, solid, and comfortable. The poem describes the estate's fields and trees, the animals and fish that provide food, the gardens with their fruits, and the local people whose gifts of their best produce are delivered by their pretty daughters, who are, like the fruits, "ripe." The description of this ample provision leads to an image of the hospitable meals served at Penshurst, where everyone, regardless of his or her status, is well fed and generously served. Jonson mentions the time when King James I himself came unexpectedly to Penshurst and found everything ready for his comfortable reception. The orderly and comfortable household represents an ideal of how life should be lived. The land's bounty supports a benevolent and generous way of life. The lord and lady of the house are at the top of a hierarchal order; they are examples of virtue, models of the right way to live. Thus the poem celebrates not just one particular household but the ideal English way of life—virtuous and abundant but not rich or proud.

Songs from Jonson's Plays

Like other playwrights of the late sixteenth and early seventeenth centuries, Jonson often placed a short lyric within his plays to be sung by and sometimes to one of the characters. Jonson's lyrics are among the most smooth and melodious in English literature. The song "To Celia" from *Volpone* is a classic expression of the *carpe diem* theme—let us enjoy the moment; time may not give us another chance. Love is "no sin" but "sweet theft." In "Slow, Slow Fresh Fount," Jonson shows his fine control of the musical effects of words, using many long syllables to create a slow pace suggesting sadness and imitating the gentle dropping of water. Similarly, "Queen and Huntress" achieves its effect from the careful placement of each word. The queen is the goddess Diana, symbol of chastity and traditionally associated with Queen Elizabeth I, who was still alive in 1601 to see the masque *Cynthia's Revels*, for which this song was composed.

To the Memory of My Beloved the Author, Mr. William Shakespeare, and What He Hath Left Us

When Hemings and Condell, two actors from Shakespeare's company, decided to publish an edition of Shakespeare's plays in 1623, Jonson provided this poem as a preface. In paying tribute to Shakespeare's genius it places him above all other playwrights, both ancient and modern, and declares him the glory of English poetry. Calling Shakespeare the "soul of the age," Jonson goes on to aver that he was "not of an age, but for all time."

Drawing on his own wide learning, Jonson alludes to many other writers and shows how Shakespeare surpasses them all. He attributes Shakespeare's superiority to Nature, meaning that he grasped and expressed essential human nature as it really is. But Jonson also credits Shakespeare with having Art, that is, learned skill and workmanship in composition. Nature and Art were Jonson's terms for the matter and the manner of poetry, which are both important, "For a good poet's made as well as born." At the conclusion of the poem, Jonson describes a vision of Shakespeare transformed into a constellation shining in the sky and shedding an inspiring influence upon the stage, which has been poorer since his death.

Pleasure Reconciled to Virtue

This is a typical Jonsonian masque, created for the celebration of twelfth night, January 6, at the court of James I. It begins with the grossly fat figure of Comus, the big-bellied image of vulgar self-indulgence, honored by a dance of figures dressed as various vessels for food and drink. Hercules enters and denounces the wallowing pleasures that Comus represents. A mountain opens, revealing the allegorical figures of Pleasure and Virtue. A chorus sings an invitation to Hercules to lie down and rest. A group of pygmies then enters. After dancing, the pygmies approach the sleeping Hercules, who awakens and frightens them all away. Mercury, the messenger of the gods, descends from the mountain and explains that the conflict between Pleasure and Virtue has ended, which brings forth the singing masquers. The rest of the masque presents alternately the songs of Daedalus, the master of art, and the dances of the masquers, the gentlemen and ladies of the court. The final song sung by all the chorus celebrates the triumph of Virtue as the only source of greatness.

In this spectacle highlighting the effects achieved by elaborate stage machinery, such as mountains opening and gods descending, plot is virtually nonexistent. The figures representing various abstract concepts merely parade onto the stage and speak their messages. The dances demonstrate that the apparently opposite figures of Virtue and Pleasure can be made to harmonize, to move together. All the courtiers and spectators take part in the climactic dance, bringing everyone into the pattern or harmony overseen by Daedalus, the grand maker of art. Such an entertainment was necessarily designed for a sophisticated, elite audience who were familiar with classical allegorical meanings and the multiple associations with the persons presented. These theatrical presentations were not commercial or professional but were the private games of a self-consciously courtly nobility.

Ode to Himself

In 1629 Jonson's play *The New Inn* was a failure. He became disgusted with the theater and in particular with what he saw as the bad taste of the London audiences. In this ode, Jonson speaks of himself as a fool for trying to please them. He uses metaphors of food and drink to depict the playgoers as merely gross consumers of foul leftovers. In the fifth stanza, Jonson determines to quit the stage and turn to lyric poetry, following the examples of the great ancient lyric poets, and to spend his final years as a poet of lofty emotions. In the final stanza Jonson imagines his fame as a poet with the more worthy task of celebrating the virtues of his king, Charles I.

ROBERT HERRICK (1591–1674)

Herrick came from a family of London goldsmiths, rich enough to send him to Cambridge when he decided, after an early apprenticeship, that the goldsmith trade was not for him. He was ordained as an Anglican minister in 1623. Herrick stayed in London for the next six years, enjoying literary society and jovial urban life as one of the "Sons of Ben." Like Ben Jonson, Herrick was strongly influenced by Greek and Roman lyric poetry. In 1627 Herrick showed his loyalty to the Royalist cause by serving as a chaplain to the Cavalier troops led by the duke of Buckingham. Two years later, he was awarded the position of vicar in the parish of Dean Priors, an obscure rural post in Devonshire. Though he lamented his exile from the stimulation of the capital, during the next fourteen years he composed a great many poems, both secular and religious. When the victorious Puritans ousted Herrick from his vicarage in 1647, he returned to London. Herrick's large collection of poems were published in 1648 in two volumes; the secular poems, *Hesperides*, and the religious poems, *Noble Numbers*. The books did not attract much attention, however, and Herrick did not write many more. During the Commonwealth era he lived in London; he was restored to his church position in Devonshire when King Charles II was restored as monarch in 1660.

Herrick's lyric poetry epitomizes classical attitudes and themes in English poetry as adapted to the scenes of country life in Devonshire. He addresses a series of imagined maidens and mistresses with names drawn from Latin verse, celebrating their beauties and calling them to seize the day, giving new vitality to the familiar *carpe diem* theme. Typically, his poems are short and light, expressing a joyful pleasure and a sense of humor.

Delight in Disorder

In this brief lyric, the poet describes the clothing of a woman from shoulder to feet. What he finds enticing is the degree of carelessness in the way these clothes are worn. In an era of elaborate and confining feminine garments, the poet enjoys seeing the careful construction of the costume somewhat violated by looseness and confusion. This description is frequently compared with that in Ben Jonson's poem *Still to Be Neat*, in which too much precision is deplored. It is also compared with Herrick's very short poem *Upon Julia's Clothes*, in which the poet is impressed by the splendor of silk fabric as it flows with the movements of the woman wearing it. In each poem, flowing garments are a pleasant attraction to male eyes.

To Virgins to Make Much of Time

This lyric of four four-line stanzas uses the familiar meter and rhyme scheme of the English popular ballad, but it expresses the essentially classical *carpe diem* idea.

> Gather ye rosebuds while ye may,
>
> Old time is still a-flying;
>
> And this same flower that smiles today,
>
> Tomorrow will be dying.

The rosebuds of the opening line suggest fresh beauty that is bound to wither soon, just as the beauty of the maidens who gather them will inevitably fade. The second stanza uses the daily rising and setting of the sun as a symbol of the rapid passage from youth to age and death. Stanza three states directly and without metaphor that youth is better than age. The poet then urges the maidens to find husbands while they can, before they begin to decline. The tone of the poem suggests an older man offering a kindly warning based on his own experience.

Corinna's Going A-Maying

To go a-maying is to go out early on the morning of May Day or May first to gather branches of whitethorn (hawthorn) blossoms, a flower symbolic of marriage, to decorate the door of one's house. This ceremony is a remnant of the pagan celebrations of spring. The poem retains suggestions of religious ceremony: the flowers have bowed to the east, the birds have sung morning prayers, and Corinna will be like the goddess Flora when she emerges from her bed. So the poet calls upon her to get out of bed and to participate in the joyful activities of the day, like other young virgins and fellows. The poet suggests that Corinna should dress herself not in jewels but in foliage; dewdrops will be her pearls today. In stanza three, the poet describes the village street all decorated with whitethorn at every entrance and suggests that not to come see this would be a sin. The stanza begins and ends with a repetition of the call "Corinna, come." The fourth stanza describes the village youth, both boys and girls, who have already completed the May Day ceremonies not only by bringing home the blossoms but even by kissing, becoming engaged to each other, and by planning their marriages. The final stanza opens with an explicit plea. The poet as lover declares that there will not be a better moment than now to enjoy love, and he warns that life is short and does not permit hesitation. The final line repeats the call "Corinna, come."

The poem is written in rapidly moving couplets, in stanzas of fourteen lines. Some lines, such as those in the opening, central, and final couplets, are five feet long, while the remaining lines have only four feet, causing a rapid return to the rhyme sound and yielding a rollicking effect.

ANDREW MARVELL (1621–1678)

Marvell was born near the northern town of Hull and graduated from Cambridge University. He then traveled abroad. Though he did not approve of or participate in the English Civil War, in about 1650 he took a job tutoring the daughter of General Fairfax, an important leader of the Parliamentary forces. In 1657 Marvell, an excellent student of languages, became an assistant to the blind Milton, the Latin secretary of the council of state. Near the end of the Commonwealth period, Marvell became a member of Parliament for the town of Hull. That position enabled him to protect Milton from rigorous penalties after 1660, when the leaders of the Commonwealth government were liable to punishment.

Most of Marvell's poetry, except for a few satires, was not published during his lifetime. Like Milton, Marvell was a Puritan poet, but his poetry is lighter and closer to the tone of Cavalier poetry. Three years after his death in 1681, his works were published in a volume titled *Miscellaneous Poems*. They did not, however, become widely read; the poetic taste of the public had changed after the Restoration. However, his witty poem *To His Coy Mistress* has been widely studied in the twentieth century. Marvell was one of the few English poets to successfully use the tetrameter or four-foot line for a wide range of effects. The tetrameter line is commonly associated with popular or comic verse.

Bermudas

In this poem Marvell imagines the Puritans, in flight from persecution by the Anglican Church authorities, discovering an unexpected island of calm and beauty. They sing praises and give thanks to God for providing this safe haven. They describe in their song the rich bounty of fruits and the comfortable shade of the island, a natural temple for worship. The tetrameter rhythm of the poem's four-foot lines suggests the beat of the Puritans' oars on the water as they row toward Bermuda.

A Dialogue Between the Soul and Body

This poem consists of four separate speeches, alternating voices of the soul and the body. Each complains that it suffers because it is joined to the other. The soul grieves that it is confined to the body, full of physical pains. The body is bothered by the restless demands of the soul. The debate is inconclusive; each speaker repeats its own position, but there is no suggestion of a reconciliation. Perhaps that was Marvell's point, but some critics have speculated that the poem is unfinished.

To His Coy Mistress

This is Marvell's most famous poem. Like other Cavalier poems it is based on the *carpe diem theme*. It is a seduction poem. The speaker is the lover who tries to convince his beloved (not a mistress in the modern sense) to put aside her concern for chastity and enjoy making love while she is still young. The speaker uses a mock-logical structure. Marvell begins by saying that if there were "world enough, and time," he would gladly be content with merely praising his beloved's beauty forever and with her refusal to accept him as a lover. But beginning with line twenty-one, Marvell points out that time is limited and that they will die, perhaps before they make love, so that her virginity would have been useless. If she dies a virgin, only the worms in her grave will enjoy her. In the final section of the poem, beginning with the word "therefore" in line thirty-three, the speaker draws the logical conclusion that the best choice is to enjoy love now, making Time serve them rather than their being its victim. Marvell develops the conceit that they will be like birds, paradoxically both "amorous birds" and "birds of prey," which grasp energetically at what they want. This paradoxical conceit is similar to the metaphysical conceits created by John Donne and his followers. Thus this poem mingles elements of Cavalier and metaphysical poetry, which were the major schools of poetry during that time.

The Mower Against Gardens

This poem speaks from the point of view of a mower, one who cuts grain in the open fields. The mower complains that the enclosed garden is a place of artificiality in which, since the fall of humankind, the sweet naturalness of plants is corrupted by gardeners who overly fertilize, force, cross-breed, graft, and transplant trees and flowers, making them unnatural and often sterile. Meanwhile, outside the garden, the fields and meadows retain their natural vitality; the "fauns and fairies" live there while only statues can exist within the garden. The two contrasting images of nature and artifice make the familiar association of civilization with corruption. The poem uses couplets, but the couplets have a slightly unbalanced quality because the first line of each has five feet while the second line has only four.

The Garden

The attitude of this poem is opposite to the one expressed in *The Mower against Gardens*. Here, the garden is a place of retirement from pointless competitive human activities. The speaker seeks solitude, repose, calm, and beauty in the garden; his only companions are Quiet and Innocence, personified as two sisters. The speaker describes the beauty of the garden, contrasting its cool loveliness to the lesser beauty of women. In the garden, his lovers are the various fruits that surround him and offer themselves to him. He is transported into an abstract mental state, a spiritual union with the garden. The poet compares his soul with a bird singing in the trees, and he celebrates his sweet solitude as the blessed state of man in Paradise before the creation of woman. Finally, the garden is described as a great sundial in which the bees keep time by moving from plant to plant.

THOMAS CAREW (1594–1640)

This poet (whose name is pronounced as if it were spelled Cary) studied classical literature at Oxford and law at the Middle Temple. Carew then became a member of the court of King Charles I, for which he wrote a masque in 1633. Carew was an admirer of both Donne and Jonson; his poetic style contains both metaphysical wit and a Cavalier tone of easy love and libertine enjoyment. Most of his poems were not published until after his death.

A Rapture

This love lyric in pentameter couplets celebrates the physical pleasures of lovemaking. In the imaginary place of love, called Love's Elysium, he and his beloved are free from the restrictions of the tyrant Honour, who would forbid lovemaking. The poet describes the beauty of his lady and his exploration and enjoyment of her beauty, using imagery of bees and flowers and of ships and harbors to suggest the act of love. They are in a realm of natural and unrestrained delight. Also in Elysium, the lover reports seeing the mythic figures of Lucrece, Daphne, and Laura, who fled from love during their lives but now, after death, are to indulge in it. The final stanza presents the poet in a more militant attitude, defending the beauty of his beloved against rivals.

An Elegy upon the Death of Doctor Donne, Dean of Paul's

This elegy was published in 1633, in an edition of Donne's poetry. Written in pentameter couplets, it celebrates the great poetic gifts of Donne. In particular, Carew points out that Donne was an energetic innovator, not content to merely rework such standard materials of Renaissance poetry as the odes of Pindar and the tales of Ovid. These are the "pedantic weeds," the old stuff that Donne swept away and replaced with wit and "giant fancy." The poem ends with a four-line epitaph for Donne as the priest not only of God but also of poetry.

JOHN SUCKLING (1609–1641)

As soldier, courtier, and man of fashion, Suckling cultivated a reputation for carelessness and ease. His poems are meant to sound natural, without the strained wit of some of his contemporaries. Suckling also wrote plays. His most famous song is from his play *Aglaura*. Near the beginning of the Civil War, Suckling took part in an unsuccessful military action in the Royalist cause; he then fled into exile and died soon after.

Song from Aglaura

This brief lyric mocks the conventional pose of the courtly lover, who is pale and silent when rejected by his beloved. The poet dismisses such a position as hopeless, saying that if the lady is not willing to love, then "the devil take her." He mocks the Petrarchan ideas of the Renaissance sonneteers.

Out upon It!

In this lyric, Suckling makes a joke of the ideal of constancy in love. Having loved the same lady for three whole days, the poet thinks he has been more "constant" than can be expected. However, he gives credit to the lady's beauty, not his own virtue, as the cause of such unusual faithfulness.

RICHARD LOVELACE (1618–1658)

A member of the king's forces during the Civil War, Lovelace came from a background of aristocratic wealth. Brave and handsome, he was considered an ideal Cavalier. However, by the end of the war, Lovelace had been wounded and suffered exile and imprisonment. He finally fell into poverty. He published a collection of his poems in 1649; another edition was published shortly after his death. Suckling's lyric poems unite images of love and war.

To Lucasta, Going to the Wars

The poet, not his lady, Lucasta, is going to war. In saying farewell, he calls war his "new mistress" but expresses his certitude that Lucasta will accept and even praise his going away, because it is for honor that he goes.

To Althea, from Prison

In this brave lyric, the poet speaks from prison, claiming that loving, drinking, and praising his king in song can be accomplished even in confinement. In the final stanza, he declares that so long as he is free to love and his soul is free, he feels as free as the angels. Thus "stone walls" and "iron bars" do not make a prison.

In the early seventeenth century, Ben Jonson and his poetic "sons" were the aristocrats of English poetry. The Cavalier poets were an attractive group of young men who risked their fortunes and their places in society, if not their lives, in gallant service to the cause of King Charles I. As poets, they strove for ease and gracefulness, mocking the moralistic attitudes of the Puritans. They accepted the carpe diem *concept that life is short and should be lived as richly as possible. Their lyrics are light, sensual, and delicious.*

Selected Readings

Bamborough, J. B. *Ben Jonson*. London: Hutchinson, 1970.

Clayton, Thomas, ed. *Cavalier Poets: Selected Poems*. New York: Oxford University Press, 1978.

Herford, C. H. and Percy Simpson, eds. *Ben Jonson*. Oxford: Clarendon, 1952–1961.

13

Early Seventeenth-Century English Literature (1603 to 1660): The Metaphysical Poets

1609	Shakespeare, *Sonnets*
1611	King James Version of the *Holy Bible* published
1611–1612	Donne, *Anniversaries: An Anatomy of the World*
1616	Donne chaplain to King James I; Shakespeare dies; Jonson appointed poet laureate; Jonson, *Works*
1621	Donne appointed dean of St. Paul's Cathedral
1622	Donne, *Sermon on Judges*
1624	Donne, prose essays *Meditations*
1625–1640	Reign of Charles I
1629	Milton, *Ode on the Morning of Christ's Nativity*
1630	Herbert begins his ministry in Bemerton
1633	Donne, *Poems*; Herbert, *The Temple*; Milton, *L'Allegro* and *Il Penseroso*
1634	Crashaw, *Sacred Epigrams*
1640	Walton, *Life of Donne*
1640–1641	Posthumous publication of Jonson, *The Underwood*

1642   The Civil War begins

1644   Crashaw flees to Europe to escape Puritans, becomes Roman Catholic

1646   Vaughan, *Poems*; Crashaw, *Steps to the Temple* and *The Delights of the Muses*

1646–1649   Charles I captured, imprisoned, then executed

1647   Cowley, *The Mistress*

1649–1653   Cromwell conducts government; theaters closed

1649   Lovelace, *Lucasta*

1650   Vaughn, *Silex Scintillians*

1651   Vaughn, *Olor Iscanus*

1653   Crashaw's *Carmen Deo Nostro* published in Paris; Cromwell assumes title
of lord protector

1656   Cowley, *Davideis* and *Poems*

*P*oets do not write poetry in order to found a new movement or "school"
of poetry. However, sometimes they do react to the poetic conventions of the
times by consciously taking a new direction. This was the case in the early
decades of the seventeenth century, when John Donne chose to mock many
of the conventions of Renaissance love poetry and to assume a new, more
aggressive tone.

JOHN DONNE (1572–1631)

During his lifetime, Donne was known primarily as a charismatic
Anglican preacher, but he did not achieve that position easily. Born into a
Roman Catholic family during a period of strong anti-Catholic feeling in
England, Donne left the church when in his twenties. He had had an unsettled
youth, studying at Oxford and Cambridge universities and at the Inns of
Court but never taking a degree. Donne then traveled in Europe. As he
needed a patron in order to survive, he became secretary to Sir Thomas
Egerton in 1598. He lost this position in 1601 because Sir Egerton disapproved of Donne's marriage to Egerton's niece, Ann More. Donne's financial and social positions were rather precarious for the next decade. King
James I insisted that he become an Anglican clergyman and blocked all other
kinds of patronage. Finally, in 1615, Donne overcame his reluctance and
took holy orders; subsequently he became a popular preacher while dean of
Saint Paul's Cathedral, London. However, he virtually stopped writing

poetry after 1615. The major works of his later years are many volumes of sermons and meditative religious writings.

Although during his lifetime Donne's poetry was circulated among courtly and literary groups in manuscript form, most of it was not printed until 1633, two years after his death. It is therefore not possible to date the poems exactly or to tell in precisely what order they were written. Most scholars assume that the more libertine, sexually daring, and cynical poems are from his early youth and that the more sincere and serious poems, including the *Holy Sonnets*, probably were written after 1600.

Because Donne's lyrics are often difficult at first reading, the reader should work through each poem several times with the help of the explanatory notes provided in most modern texts. Part of the difficulty with many of the poems results from their abruptness. The speaker often seems to begin in the middle of unexplained events. Often the setting is implied; for example, the speaker may be in the middle of a conversation or even an argument with some other person, also implied. Furthermore, the metaphors, concepts, and conceits are often unconventional and peculiar. For example, when speaking of two lovers, Donne often adds one to the other and gets the sum of one in the union of their souls. Also, in several poems Donne describes eyes as simultaneously looking out, looking into, and looking at. Concepts and metaphors that are mentioned in more than one poem obviously become clearer with each reading.

The Good-Morrow

This love lyric of three stanzas does not register the conventional complaint about a lady's coldness. Here, the lover seems to be awakening after a night in bed with his beloved. In the first stanza, he compares his previous state of incomplete awareness with his new feeling of being fully aware of beauty. The second stanza compares the small world of the lovers' room to the great worlds of explorers and astronomers. The lovers have enough world in each other. The metaphor of the world continues in the final stanza. Each lover is a hemisphere, or one-half of the world; together they make up one perfect and undying whole. Each one's face is reflected in the hemisphere of the other's eyes. The microcosm of their little world contains all the elements of the macrocosm, or great world.

Song

This poem reflects a cavalier cynicism about a beautiful woman's ability to remain faithful. The speaker begins by abruptly sending someone off to do a series of impossible tasks: to catch a falling star, to get a plant pregnant, to find out where the past has gone, and similar others. These absurd demands are meant to prepare us for the greatest impossibility of all—that of finding a woman who is both fair (beautiful) and true (faithful). In the second stanza, the poet sends us off on a trip around the world to seek such a woman among the other wonders of the world. But in the final stanza, the speaker calls off the search, saying that even if such a woman were found nearby, she would not remain true for as long as it took him to reach her.

The Sun Rising

In this poem the speaker aggressively addresses the sun as an "old fool" who should mind his own business and go wake up those who need to be wakened, such as schoolboys, huntsmen, and harvesters, because the lovers in bed do not want to get up. In the second stanza, the lover compares himself to the sun. The lover is the center of his own universe; he can eclipse the sun by closing his eyes. In his extreme subjectivity, the lover declares that he and his beloved comprise the whole world. In stanza three, the lover says that the old, tired sun can rest himself by warming only this "world" in their bed and save himself the trouble of shining on the rest. Thus, by the end of the poem the lover has completely reversed himself. He began by sending the sun away but ends by calling on the sun to focus only on himself and his lady, who comprise the whole world.

The Canonization

To be canonized is to be declared a saint by the church. This poem, whose theme seems to be Donne's disapproved marriage, begins in the worldly realm of politics and business but moves to a higher realm of mysterious love. Like the previous poems, it begins with the speaker abruptly sending away the one whom he is addressing. This other person has, it seems, objected to the speaker's love for a particular woman. The speaker responds by listing a number of more useful things that the other could turn his attention to, such as making money, getting a patron or even studying. In stanza two, the speaker continues to defend his love by pointing out that the rest of society is unharmed by it and that the lovers do not meddle in anyone else's business. The focus changes in stanza three, where the speaker begins to describe the quality of his love as a mysterious union of two into one and alludes to the legendary phoenix, which is simultaneously both male and female. He also suggests that sexual intercourse is a sort of dying from which both lovers can arise as mysterious spirits. The fourth stanza develops the concept of dying, saying that their love will live on in the poems he writes about it. In the final stanza the speaker describes a situation in which the lovers, now dead, have become saints in a religion of ideal love. Their followers beg them for a pattern of their love so that the rest of the world might follow it. Thus the isolation of the lovers in the first two stanzas has been transformed into their universal praise at the end.

The Flea

In this mock seduction poem the speaker tries to persuade the lady that her loss of virginity would be as insignificant as the bite of a flea. The speaker draws the analogy that if the flea bites him and then bites her, their blood mingles in it without sin or disgrace. He plays with the idea that the joining of their blood inside the flea is a marriage and that the flea is thus their marriage bed. Therefore, she should not kill the flea. But in stanza three she has killed the flea with her fingernail. He pretends to be shocked at her cruelty but then turns the argument to prove that just as the death of the flea is harmless, so would the loss of her virginity be insignificant. The use of an unromantic image of a flea in a love poem is a radical departure from the hearts and cupids of the love poetry of the previous century, showing how Donne replaces flowery convention with earthy and realistic imagery.

A Valediction: Forbidding Mourning

A valediction is a farewell speech. This poem may be based on a trip Donne took to Europe without his wife. The central idea of the poem is that their love is of such a quality that mere physical separation cannot affect it; therefore, she need not be afraid or cry. He begins by comparing their separation to that of the good soul leaving the body, quietly and without noise. Their separation should be a private and calm movement, like that of the revolving planets in heaven, not like the turbulence of storms and earthquakes that cause terror on earth. Because their love is more refined than mere sensual pleasure, it does not depend on each other's physical presence. Their souls can expand to cover the distance between them, like gold beaten into a thin but very large sheet. The final three stanzas develop one of the most famous metaphysical metaphors or conceits. The speaker imagines that he and his wife are like the two points of a drawing compass. The woman is the center point, staying in one place. He is the moving point that travels around but eventually comes back to where he began, pulled by her influence. Together they make a circle, the symbol of perfection and unity.

The Ecstasy

In this poem, the lover describes himself and his beloved lying together, looking into each other's eyes and holding hands but not moving. Meanwhile, their two souls advance out of their bodies and mix together, becoming one soul that is more perfect than either of their separate souls. Nevertheless, the lover admits that they also need to have bodies, that the union of souls must be expressed physically, as ordinary mortals need a book to read divine mysteries.

Elegy 19

This poem is not an elegy in the modern sense of being a poem about death but rather in the classical sense of being a reflective poem in couplets. Donne's classical model here was Ovid, whose elegies were erotic poems in Latin. In this poem Donne describes watching his lover undress as he anticipates making love to her. He mentions the various items of her clothing as she removes them, until she is left naked in the white clothes of the bed. He celebrates that nakedness, comparing it with a newly discovered land to be explored and enjoyed. He urges her to reveal herself totally, using his own nakedness as an example; he will be her "covering."

A Hymn to God the Father

Donne wrote a number of hymns, prayerlike poems to be set to music and sung by choirs during church services. In this hymn, Donne plays with puns upon his own name. When God has finished (done) forgiving the poet for all of his sins, God will still not have done (not be finished and not fully possess the soul of Donne). In stanza one, God is asked to forgive not only humankind's original sin in Donne but also Donne's own individual sins. But that will not be enough. In stanza two, God is asked to forgive the sins Donne has promoted in others and to forgive those sins that though at first resisted by Donne were often ultimately committed. Still, God will not have done all. In the third stanza, Donne expresses his fear that he will not be saved and asks that the Son of God be there after his death to save him. If that is done, then Donne will be no longer fearful and will be wholly God's. The final "thou hast done" means that God is finished with forgiving Donne and has Donne's soul completely.

The Holy Sonnets

Unlike the sixteenth-century sonneteers, who wrote cycles of love sonnets, Donne used the sonnet form to express religious emotions. As a young man he had struggled to find religious commitment, and even later, as an Anglican clergyman, he was disturbed by religious doubt. Donne wrote nineteen sonnets expressing his feelings of sin and his striving for spiritual peace; all were probably written before his ordination in 1611.

Donne uses the Italian form of the sonnet, which is made up of an octave, or eight lines with an interlocking rhyme scheme, followed by a sestet, or six lines with a different rhyme from the octave, the final two lines forming a couplet. The sonnets, like most sonnets of the Renaissance, do not have individual titles; they are referred to by their first lines.

I Am a Little World Made Cunningly

In calling himself a little world, Donne refers to the Renaissance idea that human beings have within themselves the same elements that are in the larger physical universe. He also asserts that the human being has a soul, as the universe has angels. However, the speaker of the poem feels that his world, himself, has been fouled by sin and must be cleansed before it can be saved. He calls for floods of water to drown his sin and then asks for the cleansing fire, religious zeal. In a final paradox he asserts that being consumed by fire will make him whole again.

Death Be Not Proud

This poem also develops a paradox. Personifying death, the poet accuses him of being proud of his destructive power. But the poet states that in reality death has no power, because while death takes us from life, as sleep takes us from wakefulness, it releases us to eternity. Therefore, we shall live forever while death itself dies.

Batter My Heart, Three-personed God

In this sonnet Donne speaks directly to God, calling on Him to overcome the poet's sinful nature. The poet compares himself with a town under enemy control, waiting to be liberated. In the sestet, the metaphor shifts; the poet speaks of himself as a lover engaged to God's enemy or as a prisoner of the wrong guardian. In either case, he wishes God to overwhelm him, as a woman is overwhelmed in a rape. Such an imprisonment or rape would, if done by God, result in liberation and purification from sin. Here again, the relationship is expressed as a paradox.

Devotions upon Emergent Occasions

After an illness in 1623, Donne wrote a series of Meditations in which he traced the various stages of his illness in the feelings it created. In these prose essays, Donne used some of the same language and conceits that he used in his poetry; for example, that the human being is a microcosm of the universe and has corresponding elements. These Meditations were published in 1624, soon after Donne's recovery, and were immediately well received.

The most famous is *Meditation XVII*, in which the invalid hears the church bell tolling for someone who is dying. He wonders "for whom the bell tolls" or if it could be tolling for himself. But then he considers that as the bell tolls everyone to God, dying or in health, its tolling must include himself. We are all equally summoned by God, and each one of us is involved in the passing of any other, because "no man is an island." Illness is a trouble that refines us and prepares us and makes us "fit for God." The problems of others can make us think of our own need for salvation.

These Meditations are a landmark in the development of English prose during the seventeenth century. Their quiet but intense style resulted in many memorable and oft-quoted phrases.

GEORGE HERBERT (1593–1633)

Herbert is considered the foremost of the followers of John Donne. In fact, his mother had consulted with Donne while planning George Herbert's education. Intending to be a clergyman, he achieved distinction at Cambridge University, but did not glide easily into the religious life. Like Donne, Herbert experienced spiritual struggles, some of which are described in his poetry. Eventually Herbert took holy orders and became an active and conscientious parish preacher. Before he died, he destroyed all his poems on secular topics. His poems on religious topics were published after his death in 1633. In these poems, collected in a volume called *The Temple*, Herbert, like Donne, rejects the conventional forms and phrases of Renaissance verse in favor of a more direct, even abrupt, colloquial style with images based on simple, ordinary objects. He is considered to be of the metaphysical school.

The Temple

Many of the poems in *The Temple* focus on parts of the church, such as the altar or a stained glass window. Others describe simple incidents of doubt or fear that are transformed into moments of faith.

The Altar *and* Easter Wings

These two poems are written so that the lines form the shape of the subject. *The Altar*, for example, is shaped like a church altar. Similarly, *Easter Wings*, especially if it is printed vertically as it was in the early editions, is shaped like the wings of two angels. The short lines in the center of each stanza describe man as "poor" and "thin," but in union with God, he becomes stronger and more worthy, as is shown by the increasing length of the lines.

The Collar

In this poem Herbert portrays himself in a moment of rebellion against the demanding life of Christian devotion. He expresses a longing for freedom and for pleasures and plenty. After the rebellious outburst he imagines that the voice of God calls to him, and he immediately responds with devout submission. The paradoxical "rope of sands" conceit is an image of faithful believers' voluntary submission to God.

The Pulley

The poet imagines God using a pulley to elevate souls. The poem plays with various meanings of the term *rest*; God did not give people the gift of tranquility or rest; instead He gave them all other gifts—the remainder or the rest. Herbert imagines God making the decision that restlessness should be a part of human nature so that people would strive to reach God and not be satisfied with existence in the natural world.

Virtue

The tone of this calm and sweet lyric differs from that of most of Herbert's other poems. It expresses perfect faith, acceptance, and peace. Although the day, the flower, and the season will pass away, the virtuous soul will be like a tree—permanent and unyielding but still alive and growing.

RICHARD CRASHAW (1613–1649)

At a time of increasingly militant Protestantism in England, Crashaw, the son of a Puritan clergyman, became a Roman Catholic and fled to France at the start of the Civil War. He was befriended in exile by Queen Henrietta Maria, wife of Charles I, and later was granted a post in the Catholic church in Italy. Crashaw seems to have been drawn to Catholicism by his own intensely mystical nature. He sought ecstasy in religion.

Some of Crashaw's poems follow the emblem form. That is, a printed picture of a symbolic object, such as a heart, is followed by a motto or adage, which is then followed by a poem that explains the significance of the image and its relationship to the motto. Crashaw often used imagery usually associated with love poetry, adapting it to his own intense feelings of devotion to God. Like that of other metaphysical poets, Crashaw's imagery can also be shocking and bizarre.

On Our Crucified Lord	In this poem the blood of Christ on the cross becomes his only clothing; he is "richly clad" in "the purple wardrobe" of his own blood.
On the Wounds of Our Crucified Lord	The poem describes Christ's wounds as mouths with rosy lips and as eyes yielding "ruby tears." Such extreme imagery, sometimes called baroque imagery, was ridiculed by both contemporary and later readers. While sometimes excessive, Crashaw's religious imagery also created some powerfully imaginative effects. Most of Crashaw's religious poems were published in 1652 in a volume titled *Steps to the Temple*.
The Flaming Heart	The poem comments on a picture of Saint Theresa in the act of being stabbed by a dart of holy love held by an angel. The religious ecstasy of Saint Theresa is symbolized by the wounded heart, which is an image more commonly used in love poetry. The poet first says that the picture should be altered to show Saint Theresa with the dart, because it is her example that penetrates other hearts. However, he goes on, Theresa's wounded heart is also a weapon, which the poet wants to feel in his own heart.

ABRAHAM COWLEY (1618–1667)

A Royalist during the Civil War, Cowley went into exile with the royal establishment as the queen's secretary. Back in England after the Restoration, he lived quietly in the country. Cowley's literary influence was greater than his poetic accomplishments. He was interested in the odes of the Greek poet Pindar and introduced the Pindaric ode as he understood it: lofty in language, abrupt and irregular in form. His were difficult poems. However, Dryden and other poets of the late seventeenth century adapted Cowley's extravagant form to their own purposes. In the eighteenth century, the critic Samuel Johnson described Cowley as the most important of the metaphysical poets.

Ode: Of Wit   The word *wit* has many meanings. In this poem, Cowley tries to define wit by telling what it is *not*. He surveys a series of qualities erroneously called wit, such as bombast, crudeness, shallow cleverness, puns, and word games. Then what is wit really, Cowley asks, responding that although it is hard to define, the essence of wit is recognized when we see it. True wittiness has rightness or fitness; it harmonizes with truth. The poem ends with a compliment to an unknown friend, whose poetry, Cowley avers, is an example of true wit.

HENRY VAUGHAN (1621–1695)

A Welshman, Vaughan was educated at Oxford University. He began as a law student but soon turned to medicine. He fought as a Royalist in the Civil War, after which he returned to the life of a small town physician in Wales. Vaughan was clearly influenced by the poetry of George Herbert, speaking of himself as one of Herbert's "converts." Perhaps influenced by his twin brother, Thomas, who was an alchemist and supposedly steeped in magic, Vaughan also studied the occult. Vaughan apparently underwent some sort of crisis about 1647; possibly he was gravely ill. Thereafter he focused intensely on religion, as shown in his volume of poems titled *Silex Scintillans*.

Silex Scintillans   This volume, first published in 1650, was reprinted with additional poems in 1655. The Latin title translates as "The Fiery or Sparkling Flint," indicating that Vaughan saw himself as the hard stone or flint from which divine sparks can be struck. Vaughan's lyric poems are very musical and show a strange and highly individualistic imagination.

The Retreat   This brief lyric glorifies childhood as an angel-like state of innocence and closeness to God. The central image presents life as a journey from that pure state of childhood into sensuality and sin. The poet longs for a return to innocence, but he recognizes that he is too weighted down with worldliness. He ends with the hope that death eventually will return him to his original glorious condition. The notion about the preexistence of the soul expressed in this poem is more fully presented in William Wordsworth's *Ode: Intimations of Immortality*, a much later and more well known poem.

Corruption   In this poem Vaughan imagines Adam's life after his fall from grace. As a laboring farmer after his expulsion from the Garden of Eden, Adam, the poet supposes, must have had memories of Eden and glimmerings of a nearby angelic presence. Adam's state is contrasted to that of modern human beings, who are careless, sunk in sin, and more estranged from God than Adam. At the end of the poem, an angel calls out that the time for harvesting sinners is ripe; he calls for the sickle to mow down the fields of sinners.

The World

The opening lines of this poem present a rare literary image of what eternity might look like—a circle of pure light.

> I saw eternity the other night
>
> Like a great ring of pure and endless light.

Beneath it is the shadow of time, which encloses the earth. As a contrast to the beauty of eternity, the poet presents a series of images of human types. These have lost sight of eternity and become absorbed in temporal interests. The complaining lover, the secretive statesman, the fearful miser, the self-indulgent epicure, and those who are merely materialistic fools make up the list of men who ignore the light of truth. In the final stanza, the poet warns these misguided folk that they risk losing eternity. A divine voice answers that only those who deserve eternity shall find it.

They Are All Gone into the World of Light

The poet sits alone, remembering those who are now dead and, as he imagines, enjoying a new life in heaven. He contrasts his own state of darkness with the light of eternal life. He feels some glimmerings of that light, but he calls for a better view, either in dreams or visions that God could offer him or through death so that he might fully enter into eternal light.

The metaphysical style of poetry, with its irregularities and extreme imagery, was never aimed at a broad audience. The metaphysical poets sought to express what was mysterious and strange in human consciousness. Their use of paradox and extreme images made strenuous demands on the reader's imagination, but the reward they offered was a new and surprising insight into spiritual life. In the late seventeenth century, the tide of taste changed. The poets of this group began to be neglected; their example was not followed. John Donne's literary reputation was obscure until the early twentieth century.

Selected Readings

Hammond, Gerald, ed. *The Metaphysical Poets: A Casebook.* New York: Macmillan, 1974.

Roberts, John R., ed. *Essential Articles for the Study of John Donne's Poetry.* Hamden, CT: Archon, 1975.

Roston, Murray. *The Soul of Wit: A Study of John Donne.* Oxford: Clarendon, 1974.

Williamson, George. *Six Metaphysical Poets: A Reader's Guide.* New York: Farrar, 1967.

14

Early Seventeenth-Century English Literature (1603 to 1660): The Christian Epic

1625–1640 Reign of Charles I

1629 Milton, *Ode on the Morning of Christ's Nativity*

1629–1640 Charles I reigns without Parliament

1633 Milton, *L'Allegro* and *Il Penseroso*; Donne, *Poems*

1634 Milton, masque *Comus*

1637 Milton, *Lycidas*

1638–1639 Milton makes European tour

1642 The Civil War begins; opponents of king, many Puritans among them, called Roundheads, were led by Oliver Cromwell

1642 Milton, *The Reason of Church Government*

1643 Parliament passes Ordinance of Printing requiring the licensing of printers

1644 Milton, *Areopagitica*; Milton, *Of Education*

1645 Milton, *Poems of Mr. John Milton*

1646–1649 Charles I captured, imprisoned, then executed

1649–1653	Milton appointed as Latin secretary to the Council of State; Council of State led by Cromwell; theaters closed
1651	Milton, *Defense of the English People*
1651–1652	Milton becomes blind
1653	Cromwell assumes title of lord protector
1657	Milton takes Andrew Marvell as his assistant
1658–1660	Cromwell dies, succeeded by son, who later resigns and is replaced by General Monk, who restores the monarchy
1660	Marvell uses his position as member of Parliament to protect Milton
1660–1685	Reign of King Charles II
1667	Milton completes *Paradise Lost*
1671	Milton, *Paradise Regained* and *Samson Agonistes*
1674	Milton dies

While the Royalists included a number of polished poets who created a school of lyric poetry, their opponents, the Puritans and Parliamentarians, were not as a group interested in poetry. The great exception was Milton, who endowed the Puritan concept of Christianity with epic dignity and grandeur. Milton's poetic ideas were grounded in the whole history and tradition of European literature; he transcends the age in which he lived.

JOHN MILTON (1608–1674)

The major poetic spokesman for the Puritan viewpoint in seventeenth-century England was John Milton. His kind of Puritanism, though, was not marked by the dour, narrow, suspicious attitude that later forced the closing of theaters. Milton saw himself as a follower of Spenser, whose rich imagination produced pleasurable poetry in the service of morality.

Scholars usually divide Milton's career into three periods: the youthful period of study, travel, and lyrical poetry, the middle period of prose works and public service, and the late period of retirement and the composition of his great epics.

Milton was born in London. His father, a prosperous businessman, wanted to give his son the best possible education. Milton went to St. Paul's School in London and then to Cambridge University, where in 1632 he took a Masters Degree. A student of languages, he was able to read Greek, Latin,

Hebrew, and the modern European languages. His records from Cambridge indicate that he was an outstanding student. Milton decided very early that he wanted to devote himself fully to producing outstanding poetry. Leaving Cambridge, he went to the home of his retired father in Horton, where for the next six years he wholly occupied himself with reading and studying to prepare himself for poetry. He then began to write lyric poetry. Milton toured Europe during 1638 and 1639, mainly visiting Italy. When he returned, the beginnings of the English Civil War diverted him from his poetic preoccupations, and he became a political writer for the liberal, anti-Royalist cause. During that period he produced numerous prose pamphlets in which he argued in favor of individual freedoms. When the Commonwealth government was established, Milton was given the official position of Latin Secretary to the Council of State. Because diplomatic correspondence was still carried on in Latin, this was indeed a very crucial post, close to the center of power.

Milton did not always agree with the policies of the Parliament, however. In 1644 he wrote *Areopagitica*, arguing against the new laws of censorship. About this same time, Milton married his first wife, a young woman who soon left him and went back to her family for two years before returning. Milton responded to his marital problems by writing a series of pamphlets defending divorce, which was a very radical position at the time. Partly because of his heavy load of government work, Milton went blind about 1651 or 1652, but he continued his duties with the help of secretaries. When the monarchy was restored in 1660, Milton's having held a position with the Commonwealth government was a liability. He was fined and briefly imprisoned but eventually was allowed to retire to take up his poetic career again. The last fourteen years of his life were intensely productive. During this time he wrote two epic poems and an important classical tragedy, despite his blindness and relative poverty.

On the Morning of Christ's Nativity

This ode, written at Christmastime of 1629, displays Milton's interest in music and in the re-creation of musical sounds in poetry. The poem celebrates Christ's birth as the end of the old, pagan world and the opening moment of a new era. The poet pictures the shepherds hearing the new heavenly music as the old gods shrink and fade away.

L'Allegro *and* Il Penseroso

These two poems present parallel and contrasting images of happy sociable existence and thoughtful, melancholy solitude. Written in couplets of four-foot lines (tetrameter), they create images of daylight and of happy rural scenes and activities (*L'Allegro*) and then of evening and nighttime and of scholarly study and cloudy morning walks (*Il Penseroso*). Milton shows his control of the same difficult meter to sustain two different moods.

Lycidas
This poem is a pastoral elegy—pastoral because it takes its imagery from the rural life, and elegy because it laments a death, that of a promising young poet, Edward King, referred to as the shepherd Lycidas who died too young. Classical allusions to the shepherd are blended with Christian references to Christ as shepherd of his followers. Patterned on a classical elegy, the poem includes an invocation of Muses, a description of Lycidas, an outcry against his fate, a procession of mourners, the strewing of flowers, and a final consolation, or reconciliation to his death. Milton uses the death of Edward King to raise questions about his own life: why confine oneself to study when life is so short? What will be the reward of hard work? Why do the undeserving seem to prosper more than the deserving? The figure of Lycidas, exalted at the end, is a partial answer to these questions.

Areopagitica
The title of this prose pamphlet refers to the ancient Greek Areopagus, the high court where questions of state were argued. Milton wrote this pamphlet against an ordinance of Parliament passed in 1643 that controlled the press through licensing. Milton argues that censorship takes away from the individual's ability to make an informed moral choice. He points out that God gave human beings the power of making choices as a way to exercise virtue. If choice is denied, people do not take responsibility for their own decisions; rather, they are confined to a narrow conformity of opinion, which may not always reflect the whole truth. Reform and new discovery arc cut off. Eloquent though Milton's pamphlet was, the ordinance was not repéaled.

MILTON'S SONNETS

Milton did not write a sequence or cycle of sonnets like the sixteenth-century sonneteers. Instead, he occasionally wrote sonnets during his youth and middle years, some on public issues and some very personal. Milton preferred the Italian sonnet form, consisting of an octave and a sestet, to the English form, which ends with a couplet.

On the Late Massacre in Piedmont
In this sonnet Milton express grief and outrage at the slaughter of a group of Protestants living in northern Italy.

When I Consider How My Light Is Spent
This sonnet, written soon after Milton became blind, expresses his frustration at being deprived of the ability to use his "talent" for writing. The voice of personified Patience answers that by submitting to his fate the poet will best serve God.

Paradise Lost

The mature Milton used the full range of his classical and biblical learning and of his political and personal experiences to write this comprehensive epic poem. Rising above the usual epic hero, who depends on cleverness and physical courage, Milton created in Adam a Christian hero of conscience. Adam is heroic in his acceptance of guilt. At first the most impressive figure in the poem is Satan, who is as attractive as he is evil but who diminishes in stature as the epic progresses, gradually becoming a figure of meanness and spite.

Milton employed blank verse, which prior to this was used mostly for drama, because he had a lengthy and complex story to tell and needed the flexibility that rhymeless lines offer.

STRUCTURE OF *PARADISE LOST*

The poem has twelve books. The story begins with the expulsion from Heaven of Satan and his crew of rebellious angels and ends with the expulsion of Adam and Eve from Paradise. But Milton describes many events that preceded the main action, working them into a pattern of parallel and contrasting scenes. For example, the debate in Hell about how to oppose God is contrasted to a debate in Heaven about how to counteract Satan's seduction of human beings. The unholy trinity of Satan, Sin, and Death is a grotesque parallel to the holy trinity of God, Mary, and Christ.

Milton's purpose, stated early in Book I, is to explain why God, being good, allows evil to plague people's lives. His Puritan theology stresses the importance of individual moral choice. To be virtuous, people must be able to choose from among both good and evil actions, but even if they choose evil, they still may obtain mercy and forgiveness by repenting.

MILTON'S STYLE

Milton's style is not easy. His sentences tend to be long and complicated, especially where he imitates the twisted reasoning of one of the fallen angels. Milton had a vast vocabulary and frequently used a term to exploit the meaning of the Latin root word as well as the English meaning. The modern reader should expect to have to read slowly and to reread frequently.

The work contains many epic similes, or extended comparisons where the poet abandons the narrative line temporarily while he brings in an image, situation or brief incident from some other context in order to suggest its parallel with or similarity to the main action. These epic similes are usually introduced by a phrase such as "as when" or "as whom," and the transition back into the main story line is usually marked by the word "so."

Also, Milton frequently includes a long catalog of lofty-sounding names with accompanying descriptive terms. These rhetorical devices are unfamiliar to most modern readers, but once they are pointed out, the reading becomes less difficult.

Book I. Book I begins with the poet's invocation for help from the Heavenly Muse and his statement of purpose (to "justify the ways of God to men"). The narrative then describes Satan and his band of fallen angels, now demons, lying prostrate on the burning lake of Hell, having just fallen there after an unsuccessful battle against God in Heaven. Satan, huge and shining, raises his head and speaks to his chief follower, Beelzebub. (Milton has given the demons the names of pre-Christian pagan gods, assuming that these false gods were really demons.) Satan complains about their fall and expresses his continued hatred and resistance. He picks himself up and flies to solid ground, then calls to his troops and mocks them to rouse them from the effects of their long fall.

Milton gives a catalog of the most notable devils, including Moloch, Chemos, Astoreth, Thammuz, and Belial.

The demons assemble on the shore, and Satan makes a speech, blaming God for having tempted them to rebel and promising that the battle is not over. Book I ends with the building of Pandemonium, a new palace for Satan and all the demons.

Book II. Book II opens with a debate among the chief demons in Pandemonium about the best strategy for resisting God. Beelzebub reports a new creation, the universe, with earth and humankind at the center, which seems to be the most vulnerable place for attack. Everyone else is afraid to go, so Satan sets out through the gates of Hell to investigate the weakness of earth and Man. But at the gate, he is confronted by Death, an ugly, shapeless monster who refuses to let him pass. As Death and Satan begin to fight, they are stopped by Sin, a foul female figure. Sin explains that she is actually the daughter of Satan, born out of his side when he conspired against God and later made pregnant by him. She has given birth to hideous Death. Sin holds the key to the gate of Hell. She opens it to let Satan out, but cannot close it again. Satan makes his way toward the world, which hangs on a golden chain from the gate of Heaven.

Book III. In Book III the scene shifts to Heaven, where God consults with his son about the fate of human beings. God foresees that they will sin, but his son volunteers to go to earth and redeem humankind by sacrificing himself. Pleased by this offer, God bestows on his son all his powers on earth. There is a celebration in Heaven, but meanwhile Satan is surveying the earth.

Book IV. In Book IV Satan sneaks onto the earth and locates Paradise, where he sees the beautiful Adam and Eve. Assuming the shape of a lion, he hears them speak about the forbidden fruit. Satan reacts with jealous spite. Then the angel Gabriel is dispatched to seek out Satan and to get rid of him.

Books V and VI. In Books V and VI, the angel Raphael, sent by God, visits Adam and Eve to warn them of Satan's evil intentions. He stays to lunch with them, and in response to Adam's questions, he tells the history of how Satan warred against God in Heaven.

Book VII. Book VII begins mid-point in the epic with the word *descend*. Raphael continues his history, describing how God created the universe, Adam, and Eve in seven days. Milton asserts that God's intention was to replace the fallen angels with new spirits, the souls of virtuous people.

Book VIII. In Book VIII Adam responds to Raphael's narration with the story of his own creation, from his point of view, and the subsequent birth of Eve from a rib taken out of his side. She was created as a cure for his solitude. Finally, Raphael departs.

Book IX. Book IX contains the crisis of the poem. Satan has reentered earth and slips into the body of a snake. Meanwhile, Eve complains to Adam that when they work together in the garden, they too often stop to talk and do not get much done. She wants to work separately. Adam protests, reminding her of the danger Raphael has warned them about, but Eve is stubborn because she does not like to be thought of as weak and untrustworthy. They agree to meet at noon. Finding her alone, Satan, as the snake, convinces Eve that he has learned to speak, unlike other animals, by eating a special fruit. Eve is eager to see it, but when they arrive at the Tree of Knowledge of Good and Evil, she recognizes it as the forbidden fruit. Satan persists and with flattery and false reasoning finally convinces her that there is no danger. She eats, gorging herself and becoming drunk. She then staggers back to Adam, telling him what she has done and offering to share the fruit with him. She lies to Adam by saying that she ate of the fruit for his sake. He realizes that she has fallen, but he eats the fruit regardless, not wanting to be separated from her again. They immediately begin to make love. But when they wake up the next day, they begin to bicker, blaming each other and hiding their shame with fig leaves.

Books X, XI, and XII. The remaining Books, X, XI, and XII, show the aftermath of Adam and Eve's fall. Adam and Eve repent, but must now suffer. Adam must work for survival and Eve will endure the pains of labor and difficult childbirth. The angel Michael, however, gives them some hope with a vision of the future. Meanwhile, Sin and Death are rejuvenated and find easy passage onto the earth. In the final scene, Adam and Eve regretfully leave Paradise and move out into the harsh climate of the world.

Paradise Lost was always difficult because of its complexity and many obscure allusions. However, those able to understand it at the time recognized at once that it was a monumental work. Many images and phrases from this poem have become a part of the poetic heritage of the English language. In the eighteenth century, Addison wrote a series of essays in *The Spectator* to help readers understand and enjoy *Paradise Lost*.

In 1671, three years before he died, Milton published both *Paradise Regained*, an epic in four books completing the story of *Paradise Lost* by showing Christ's redemption of humankind, and *Samson Agonistes*, a tragedy on the model of a Greek classical drama.

Samson Agonistes

Scholars are not certain when Milton actually composed this drama. It probably was written after 1660, (when Milton suffered defeat along with the Commonwealth government,) but well before its publication in 1671.

THE MILTON-SAMSON PARALLEL

Milton's story of Samson tells of a defeated, blind, and disgraced hero who nevertheless remains faithful to his God, thus paralleling Milton's own situation. The story of Samson is found in the Bible, in the Book of Judges, chapters 13 through 16. Samson was a hero of superhuman strength. The secret source of his strength was in his thick and long hair. The Philistine woman Delilah seduced Samson into revealing this secret, after which she cut his hair and betrayed him to her people, the Philistines, who were enemies of the tribe of Dan, Samson's folk. Milton made two important changes in the biblical story. First, he made Delilah the wife rather than the mistress of Samson, rendering her betrayal even more criminal. Second, Milton added a scene in which Samson's father, Manoa, tries to ransom his son from captivity. Milton has blended Christian and classical Greek elements in this play. The structure is like that of a Greek tragedy, containing a chorus and focusing on the ultimate moment of the hero's career. Everything takes place in one day, and the final violence is not represented but is reported by a messenger. As a Christian story, the play describes temptation leading to a fall, suffering and doubt, the renewal of faith and subsequent redemption, and finally joy and the assurance of salvation.

Prologue. The drama begins in defeat. The blind Samson in soliloquy laments his condition as a captive slave of the Philistines, "eyeless in Gaza," the city of his enemies. He asks why God has let this happen to him. Resting in the open air, because it is a holiday, Samson seems half dead.

The Chorus enters. They are old friends from the tribe of Dan who have come to visit and comfort Samson. They lament his fallen condition and retell some of his former heroic deeds.

Scene I. In scene I Samson's father, Manoa, arrives and sympathizes with his son, blaming God. But Samson blames himself, telling how he allowed Delilah to discover his secret. Samson's chief sorrow is that he has failed his God, and he now feels useless. He does not want to be ransomed and live an idle life, as Manoa suggests. The Chorus sings an ode questioning God's fairness.

Scene II. Scene II begins as Delilah visits Samson, pretending to feel repentance for her betrayal of him and claiming that the pressures put on her by the Philistines were too great to resist. Samson is roused to anger, particularly when she reaches out to touch him. The Chorus then discusses the danger of loving a woman; they are puzzled by women's motives.

Scene III. In scene III the giant Harapha of Gath comes to taunt and mock Samson, boasting of his own deeds. Further aroused, Samson offers to fight Harapha, even blind, inside an enclosure. Harapha charges that Samson uses magic to win. But Samson cites God as his source of power and repeats his challenge to fight as God's champion. Samson begins to feel rejuvenated and hopeful. Harapha goes away muttering vague threats. The Chorus is pleased to see Samson once again fearless; they celebrate his revival.

Scene IV. In scene IV some officers come to take Samson to the arena where games are being played to celebrate the holiday. The crowd wants Samson to display his amazing strength. At first Samson refuses to enter into the celebrations of a false god, the god of the Philistines, but then he begins to change his mind. He senses that this may be an opportunity and agrees to go. This is our final view of Samson. The Chorus expresses hope based on Samson's change of mood; they pray for him.

Scene V. In scene V, the final scene, Manoa returns, full of hope because he has arranged to ransom Samson and take him home. There is loud noise from the arena. Then a messenger enters; he is fleeing the scene of the temple and reports how Samson has, after his display of strength, taken the opportunity while resting between two pillars of the temple to push them apart, thereby bringing down the temple on the heads of the major Philistine chiefs, thus killing them. Samson has also been killed, but he has had his revenge.

The Chorus expresses the irony of Samson's fate, but they see his act as a triumph. Even Manoa does not lament but feels joy and relishes the victory. The Chorus sings "all is best" and ends with "calm of mind, all passion spent."

This play was a closet drama: that is, it was intended to be read rather than performed. It is a poem in the form of a tragedy and comes closest to revealing Milton's own complex feelings of despair and acceptance not only of his blindness but also of the political defeat of the Commonwealth government to which he had been attached.

In his great epic poem Paradise Lost, *Milton wrote the only complete epic poem in modern English. In it he consolidated on a grand scale various poetic forces active since the beginning of the Renaissance. It was both learned and familiar. The complexity of the poem kept it from being widely read, but it nevertheless influenced subsequent poets. Dryden wrote an opera based on*

Paradise Lost. *Pope's mock-heroic poetry contains many Miltonic echoes. Later poets such as Wordsworth and Keats learned by studying Milton's works. Milton's images of Paradise, Adam and Eve, and Satan have become a part of the body of English poetic imagery. The dignity of Milton's blank verse encouraged the use of blank verse in the nineteenth century. Thus Milton stands out as a powerful individual talent. He fulfilled his early ambition to accomplish great things in English poetry, despite the long delay caused by his public service and despite his blindness in his later years.*

Selected Readings

Nicolson, Marjorie. *John Milton: A Readers' Guide to his Poetry.* New York: Farrar, 1963.

Patrides, C. A. and Raymond B. Waddington, eds. *The Age of Milton: Backgrounds to Seventeenth-Century Literature.* Totowa, NJ: Barnes, 1980.

Richardson, J. *Explanatory Notes and Remarks on Milton's "Paradise Lost".* New York: AMS, 1973.

Wilson, A. N. *The Life of John Milton.* New York: Oxford University Press, 1983.

15

Early Seventeenth-Century English Literature (1603 to 1660): Development of the Drama

1603–1625	Reign of James I, first Stuart monarch
1604	Shakespeare, *Othello*; Marlowe's *The Tragical History of the Life and Death of Doctor Faustus* published
1606	Shakespeare, *Macbeth*; Jonson, *Volpone*
1613–1614	Globe Theatre in London burns and is rebuilt
1614	Webster, *The Duchess of Malfi*
1644	Globe Theatre torn down

*O*nce the monarchy had been challenged by the Puritan forces of Parliament, questions about the nature of society and the legitimacy of power were open for debate. In the theater, images of heroism were increasingly displaced by images of trickery and betrayal. The violence and sensationalism of the drama came to an abrupt end with the closing of the theaters in 1640.

EARLY SEVENTEENTH-CENTURY DRAMA

During the early years of the seventeenth century, those playwrights who had emerged and prospered during the reign of Queen Elizabeth I continued to write, Shakespeare and Ben Jonson among them. But the theater began to change after the accession to the throne of James I. Puritan dislike of the theater as a place of lies and sinfulness began to influence it and to keep away more and more of the middle-class audience that had been its mainstay. Meanwhile, the court of James I became a center for self-indulgent behavior. Courtiers became mere flatterers, and the court theater was aimed at a more narrow, elite audience. Theater productions tended to lose touch with the broad texture of English life and looked to sources in Spain and Italy for more sensational dramatic ideas. Plots based on revenge, sordid intrigue, violence, and terror were used to excite the rather jaded tastes of this new group of spectators. Tragicomedy, for example, as developed by Beaumont and Fletcher exploited the theatricality of dire situations before patching on a happy ending. Comedies became generally less romantic and more satiric. In tragic plays, themes of betrayal, adultery, and incest made the stage even less tolerable to Puritan preachers, so that one of the Puritans' first acts on gaining power in 1642 was to close down the theaters.

BEN JONSON, PLAYWRIGHT

One of the outstanding writers of comedy during this period was Ben Jonson, the same writer who headed the school of lyric poets known as "Sons of Ben." His satiric comedies use humor characters. These are simple, one-dimensional characters who display a single bias or inclination of personality. They act the same and pursue the same purpose no matter how their situation develops or changes. Jonson's two most famous comedies were *Volpone*, produced in 1605, and *The Alchemist*, produced in 1610.

Volpone, *or* The Fox

Jonson combines medieval and classical elements smoothly in this play. Influenced by the medieval beast fable, he creates the following allegorical animal names:

> Volpone is a fox in his shrewd deviousness.
>
> Mosca is a fly that is elusive and exploits others.
>
> Voltore, the vulture,
>
> Corbaccio, the raven,

and Corvino, the crow are all birds that eat dead meat.

But the play is constructed tightly according to the classical unities of time, place, and action, supposedly derived from the dramatic criticism of Aristotle. The play uses situations of urban decadence suggested by the classical satires of Horace, Juvenal, and Lucan. Jonson combined all these elements and set the play in Venice, a city that to the English represented the evil effects of commercial wealth, of money gotten through trade and manipulation rather than from productive lands. This play makes an interesting contrast to Jonson's poetic image of the good English way of life in his poem *To Penshurst*. *Volpone* is written in blank verse with some prose.

ACT I

Act I opens with Volpone gloating over his wealth, admiring it to the point of worship. He especially enjoys the fact that he has done no actual work to amass his fortune. Playing sick, Volpone is visited in turn by three fortune hunters: the lawyer Voltore, the old man Corbaccio, and the merchant Corvino, each of whom gives Volpone rich gifts in hopes of being named his heir. Mosca, who is Volpone's servant and spokesman, assures each of the fortune hunters that he is the only one named in Volpone's will. Meanwhile, Volpone encourages them by pretending to be at the point of death. Between their visits, Mosca and Volpone mock the three as fools.

ACT II

Act II introduces the English gentleman Sir Politic Would-be, who foolishly pretends to know all sorts of state secrets and to consult with the great ministers of state. Sir Politic is easily impressed by Volpone, who has come to him disguised as a mountebank, a street seller of fake medicines. Volpone makes a long sales pitch under the window of Corvino's pretty wife, Celia, whom Volpone wishes to seduce. But Corvino returns home and chases Volpone and his followers away. At home, Volpone confesses to Mosca that he is in love with Celia and asks Mosca to contrive a plan whereby he, Volpone, can seduce her. Meanwhile, Corvino is in a jealous rage at his wife, Celia, for having looked out her window. His threats to her are interrupted by the arrival of Mosca, who claims that the doctors attending Volpone have prescribed that for his health's sake he sleep with a young healthy woman. After much hesitation, Corvino decides to assure himself of Volpone's favor and fortune by lending his wife for the prescribed medicinal visit to Volpone's bed. Corvino is assured by Mosca that Volpone is impotent.

ACT III

Act III begins with a soliloquy by Mosca, justifying his role as parasite. Mosca seeks out Bonario, the son of Corbaccio, and reveals to him that his father is about to disinherit him. Meanwhile, Volpone, eagerly awaiting a visit from Celia, is visited instead by the unattractive and very talkative Lady Would-be, who tortures him with a flow of chatter until Mosca returns and gets rid of her. Bonario comes, expecting to stop his father, Corbaccio, from changing his will to favor Volpone. This plan is interrupted by the arrival of Corvino, who has finally brought his wife, Celia, to be old Volpone's comforter in his final sickness. Celia resists with tears and pleading, but she is left alone with Volpone. Volpone instantly jumps out of bed, full of vigor and seductive flattery. At this point, he sings the famous lyric "Come, My Celia," promising her that their lovemaking will be secret. He tempts her with jewels and luxuries, gorgeously described, but she resists. Volpone then attacks her, and the concealed Bonario responds to her cries for help, preventing the rape. Bonario and Celia rush out to call for legal help. Mosca rushes in to lament the backfire of his plots with Volpone. Corbaccio and Voltore then show up, hoping to advance their own interests. Mosca manages to reconcile all the competing claims with some quick and clever lies, but the situation is precarious.

ACT IV

When act IV begins, Sir Politic is giving silly advice and explaining foolish plans to get rich, all for the benefit of Peregrine, a young English traveler who pretends to be impressed. The jealous Lady Would-be discovers them together and assumes that Peregrine must be a woman in disguise, until she is put straight by Mosca.

The next scenes take place at the court, where Voltore is accusing Bonario and Celia of a plot against the life of Volpone. The three hopeful heirs of Volpone—Voltore, Corbaccio, and Corvino—conspire to lie in support of the accusations against Celia and Bonario. Volpone is carried in on his bed to move the court's sympathy. Mosca manages with skillful lies to make Voltore, Corbaccio, and Corvino believe that each is the only person bound to inherit Volpone's wealth.

ACT V

Act V begins at Volpone's house, where Volpone and Mosca congratulate each other on their success at court and launch a new trick, a false report of Volpone's death. They plan that when the three hopeful legatees come to verify the report, Mosca will greet them in rich robes and show them a will naming himself as sole heir. Volpone will hide behind a curtain to enjoy the sight of their anger and despair at having been left out of his will. The trick works; each man is confronted by Mosca with the truth of his own evil plots to inherit Volpone's wealth. The cheating of each one is asserted to be merely justice. But Volpone wants to push the joke even further by going out in disguise to hear what outrageous things will be said about him by those who believe him dead. Meeting Corbaccio, Corvino, and Voltore in the street, the disguised Volpone mocks them with congratulations on their supposed recent inheritances, then pretends to pity them for having lost out to Mosca. But Volpone goes too far. Voltore, in reaction, confesses and accuses Mosca in court of creating the slanders against Bonario and Celia, who are really innocent. This crisis makes Volpone summon Mosca to court, but when Mosca persists in the lie that Volpone is dead and that he, Mosca, is his heir, Volpone throws off his disguise and the truth of all the plots comes out. Each scoundrel is to be punished according to his crime: Mosca is to be a galley slave, Volpone is to be imprisoned, Voltore is to be banished, Corbaccio's wealth is to go to his son, Bonario, and Corvino is to stand in the pillory. Jonson has created a moral conclusion; the play demonstrates the awful outcomes of greed and, in Volpone's case, lust.

JOHN WEBSTER (1580–1625)

Very little is known about Webster's life. Because he often collaborated with other playwrights, it is not even known for sure how many plays he wrote. And because he borrowed heavily from the ideas of other writers of his time, it is difficult to know which plays should be attributed to him. But the plays *The White Devil* and *The Duchess of Malfi*, probably written during 1613 and 1614, are surely both his works. Both dramas have plots of horror and revenge, and both plots present women of intense passion, one evil and the other a victim.

The Duchess of Malfi

This play is set in several cities of Italy, a land linked to dark intrigue and immorality in the mind of most seventeenth-century English people. As southerners and as Catholics, the Italians were presumed to be less rational and more passionate than the sober English. The Duchess's unconventional choice of her steward as husband would be more believable among those foreigners, although the dignity of the Duchess becomes the one redeeming force of the play. As for the rest, Webster creates images of power as cruel, corrupt, and irrational.

ACT I

Act I begins as the Duchess says farewell to her two brothers, Ferdinand, duke of Calabria, and the Cardinal. The Duchess is a widow, and both of her brothers suspect that she wants to remarry, which would introduce a rival power in Amalfi. The brothers arrange for the melancholy Bosola to become chief of the Duchess's horsemen and to act also as their spy. Once her brothers have left, the Duchess calls Antonio, her household steward, to her chamber, where she reveals her love for him. They marry privately by mutual consent.

ACT II

In act II, Bosola, suspecting that the Duchess is pregnant, offers her some apricots. She eats them greedily and immediately goes into labor. Antonio, in order to conceal the birth, locks up the household, saying that a robbery has taken place and that the apricots were poisoned. Bosola, however, discovers that the Duchess has given birth to a son. He sends this news to her brother, the Cardinal, who has meanwhile seduced Julia, the wife of an old courtier, Castruccio. Ferdinand has received news of the birth from Castruccio, and in a fit of rage, he threatens to murder both the Duchess and her unknown lover.

ACT III

Act III begins some years later. The Duchess and Antonio now have three children. So far, her brothers have taken no action against her, but now Ferdinand has come to Amalfi to discover who the father is. Ferdinand confronts the Duchess, who admits to marriage but continues to conceal the identity of her husband. The Duchess then plots to save Antonio. She falsely accuses him of theft so that she can abruptly send him away. But Bosola, although he hates to betray the Duchess, as the Cardinal's spy will report what he has discovered, that Antonio is the husband and father. The Cardinal has the Duchess and Antonio banished from Anconia, the region where they had hoped to find safety. Antonio takes their elder son and flees to Milan. Bosola takes the Duchess and her younger children as prisoners back to Amalfi.

ACT IV

Back in her own castle in act IV, the Duchess is cruelly tortured by Ferdinand, who shows her wax figures of the corpses of her husband and children. She despairs and longs for death; even Bosola pities her. Ferdinand has her visited by a troop of madmen, but she retains her sanity. Bosola oversees her execution by strangulation. This is a sensational moment on the stage, a terrifying scene. It is followed by the strangling of her servant woman and of her two younger children. But when Bosola claims his reward from Ferdinand for having carried out his order of execution, Ferdinand rejects all responsibility for the action and refuses to pay. Bosola now feels great regret and pity, as well as anger that he has been used to do these terrible deeds and then rejected. He decides to go to Milan in the hope of preventing disaster to Antonio.

ACT V

Act V is set in Milan. The now remorseful Ferdinand has gone mad. The Cardinal, pretending not to know the Duchess has been murdered, hires Bosola to kill Antonio. Bosola uses the Cardinal's mistress, Julia, to discover that the Cardinal not only knew of the murders but also ordered them. Bosola pretends to accept the Cardinal's instructions to kill Antonio, but instead he intends to kill the Cardinal. However, in the dark he mistakenly stabs and kills Antonio, thinking he is the Cardinal. Bosola, carrying the corpse of Antonio, then confronts the Cardinal. Bosola stabs the Cardinal, the mad Ferdinand rushes in and stabs at both his brother, the Cardinal, and then at Bosola, who stabs back at Ferdinand. There is a general slaughter and dying confessions of guilt. Bosola claims he has done justice in killing the Duchess's brothers, Ferdinand and the Cardinal. The play ends when the surviving son of the Duchess and Antonio is carried on stage as the heir to the future.

This play, with its murky scenes of strangulation and stabbings, its suggestions of lust in the Cardinal and of incestuous jealousy in Ferdinand, illustrate all the tendencies that Puritan critics found shocking and disgusting in the drama of the day.

Some modern critics have remarked that when the Puritans closed the theaters, drama was already in a decline. Certainly there had been changes since the high point of Renaissance drama at the turn of the century. The foreign settings were a mark of the disengagement of drama from the issues of English history, politics, and everyday English life. Playwrights exploited sensational effects to appeal to a more jaded and sophisticated audience. They had great technical skill, but the atmostphere in these plays, even comedies, was dark and dour.

Selected Readings

Bamborough, J. B. *Ben Jonson.* London: Hutchinson, 1970.

Peterson, Joyce E. *Curs'd Example: The Duchess of Malfi and Commonweal Tragedy.* Columbia: University of Missouri, 1978.

16

Early Seventeenth-Century English Literature (1603 to 1660): Prose

1597	Bacon, *Essays*, first edition
1603	Bacon knighted; Florio, *Translation of the Essays of Montaigne*
1603–1625	Reign of James I, first Stuart monarch
1605	Bacon, *Advancement of Learning*; Gunpowder Plot by Roman Catholic extremists to blow up Parliament fails but plot deepens anticatholic feelings
1609	Bacon, *De Sapientia Veterum*; Kepler, German astronomer, publishes first two laws of planetary motion
1612	Bacon, *Essays*, second edition
1614	Raleigh, *History of the World*
1614–1620	Napier of Scotland, Burgi of Switzerland propose system of logarithms; Biggs of England modifies method by proposing ten as base
1615	William Harvey lectures on the circulation of blood
1616	Shakespeare dies
1618	Bacon, lord chancellor; Thirty Years' War begins in Europe
1620	Bacon, *Novum Organum*
1621	Burton, *Anatomy of Melancholy*; Bacon indicted for bribery
1622	First English newspaper *The Weekly News*, published

1625	Bacon, *Essays*, complete edition
1625–1640	Reign of Charles I
1626–1627	Bacon, *Sylva Sylvarum* and *The New Atlantis*
1633	Donne, *Poems*; Herbert, *The Temple*; Milton, *L'Allegro* and *Il Penseroso*
1637	Descartes, *Discourse on Method*
1640	Walton, *Life of Donne*
1641–1642	Browne, *Religio Medici*
1642	Civil War begins
1649–1653	The Commonwealth, an experiment in republican government, tried, with political power in a one-house parliament; Council of State led by Cromwell conducts government operations; theaters closed
1651	Hobbes, *Leviathan*; Milton, *Defense of the English People*
1653	Cromwell assumes title of lord protector; Walton, *The Compleat Angler*; Osborne, *The Letters of Dorothy Osborne*
1658–1660	Cromwell dies, succeeded by son, who resigns and is replaced by General Monk, who restores the monarchy

No major literary forms were developed in prose during the seventeenth century, though nonliterary public discourse and private meditation both required an English prose less ornate than the artificial courtly prose of the Renaissance. In sermons, political tracts, and essays, writers sought to produce a style both dignified enough to adorn their thoughts and simple enough to reach a large audience. Both pulpit oratory and classical rhetoric influenced the style and the tone of the new prose. As the century progressed, a plainer, more natural style that somewhat imitated ordinary speech began to become the dominant manner of writing.

THE BIBLE

The one great exception to the trend toward natural simplicity of expression was the Authorized Version of the *Holy Bible*, commissioned by King James I to correct and supersede the *Geneva Bible*. Written by a committee of scholars and intended for use by every literate English Christian, the new Bible maintained the lofty and lyrical sound that developed during the Renaissance. Striving for accuracy, these scholars were nonetheless conservative in their choice of expression, thus helping the English language retain some of the flavor of the diction and phrase from the Tyndale translation of the early sixteenth century. The scholars were particularly concerned that the Psalms should sound like the lyrical poems that they originally were. The Authorized Version, or, as it is now known, the King James Version, was completed in 1611.

PROSE STYLES

Nonbiblical prose allowed for greater individuality in style. Each major prose writer of the period is readily recognizable by his characteristic phrasing, but they all have certain qualities in common. First, they all used copia, or the quality of fullness. If a thing could be said in two or three different ways, the prose writer of the early seventeenth century was likely to use all three, piling them up one upon another. If the resulting passage seems to move slowly, it also has an intensity and richness. Secondly, references to authorities are constantly made. Allusions to ancient, biblical or historical spokesmen and summaries of their thoughts became part of the evidence used to convince the reader. Quotations in various languages also were signs of solid learning and deep investigation. Thirdly, the style of most seventeenth-century prose writers was highly metaphorical. These writers tended to see similarities and correspondences in widely diverse aspects of the subjects they discussed. The writers particularly loved paradoxes. Finally, they felt compelled to be thorough. This was the era of the verbal anatomy. An anatomy is a complete, exhaustive, and systematic treatment of a subject. Subjects such as melancholy were dissected in a manner to show its every aspect and to lay bare the inner structure of the thing. Not every seventeenth-century writer has each of these stylistic traits in equal measure, but together they made up the essentials of early seventeenth-century prose style and demonstrate how different it was from the leaner, more efficient prose of later centuries. After Dryden in the Restoration period, modern prose style begins to evolve.

FRANCIS BACON (1561–1626)

After receiving legal training Bacon entered government service while Elizabeth I was still Queen of England. During the reign of King James I, Bacon rose to be lord chancellor of England. At the height of his power, he was accused of taking bribes and of neglecting his responsibilities. Bacon confessed, retired, and spent the last five years of his life engaged in scientific experimentation. Bacon is known as a philosopher, "the father of English empiricism." Empiricism is the systematic study of natural phenomena by direct observation and controlled experiment. This was a new way of finding truths, the opposite of speculation and very different from traditional, logical deduction and the interpretation of authorities, which had characterized the scholastic philosophical method of medieval times.

The Advancement of Learning

Bacon wrote various types of prose. In his treatises *The Advancement of Learning*, written in 1605, he describes a future utopian society based on scientific investigation. But Bacon's most important literary writings are his *Essays*. Bacon introduced the essay form into English, following the example of the sixteenth-century Frenchman Montaigne.

Essays

Bacon wrote, revised, and added to his collection of essays, producing three different editions in 1597, 1612, and 1625, spanning his entire career. His *Essays* are brief, direct, and highly concentrated. Each essay begins with a general assertion about the topic; this serves as its title. Many essays consist of only two or three long, fully packed, and densely argued paragraphs. The tone is impersonal; unlike most seventeenth-century prose writers, Bacon does not digress much nor wander into speculative byways. He is brief and highly focused. He asserts general truths as if his observations become rules by the very act of his stating them. Yet Bacon is frequently insightful and stimulating, as when he declares in his essay *Of Marriage and Single Life* that "he that hath wife and children hath given hostages to fortune; for they are impediments to great enterprises." Bacon combines the metaphor of hostage giving with the plain and perhaps self-evident truth that spouses and families do drain off energies that might otherwise go into great accomplishments. Bacon does not use autobiographical instances but instead he analyzes the collective experience of humanity as he has observed it.

ROBERT BURTON (1577–1640)

Burton, a widely read and learned man, spent his entire adult life at Oxford University. He had no other interest but books, no other activities than reading, studying, and writing. Traditionally, such a life was supposed to lead to melancholy, so in choosing that disease for the subject of his one great book, Burton was also studying himself.

**The Anatomy
of Melancholy**

This vast treatise was first published in 1621, but Burton continued to add to and to revise it through five editions. As an anatomy, its aim was to cover the topic completely. The treatise has three main parts. Part I defines melancholy and discusses its causes and symptoms. Part II is about various cures and remedies, and Part III takes up the special problems of two different and distinct types of melancholy: religious melancholy and love melancholy. Each part of the anatomy is systematically divided into sections, numbers, and subsections. Burton's style is marked by copia. He piles up every learned opinion and every instance or example that has relevance to the question at hand, as if the accumulated evidence, even if contradictory, must yield some core of truth. Burton included many lists, multiple allusions, and quotations.

PART I

In Part I, Section I, Subsection II, Burton lays out the ancient theory of humors, which provides the basic assumptions behind his study of *one* of the humors, that of cold and dry melancholy. Tied to book knowledge, Burton's compilations cannot move beyond ancient and medieval scholarship into the realm of the new science. But paradoxically, the psychology of Burton himself, his quirks and mental habits, are intimately revealed by his book.

IZAAC WALTON (1593–1683)

Walton was a tradesman and a devoted Anglican, a member of John Donne's parish. Although Walton is usually associated with his book about fishing, *The Compleat Angler* (1653), he is more important as an early writer of biographies. He wrote accounts of the lives of five contemporaries who were important either as poets or as pious and influential clergymen of the Anglican church. Walton wrote at a time of deep religious divisions, and the tone of his biographies tends to exalt his subjects as examples of piety. His subjects included John Donne, Richard Hooker, George Herbert, Robert Sanderson, and Henry Wotton.

**The Life of Dr.
John Donne**

First completed in 1640, nine years after Donne's death, the biography was revised several times. The fourth edition was published in 1675. Walton knew Donne well and creates an impressive, saintly figure, citing Donne's piety, his good works, and especially his exemplary death. Donne is quoted by Walton, effectively but perhaps not too accurately, to show how a man of God, having complete faith, welcomes death, putting aside all earthly concerns and patiently waiting to be taken. Walton's purpose was to memorialize Donne as a hero of the Anglican faith.

THOMAS BROWNE (1605–1682)

Sir Thomas Browne was a physician. He had studied medicine at the most respected European medical colleges in Italy, France, and Holland, and he was a disciple of Francis Bacon and the new empirical science. On the other hand, Browne was also an antiquarian, one who studies or collects antique artifacts and books. He was fascinated by old beliefs, old superstitions, and prescientific ideas and practices.

Pseudodoxia Epidemica or Vulgar Errors

In this study Browne explored a wide range of myths and false beliefs not merely to expose them as wrong but also to satisfy his own curiosity. Sir Browne was open minded and tolerant; he loved to speculate, but he was also a man of faith.

Religio Medici

This Latin title translates as "the faith or religion of a physician." As scientific thinkers, doctors had a reputation for skepticism, but Browne asserts his belief in orthodox Christianity and his adherence to Protestantism and the Church of England. Nevertheless, he had a broad tolerance for other varieties of Christian belief. Browne's style is poetic and varied. He achieved both lofty effects and intimacy. He saw himself as the microcosm and therefore studied himself to find out the nature of all humankind, moving easily from his own ideas, dreams, and memories into general statements about the mental and spiritual life of all. This work was originally circulated for several years in manuscript not intended for publication, but after an unauthorized version was printed in 1642, Browne had a correct edition published the following year.

THOMAS HOBBES (1588–1679)

After attending Oxford University, Hobbes was patronized by important people of the day, especially by Francis Bacon, whose secretary and disciple Hobbes had become. He applied the type of systematic and skeptical thinking that Bacon advocated to the study of the nature of the individual and of the relationship of the individual to the state. Hobbes was a materialist; he saw the world as operating mechanically, and he did not believe in souls or spirits. His radical philosophy made him the focus of controversy from the time of the publication of his treatise *The Leviathan* until the end of the century.

The Leviathan　　This philosophical work, published in 1651, argues from the nature of human beings to the necessity for their subjugation to a ruler. Hobbes asserts that the state is the larger body, incorporating all people into one unified being that he refers to as a great whale or the leviathan. Hobbes sees people as lacking free will but driven by desires and appetites. In a state of nature, lacking government, the life of the individual is an unceasing competition with others; therefore life is, as he says, "solitary, poor, nasty, brutish, and short." In order to improve their security, people band together by mutual consent to form commonwealths and place a single ruler, a king, at their head. Thus Hobbes justifies monarchy not on the old ground of divine right but on the new basis of reason.

Hobbes's prose style is vigorous and witty. He writes directly, raising and giving rational answers to rhetorical questions, moving step by logical step to seemingly inevitable conclusions. Hobbes is contemptuous of fools and weak notions, sweeping them aside to get to the heart of the matter. The rationalism and materialism of Hobbes were shocking to many of his contemporaries, who could not replace their concept of the individual as made in God's image with that of a mechanical being driven by needs and desires.

DOROTHY OSBORNE (1627–1695)

This seventeenth-century woman became known when her letters were published in the late nineteenth century. She wrote during a lengthy courtship to William Temple (later a patron of Swift). Family disapproval on both sides made marriage impossible for six years, during which time they corresponded secretly.

The Letters of Dorothy Osborne　　Her letters anticipate the great era of personal letter writing during the next century, when such compositions were raised to the level of art. The mocking wit and playful tone of her letters hide the stress she felt from family pressure to marry a great fortune. Her surface calm implies great self-control, which was the only assurance that her suitor, Temple, had that she would not allow herself to be bartered away to a more wealthy man. Meanwhile, social correctness would not allow her to admit that Temple was more than a "friend" for whom she feels "kindness." Thus Osborne's writing mediates between her genuine feelings of love and longing, which she must express only covertly, and the restrictions of social forms that would not permit her to have any feelings at all until a proper husband could be found to receive them. The grace with which she handles this quandary and still retains her lover's interest gives literary value to what was intended only as personal communication.

Despite the political unrest and civil strife that disrupted English society in the first half of the seventeenth century, writers of this period were active and productive. Some, like most playwrights and the Cavalier poets, tried to extend the great accomplishments of the Renaissance. Others reacted against the conventions of the last age and tried new forms; the metaphysical poets exemplify this tendency. Meanwhile, the great poet Milton stood outside both of these trends, creating epic poetry that transends its era.

The hold of ancient ideas was loosening; new philosophies based on present experience made new images and concepts relevant. Prose forms began to be developed to cope with the flow of new ideas. Generally, the era saw a movement away from heroics and idealism toward a more cynical, realistic, and sophisticated attitude toward human actions. The sureness of Elizabethan lyricism was replaced by smooth but mocking seductions in verse.

The many varied styles of the early and mid-seventeenth century made English prose a stronger and more flexible medium, ready to express the controversy, reevaluation, and new scientific thought provoked by the restoration of the monarchy in 1660. No one could avoid controversy; all opinions were under some attack, and all opinions had to be reexamined in order to be defended by their believers. Soon after the new king, Charles II, organized his court, he established the Royal Society. One of their first duties was to purify and perfect English prose as a medium for modern thought.

Selected Readings

Wedgewood, C. V. *Seventeenth-Century English Literature*. London: Oxford University Press, 1950.

17

Restoration Literature (1660 to 1700): Restoration Period

1660	Restoration of monarchy
1660	Dryden, *Astraea Redux*; two companies of actors chartered: the King's Players and the Duke's Players
1660–1669	Pepys's *Diary* written (published 1825)
1660–1685	Reign of King Charles II
1661–1662	Philips, *To My Antenor, March 16, 1661*
1661–1665	Clarendon Code passed: reestablished Church of England and passed restrictions on both Roman Catholics and Dissenters or Nonconformists
1662	The Royal Society for Improving Natural Knowledge founded, replacing the Philosophical Society
1663	Butler, *Hudibras*; Drury Lane Theatre built
1664	Etherege, *Love in a Tub*
1665	Moliere, *Tartuffe*
1666	Bunyan, *Grace Abounding*; Historic fire of London
1667	Dryden, *Annus Mirabilis*; Milton, *Paradise Lost*
1668	Dryden, *Essay of Dramatic Poesy*; Dryden named poet laureate
1669	Pepys makes final entry in his diary

1672	Newton, *A Letter Containing His Theory about Light and Colors*
1672–1674	Wycherley, *The Gentleman Dancing Master* and *The Country Wife*
1673	Parliament passes the Test Act
1677	Behn, *The Rover*
1678	Bunyan, *Pilgrim's Progress, Part I*
1679	End of censorship of the press; Rise of Whig and Tory parties
1680	Rochester, *The Disabled Debauchee*
1681	Dryden, *Absalom and Achitophel*
1684–1687	Behn, *Love Letters between a Nobleman and His Sister*
1685–1688	Reign of James II; Catholic-Protestant conflict increases
1687	Newton, *Principia Mathematica*; Dryden, *The Hind and the Panther*
1688	The "Bloodless" or Glorious Revolution; Parliament regains power, offers crown to William of Orange
1688	Behn, *Oroonoko*
1689	Parliament passes Bill of Rights; the Toleration Act granting some freedom of worship is passed
1689–1702	Reign of William and Mary
1690	Locke, *Two Treatises of Government* and *Essay Concerning Human Understanding*
1690–1692	Salem witchcraft trials and executions in Massachusetts Colony
1691	Purcell's opera *King Arthur*
1693	Congreve, *The Old Bachelor* and *The Double Dealer*
1694	Astell, *A Serious Proposal to the Ladies*
1695	Congreve, *Love for Love*
1698	Collier, *A Short View of the Immorality and Profaneness of the English Stage*
1700	Congreve, *The Way of the World*; Dryden, *The Secular Masque* and *Fables Ancient and Modern*; Astell, *Some Reflections upon Marriage*; death of Dryden

*T*he Restoration period is so called because it was marked by the restoration of the monarchy. With the weakening of the Commonwealth government after the death of Oliver Cromwell, the consensus in England was to return to royal rule. Parliament restored to the throne King Charles II, a Stuart and the Protestant son of the former King Charles I, who had been beheaded by the Puritans in 1649. From his exile in Europe, Charles II brought into

England a lively and showy group of courtiers who had developed sophisticated literary tastes while abroad. The king, called "the Merry Monarch,"
restored patronage of the arts. The post of poet laureate was officially
created. The Puritan ban on theatrical productions was lifted, and two new
"legitimate" theaters were established, the Theatre Royal at Drury Lane
and the Duke's Theatre in Dorset Garden.

Even though England was again a monarchy, the political divisions that
had caused the revolution continued to agitate the public; the danger of a
new civil war seemed very real. Parliament still competed with the king for
power, and religious divisions still persisted. Organized political parties
eventually developed:

> the Tories: conservative, Church of England Anglicans and
> Royalist supporters

> the Whigs: middle-class supporters of parliamentary power,
> and politically more tolerant of the various religious fac-
> tions dissenting against Anglican rule

In this climate of social tension, many writers also became involved in
partisan activities. Some reinforced the images of royal grandeur while others
attacked the court as a center of immorality and corruption. Diehard Puritans,
called Dissenters because they would not accept the king as head of the
church, produced literature aimed at a broad audience of noncourtly readers.
The spirit of dissent was also expressed by philosophers of the new sciences
and of the antiauthoritarian ideas of the Enlightenment.

After the death of Charles II in 1685, his Roman Catholic brother James
II ruled briefly and badly, provoking by his rigid intolerance the crisis of the
"Bloodless" or Glorious Revolution of 1688. James II fled to France without
abdicating, and when Parliament declared the throne vacant, he was replaced
by the Protestant monarchs William of Orange, a Dutch ruler, and his wife
Mary, one of James I's daughters. Under their joint leadership and the
ascendancy of the Whigs, the tone of court life and of the government changed.
Calm was regained and the self-indulgence of "the Merry Monarch" was
replaced by a more modest and sober demeanor acceptable to the Parliament,
to the city of London, and to most of the populace.

LITERARY FORMS

**Restoration
Prose**

Before the Restoration, narration, the telling of a story, was no longer
found in epic or poetic romance. (The great exception was Milton's *Paradise
Lost*, an epic narrative poem he planned to write earlier in the century but
postponed until after his service to the Commonwealth government.) During

the Restoration period narration began to emerge in prose. The new prose narrative developed from forms not considered literature: personal and instructive writings, diaries, autobiographical accounts, and essays or letters of religious instruction. These forms were not written for aristocrats but for common people. They focused on actual events and on the ordinary person's experience. A simple and exact prose was also needed to communicate the scientific and philosophical ideas being explored at the time. One of the projects of the Royal Society, a scientific academy chartered by Charles II, was to rid the language of a confusing excess of imaginative metaphors and other fanciful expressions. The Royal Society sought to make English an effective intellectual tool.

Restoration Poetry

Poetry also took other directions. The imaginative, emotional lyric became less central to literature, gradually being limited to songs for plays, seduction poems mocking the conventions of courtly love, and odes to celebrate important persons or occasions. A polished sound was valued more than depth of feeling; *easy* and *natural* were terms of praise for lyric verse of this period. In contrast, the poetry of politics and criticism was satiric, treating its subjects with irony or ridicule, especially in mock-heroic verse and political allegory. Dryden in particular employed the heroic couplet (two rhyming lines of iambic pentameter), which was well adapted to witty and pungent statement. For example:

> Great wits are sure to madness near allied,
> And thin partitions do their bounds divide.

Each line has five feet, with an unstressed syllable followed by a stressed syllable. The lines rhyme and form one complete sentence. But the sentence has two parallel parts, so that each line restates the idea of the other in different terms.

Restoration Drama

The most spectacular developments of Restoration literature took place in drama. Playwrights experimented with various forms, trying both to recapture the imaginative richness of the great dramas of the Elizabethan era and to imitate the more restrained and regular qualities of neoclassical drama that was being developed at the same time in France by Racine, Corneille, and Moliere. The English playwrights were writing for an elite group rather than for the popular audience that Shakespeare and his contemporaries aimed at. The Restoration playwrights created two main theatrical forms: the heroic drama, which was full of violent action and bombastic speeches; and the satiric comedy of manners, with witty dialogue and complex plots. The conflicts in both kinds of plays tended to arise from rivalries for power and jealousies in love. In many of these plays honor or duty was in conflict with love.

The portrayals of female roles by actresses made those roles more important. (Nell Gwynn, one of the most glamorous actresses of the era, became one of King Charles II's mistresses.) Other innovations such as elaborate painted scenery and gorgeous costumes appealed to the upper-class audiences. The early Restoration comedies especially reflected the attitude of sexual adventurousness that prevailed in the Stuart court. For that reason, late in the century the theaters again came under attack by the clergy. During the reign of William and Mary a more middle-class audience began to patronize the theater. The heroic style faded and comedies became less scandalous. Nevertheless, in 1698 the clergyman Jeremy Collier was moved to write an attack on the stage called *A Short View of the Immorality and Profaneness of the English Stage.* Playwrights were alarmed, but much of the public supported Collier, and the forces of reform gained even more influence over the subject matter of plays.

Restoration literature was marked by brittle wit, high polish, and suggestive or immoral situations. Despite the beginnings of a plainer popular literature, most writers of the era focused on the artificial and the glamorous. One of their persistant themes was the disparity between appearance and reality. Dissembling and falsehood were seen as necessary or inevitable strategies to conceal and restrain natural desire and competition. Disguise was a common device, but the appearance of naturalness was widely sought after. Such a self-contradictory mode was bound to yield to more rational and more moral influences toward the end of the era.

Selected Readings

de Sola Pinto, Vivian, ed. *Poets of the Restoration, 1653–1700.* New York: Barnes, 1966.

Moore, Cecil A., ed. *Restoration Literature: Poetry and Prose, 1660–1700.* New York: F. S. Crofts, 1934.

Persson, Agnes V. *Comic Characters in Restoration Drama.* The Hague: Mouton, 1975.

18

Restoration Period (1660 to 1700): John Dryden

1659	Dryden, *Heroic Stanzas*
1660	Restoration of monarchy; Dryden, *Astraea Redux*
1660–1685	Reign of King Charles II
1663	Drury Lane Theatre built
1665	Dryden, *The Indian Emperor*
1666	The historic fire of London
1667	Dryden, *Annus Mirabilis* and *All for Love*; Milton, *Paradise Lost*
1668	Dryden, *Essay of Dramatic Poesy*; Dryden named poet laureate
1678	Popish plot intensifies English fears of Roman Catholics
1681	Dryden, *Absalom and Achitophel*
1682	Dryden, *Mac Flecknoe*, *The Medal*, and *Religio Laici*
1683	Dryden and sons convert to Catholicism
1685–1688	Reign of James II; Catholic-Protestant conflict increases
1687	Dryden, *The Hind and the Panther*
1688	The "Bloodless" or Glorious Revolution
1689–1702	Reign of William and Mary

1689   Parliament passes Bill of Rights; the Toleration Act granting some freedom of worship is passed

1696   Dryden, translation of Virgil

1697   Dryden, *Alexander's Feast*

1700   Dryden, *Secular Masque* and *Fables Ancient and Modern*; death of Dryden

*T*he Restoration period is also sometimes referred to as the "Age of Dryden" because he was the most prolific and influential writer of the era. Dryden wrote in all the major genre. His output consisted of literary criticism in prose, songs and odes in verse, epics and mock-epics, satires, and a wide variety of plays. Novelty and variety were two of Dryden's main purposes in writing; he sought to please his readers by giving them what was new and surprising but not shocking. Dryden became the literary authority of London. By the end of his career, even though he had lost his official court positions, he held court himself at Will's Coffee House, where young, aspiring poets and playwrights came to ask his advice and help.

JOHN DRYDEN (1631–1700)

Dryden was from the landed gentry rather than the aristocracy; his family had favored Cromwell during the Civil War. Dryden married the daughter of an earl and sought the favor of Charles II, who in 1668 appointed him the first official poet laureate. Because he lacked inherited wealth, Dryden worked as a professional man of letters, earning money both from the king and from the theater, adapting his production to the changing demands of each. Dryden explained and defended his various experiments in the heroic drama in a series of prefaces to the published versions of his plays. These *Prefaces*, along with his *Essay of Dramatic Poesy*, laid the foundation for the genre of literary criticism.

When political tensions grew during the 1680s, Dryden served Charles II by composing an influential satire, *Absolom and Achitophel*, which helped shift public opinion in favor of the Tory position and thus helped avert a political crisis. However, after the death of Charles II and the exile of James II, Dryden, a new convert to Catholicism, was out of favor with the Protestants in power. He lost his laureateship and went back to grinding out plays. Dryden also made translations, most notably of Virgil's *Aeneid* and Chaucer's *Canterbury Tales*. Among his last works are two great odes for Saint Cecelia's day and *The Secular Masque*, celebrating the end of the century.

Essay of Dramatic Poesy

Early in the Restoration period, Dryden and his fellow playwrights debated among themselves which dramatic tradition they should follow. By the time the theaters reopened, the acting companies and the playwrights of the last age had disappeared; a fresh start was needed. In 1668 Dryden wrote his *Essay of Dramatic Poesy* as a contribution to the general debate. The characters in the essay are four young men of London, each of whom takes a different position on drama. Crites praises the ancient playwrights of Greece and Rome. Eugenius agrees that the ancient playwrights were great but holds that modern playwrights have the advantage not only of reading them but also of all the learning and literature that has developed since ancient times. Next, Lisideius holds that the playwrights of France have excelled because they write more orderly and regular plays, observing the unities of time, place, and action. Finally, Neander, who represents Dryden himself, takes the position that their own native English tradition is best. He cites Shakespeare and Jonson as the best of the tradition and worthy of imitation. The *Essay of Dramatic Poesy* ends inconclusively; there is no winner of the debate, but all the current ideas about dramatic theory have been set out and compared.

Song from Marriage a la Mode

This song is a typical Restoration lyric poem, one of the many songs that ornament Dryden's plays. Its wit and smoothness are extensions of the light-hearted Cavalier style of earlier poetry of the century. Intended to be sung by a woman, this lyric poem song takes the *carpe diem* or "live and love for today" theme to an extreme, suggesting that marriage is only a temporary interruption in the free sexual life of two rather jaded lovers. The ideal of eternal faithfulness in love is mocked; immediate pleasure is established as the new goal. It is, however, important to notice that this song *begins* the play; by the last act the married couple has taken enough amorous risks to convince them that fidelity is preferable after all. The song raises the theme question; the rest of the play answers it.

Absolom and Achitophel

Because Charles II had no legitimate children, the heir to the English throne was his brother James II, who was unacceptable to the majority of the population because he was a Roman Catholic. In 1681 this problem reached a crisis when the Whig party in Parliament acted to exclude James II from royal succession and to replace him with the duke of Monmouth, an illegitimate son of Charles II with an attractive but easily influenced character. Dryden's poem, written in the midst of this struggle, argues allegorically for the Tory position of acceptance of James II and submission to the principle of the divine right of kings to rule.

The poem is written in epic style with heroic couplets. Using parallels to a biblical incident, the poem compares King Charles II with King David and Monmouth with David's rebellious son Absolom. The villain,

Achitophel, represents the powerful Whig leader, the earl of Shaftesbury, as a clever and dishonest plotter who tempts the son to seize his father's throne. The most impressive passages in this long and complex poem are Dryden's mocking portraits of the central characters in the conspiracy against the king and the self-revealing speeches he creates for each of the two figures of the title. The most dramatic scene, Achitophel's temptation of Absolom, hints at the seduction of Eve by Satan in Milton's *Paradise Lost*. Achitophel's speeches are full of flattery and misleading reasoning. Achitophel suggests that the king desires to be overthrown by young David, as a sort of "pleasing rape." In response, David laments that his rank by birth is not so high as his ambition for power. He declares that "Desire of greatness is a god-like sin." Using twisted arguments like these, the two rebels show the folly of their position. Toward the end of his poem, Dryden speaks directly to the reader, arguing in favor of stability and continuity in government. He gives King David (Charles II) the last word, an impressive and triumphant assertion of royal power. The poem was effective enough to sway public opinion and help calm the crisis.

Mac Flecknoe

In this burlesque, mock-heroic poem written in heroic couplets, Dryden attacks a rival playwright, Thomas Shadwell, for the sins of self-importance and dullness. Shadwell is pictured as the heir of an even worse poet, Richard Flecknoe. (Mac means "son of.") At the beginning of the poem, Flecknoe nominates Shadwell to succeed him on the throne of Dullness. The action in the poem is a mock-heroic procession through the streets of London, ending at a coronation ceremony full of boring speeches. The way is strewn not with flowers but with pages of old, trashy books. Addressing his heir, Flecknoe advises him: "Trust nature, do not labour to be dull." The absurd ending has the long-winded Flecknoe falling through a trap door of the coronation stage, a trick Dryden borrowed from one of Shadwell's own plays.

Alexander's Feast *and* A Song for Saint Cecilia's Day

A few years before his death Dryden wrote these two highly emotional odes in irregular stanza form for annual celebrations of the feast day of Saint Cecilia, the patron saint of music. Each was set to music for a chorus to sing. *Alexander's Feast* demonstrates the power of music to awaken and to shape the emotions. One character, the musician Timotheus, controls the feelings of Alexander the Great by varying the mood of his song. Alexander feels pride, joy, sadness, love, and rage in rapid succession, showing that the ultimate power lies with the artist rather than with the soldier or military hero.

To the Pious Memory of the Accomplished Young Lady Mrs. Anne Killegrew

In creating an elegy on the death of Anne Killegrew, the daughter of a friend, Dryden used the form of the Pindaric ode as it had been introduced into English by Abraham Cowley. This was an irregular form that only approximated Pindar's. The subject, Anne Killegrew, was a young woman who wrote poetry and painted. Dryden uses her early death by smallpox as an occasion to consider the state of the arts in England at that time. In contrast to the pure poetry written by Anne, Dryden portrays most poetry and drama of the time as fallen or decadent. He laments the corruptions of the "adulterate age" and the "pollution of . . . the stage." Meanwhile, he depicts Anne as being received into heaven and becoming a bright star. Dryden lavishly praises Anne's poetry; she has conquered this realm as well as that of painting. Dryden describes landscapes and royal portraits painted by Anne Killegrew. Finally, he imagines that on the final day of judgment, she will be first among the sacred poets who will rise into heaven.

DRYDEN'S PLAYS

Dryden produced over thirty plays for the Restoration stage. He was an important influence on the drama, even though none of his plays satisfies modern tastes enough to be revived. His first play was *The Wild Gallant* (1663), a witty play about a young libertine fortune hunter.

Dryden went on to write lavish spectacles such as *The Indian Queen* (1669) and humor comedies such as *Sir Martin Mar-All* (1667). He collaborated in creating operas based on Shakespeare's *The Tempest* and Milton's *Paradise Lost*. But Dryden's greatest innovation was the heroic play. The most famous of these was a long, two-part, action-packed drama, *The Conquest of Granada* (1770–1771), which had a flamboyant, boasting hero and many sudden turns of plot. This play was later satirized for its excesses in a play called *The Rehearsal* by the duke of Buckingham and others, in which Dryden appears as a foolish playwright named Mr. Bayes. The best of Dryden's heroic plays was *Aurenge-Zebe* (1675), which was based on the recent history of India. This is also the last of Dryden's heroic plays written in couplets. He then wrote *All for Love*, or *The World Well Last*, a blank-verse tragedy based on Shakespeare's *Antony and Cleopatra*. Dryden said that of all his plays, *All for Love* was the one he wrote for himself rather than for the pleasure of his audience. The most notable of Dryden's comedies is *Marriage à la Mode* (1672), which has two separate plots, one satiric and one romantic, both joined by the idea of love purified because of being challenged by outside forces.

Along with his great output of plays, Dryden wrote a number of essays and prefaces on his dramatic theory, explaining and defending the choices of situation, structure, and verse form he had made.

*A*s *a professional poet and man of letters, Dryden believed he had an important function in English society. As poet laureate, he served the king, not only by providing entertaining plays but also by writing forceful political satire to advance the king's cause. As poet he not only wrote songs and odes for special occasions, but he also upheld the standards of good poetry by praising what was worthy and mocking what was dull or pompous. As one who wanted to advance the state of English letters, Dryden translated not only classical Latin authors but also the tales of Chaucer, teaching his contemporaries to enjoy their own poetic ancestor. Dryden introduced an easy and familiar prose style and made literary criticism accessible and interesting. As Samuel Johnson later said of Dryden's influence on English literature, "He found it brick and left it marble."*

Selected Readings

de Sola Pinto, Vivian, ed. *Poets of the Restoration, 1653–1700.* New York: Barnes, 1966.

Hopkins, David. *John Dryden.* Cambridge and London: Cambridge University Press, 1986.

Moore, Cecil A., ed. *Restoration Literature: Poetry and Prose, 1660–1700.* New York: F. S. Crofts, 1934.

Van Doren, Mark. *John Dryden: A Study of His Poetry.* Bloomington: Indiana University Press, 1960.

Wasserman, George R. *John Dryden.* New York: Twayne, 1964.

19

Restoration Period (1660 to 1700): Minor Poetry and Prose

1651 Hobbes, *The Leviathan*

c. 1652 Pepys studies shorthand from Shelton's *Tachygraphy*

1660 Restoration of monarchy

1660 Pepys among those who escort King Charles II home from exile; Dryden, *Astraea Redux*; Marvel uses position as member of Parliament to protect Milton

1660–1669 Pepys's *Diary* written (published 1825)

1660–1685 Reign of King Charles II

1661–1662 Philips, *To My Antenor, March 16, 1661*

1662 The Royal Society for Improving Natural Knowledge founded, replacing the Philosophical Society

1663 Butler, *Hudibras*, Part I; Drury Lane Theatre built

1665–1667 Behn spies against Dutch during English-Dutch War

1666 Bunyan, *Grace Abounding*; historic fire of London; Pepys joins King Charles II in royal barge to inspect damage to city

1667 Dryden, *Annus Mirabilis*; Milton, *Paradise Lost*

1668 Pepys defends naval administration in House of Commons

1669	Pepys makes final entry in his diary
1672	Newton, *A Letter Containing His Theory about Light and Colors*
1677	Behn, *The Rover*
1678	Bunyan, *The Pilgrim's Progress*, Part I
1679	End of censorship of the press
1680	Rochester, *The Disabled Debauchee*
1684–1687	Behn, *Love Letters between a Nobleman and His Sister*
1685–1688	Reign of James II; Catholic-Protestant conflict increases
1687	Newton, *Principia Mathematica*
1688	The "Bloodless" or Glorious Revolution; Parliament regains power
1688	Behn, *Oroonoko*
1689	Parliament passes Bill of Rights; the Toleration Act granting some freedom of worship is passed
1689–1702	Reign of William and Mary
1690	Locke, *Two Treatises of Government* and *Essay Concerning Human Understanding*; Pepys vacates his post with the Navy; Pepys, *Memoires Relating to the State of the Royal Navy 1679–1688*
1690–1692	Salem witchcraft trials and executions in Massachusetts Colony
1694	Astell, *A Serious Proposal to the Ladies*
1700	Astell, *Some Reflections upon Marriage*; death of Dryden

While Dryden dominated the literary scene, many other writers used poetry and prose to explore the social and intellectual controversies of the era. Puritan conservatism, exemplified by Bunyan, was mocked by the poet Butler. Rochester spoke for the cynical and disillusioned aristocracy while Behn exploited sensational themes. As these writers demonstrate, the various factions and conflicting life-views generated a literature marked by the forceful expression of ideas. Each writer tried to clothe his or her ideas in as appealing a form as possible, and each one achieved popularity or, at least, notoriety. Rochester and Behn especially became known as much for their free and unconventional life styles as for the content of their writings. Even the Puritan preacher Bunyan, who was imprisoned for religious dissent, made his life of sin and redemption the basis for his allegorical prose. In this era, it seems, there was no neutral position; the poet could not stay aloof from politics and moral controversy.

The nonliterary prose of the Restoration reflects the writers' awareness of being part of a new age. The debate about authority and power, which had been part of the revolutionary era, continued to influence concepts about the individual's role in society and relationship to nature. It became more possible to look at human life in radical ways or, like Pepys, to abandon preconceptions about the limits of one's role. It is not surprising, therefore, that one of the first advocates for women's liberation emerges during this period.

SAMUEL BUTLER (1612–1680)

Immediately after the Restoration, the most popular anti-Puritan writer was the satirist Samuel Butler. A staunch Royalist and conservative, Butler had held minor public posts during the Commonwealth era. His rough and partisan satire won him temporary fame during the 1660s, but he was not a polished courtier. His later years were spent in obscure poverty.

Hudibras

This popular burlesque appeared in several installments in 1663 and 1664. Using a four-foot line in couplets to create a jogging, antiheroic effect, Butler creates a dull and foolish Puritan knight, Sir Hudibras, and sends him out on trivial adventures, such as trying to stop the sport of bear-baiting, the kind of village entertainment of which Puritans disapproved.

Hudibras represents the wrong-headed, false courage of the champions of the Commonwealth government. Published after the restoration of the monarchy, this poem enjoyed particular success among Royalists. It exposed what Butler saw as the shallow reasoning and pointless actions of the Presbyterian and the Independent sects during the Civil War.

JOHN BUNYAN (1628–1688)

The son of a poor tinker, (that is, a traveling mender of pots and pans,) John Bunyan produced one of the most popular and influential books of the Restoration period *The Pilgrim's Progress*. As a devout Puritan, Bunyan wrote about the experiences of the soul. He became a Dissenting sect minister and was imprisoned after the Restoration for continuing to preach. During one period in prison, Bunyan wrote a more general and allegorical treatment of the salvation of the soul.

Grace Abounding to the Chief of Sinners

In this autobiographical book Bunyan presents himself as a child, full of sin and fearful of punishment, then as a youth experiencing spiritual enlightenment. He examines his thoughts and feelings, his satisfaction and joy when he feels saved, then his fear and torment when he realizes his own wickedness. Bunyan believes that sudden thoughts that come into his mind are direct messages from God.

The Pilgrim's Progress

This simple book had an immediate appeal to a wide range of readers. The plot involves a journey, a pilgrimage to salvation. The allegorical characters, such as Obstinate, Pliable, and Mr. Badman, engage in lively and realistic dialogue. Christian, the central character, passes through such dangerous places as the "Slough of Despond," a bog or swamp of despair; and "Vanity Fair," a corrupt marketplace, before reaching his goal, the "Celestial City." This book became standard reading for children in England and in the United States for the next two centuries.

KATHERINE PHILIPS (1632–1664)

Born within a year of Dryden, Katherine Philips shared her contemporary's interest in poetic correctness and formal polish. During her lifetime, Philips was most celebrated for her elegant translation of a tragedy by the French playwright Pierre Corneille. Most of her poetry was not published in an authorized version until after her death. Married at sixteen, Philips lived at the remote Welsh country estate of her husband. She enjoyed the literary companionship of a cultivated group who called themselves the Society of Friendship. Idealizing friendship as the most perfect, pure, and exalted of human relationships, they addressed each other in letters and in verse using classical poetic names. Philips's name was Orinda, and the excellence of her poetry earned her the title of "the matchless Orinda." She died in London of smallpox at the age of thirty-two.

To My Excellent Lucasia, on Our Friendship

This is one of several poems addressed to Philips's close friend, Anne Owen, called Lucasia. In this lyric, the poet asserts that their friendship exists as the union of two souls. The union is more perfect than a marriage because it is not physical but spiritual and can therefore be immortal.

To My Antenor, March 16, 1661

Antenor was the poetic name for Philips's husband, James. He had been depressed over legal and financial difficulties and was apparently considering suicide. In this brief lyric of thirteen couplets, the poet/wife pleads with him not to think of death, not to run away from the storms of life but to endure them bravely. She suggests that their troubles will end soon, and she offers hope that Providence will rescue them from their misfortunes.

APHRA BEHN (1640–1689)

A farmer's daughter from Kent, Aphra Johnson made a journey with some of her family to Suriname in South America, where she saw the cruel treatment of black slaves. Back in London about 1658, she married a merchant of Dutch decent named Behn, who died shortly afterward of the plague. Aphra found employment as a spy against the Dutch during the English-Dutch war of 1665 to 1667, but she remained poor, even being confined in debtor's prison. She began to write verse, using the pseudonym Astrea, but her first success as a professional writer was as a playwright in 1670. She wrote lusty, bawdy comedies, the best of which was *The Rover* (1677). She also wrote novels that achieved great popularity. But Aphra Behn was famous for her life style as well as for her literary works. She never remarried, and she believed in sexual freedom. Partly because of her notorious life, her accomplishments tended to be ignored after her death up until the present time.

Oroonoko, *or* The History of the Royal Slave

Written in 1688, this short novel has been called the first philosophical novel in English. It is based on Behn's observations in Suriname, which made her an early advocate of the abolition of slavery. It is a heroic love story about a noble black prince and his fantastic adventures while trying to rescue his beloved, who has been taken away to the harem of the king.

In the second part of the novel, Oroonoko has been taken as a slave. Not accepting his slave status, he organizes a rebellion, but he is recaptured, tortured, and killed. Oroonoko, who represents honesty and moral courage, is in contrast to the decadent and degenerate plantation owners. He is not, however, a noble savage, because Oroonoka is educated and has absorbed European ideas.

Love Letters between a Nobleman and His Sister

This early epistolary novel was based upon an actual scandal. First published in three volumes during 1684 to 1687, it is the story of a young aristocratic man, called Philander, who seduces his wife's sister, Sylvia. According to the standards of that time, this was an incestuous relationship. The first part traces step by step the gradual yielding of Sylvia to the pleading arguments of Philander. After the seduction, the couple flees to France, where Philander becomes involved in political activities in support of the royalist cause. Gradually, Sylvia becomes corrupt, mercenary, and promiscuous. Eventually she marries, and her husband becomes her accomplice in a sordid practice of using her beauty to attract and exploit naive young gentlemen. Ultimately, she sinks into the obscurity of a life of crime.

The last part of the novel, which is narrated without the use of letters, tells of the capture of Philander, who ends up imprisoned in the Bastille in Paris.

JOHN WILMOT, EARL OF ROCHESTER (1647–1680)

This aristocratic poet, usually called simply Rochester, was notorious as one of the most wild and indecent young men of the court of Charles II. He was the epitome of the libertine. Often lusty and profane, his poetic works were not intended for publication, but they were widely circulated in copies made by the members of his elite court circle. His poems were admired for their daring wit and smooth style.

The Disabled Debauchee

The speaker in the poem is an older man who has wasted his strength and health in too much womanizing. Although worn out and disabled, he admires young men still capable of debauchery and urges them on. He enjoys observing young rakes in action as an old admiral enjoys watching a sea battle.

A Satyre Against Mankind

This is a more influential poem, a formal verse satire in heroic couplets. Here, the poet as satirist ridicules human beings by comparing them, unfavorably, with animals. Although people have reason, which animals lack, they use their reason only for foolish or bad purposes. They speculate on matters beyond what they can understand. Beasts, he claims, have more common sense and do not prey on each other except from necessity. Rochester generally does not believe in human virtues, viewing them as more apparent than real. People are afraid to be seen as cowards; therefore they act brave.

SAMUEL PEPYS (1633–1703)

Although his family background was Puritan rather than royalist, Pepys (pronounced "Peeps") was able to keep his position in the admiralty office after the Restoration. Like most English people, he was eager for a return to ordered government. As a conscientious and innovative civil servant, Pepys advanced within the naval bureaucracy to a position of influence and power. He organized a budgetary system that minimized corruption and enabled sailors to be paid more regularly. Pepys never intended his diary for publication. In fact, he wrote it in a shorthand code that was not deciphered for about 120 years.

The Diary

Pepys was a self-made man, rising by hard work and loyal service to become secretary of the admiralty. *The Diary* is more than a record of Pepys's worldly success; it is also a record of the ups and downs of his domestic life, including problems with servants and his relationship with his wife. *The Diary* includes entries about his love of music and his interest in both the theater and new books and about his association with the Royal Society. In 1660 Pepys accompanied the party that escorted home from exile the restored King Charles II. He witnessed and reported to the king on the 1666 Great Fire of London. Because Pepys was aware of and involved in so many aspects of city and court life, his *Diary* for the years 1660 to 1669 is a valuable historical document as well as an intimate view of a Restoration man. When Pepys finally was forced to abandon his diary because of failing eyesight, he felt as if a part of himself was being lost.

PHILOSOPHICAL PROSE

The Restoration saw the further development of philosophy in England. Early in the seventeenth century, the ideas of Bacon and Descartes had stimulated a new spirit of scientific observation and experiment. Thinkers began to clear away centuries of scholarship based on ancient texts. They tried to reexamine without prejudice all of nature, including human nature, seeking the essential, self-evident truths.

MARY ASTELL (1666–1731)

The prose of Mary Astell is sharp, mocking, and familiar in tone. While not an abstract thinker, she is part of the debate about the natures of men and women that took place during the Enlightenment. Although Astell's works were all published anonymously, she was an early champion of women's causes, and her arguments influenced the early feminist discussions.

Some Reflections upon Marriage

In this her best-known writing, Astell questions contemporary assumptions about the basis for a good marriage. She even questions the presumed necessity of marriage for the intelligent woman. Astell ridicules the conventions of courtship and cites the faithful and conscientious wife as a "new hero and martyr."

JOHN LOCKE (1632–1704)

From a Puritan family background, Locke was educated at Oxford and became a physician, although he never established a general medical practice. He lived a quiet and contemplative life. He was supported by the patronage of the great Whig politician the earl of Shaftesbury, who was heavily influenced by Locke's liberal ideas about government. During the political controversies of the 1680s that led up to the Glorious Revolution of 1688, Locke lived quietly in exile in Holland, where the atmosphere was more tolerant. Locke published all of his most important works in the year 1690, soon after his return from Holland.

Two Treatises of Government

Like Hobbes, Locke sees government as a necessary contract. Locke, however, sees individuals as more rational beings who could consent to be governed.

FIRST TREATISE

In the *First Treatise* Locke disproves the principle of the divine right of kings to rule. No one, he avers, has an absolute right to power.

SECOND TREATISE

Locke claims in the *Second Treatise* that by natural law, all human beings are free and equal. If they behave rationally, they will not harm one another. They all have rights to "life, liberty, and property." They create governments to protect these natural rights. Thus the government serves their interests, but when it does not serve them, they have the right to change it for a better government. These ideas of Locke were incorporated later in the formulation of the U. S. Constitution. Locke was much more optimistic than Hobbes about the abilities of the ordinary individual.

Essay Concerning Human Understanding

This influential essay examines how the mind becomes stored with ideas. Starting in infancy, the mind receives sensations from the outside world. When many sensations have accumulated, the mind begins to compare and combine them by the mental process of reflection. The person develops simple ideas drawn from sensations into more and more complex ideas by reflecting on his or her own experience and by education. The process is the same for all individuals, although the particular experiences and education vary. This variation results in people's different abilities.

Locke's method is empirical. That is, he looks into his own mind and observes his own experience as the basic evidence. He observes how children think and studies the effects of being deaf or blind on how the mind works. As proof of his theories, he suggests that his reader consult his or her own mental experiences to see if they are similar.

Locke's description of the gradual and cumulative process of proceeding from simple to complex ideas became the basis for presenting literary characters' development from childhood to maturity, especially in the eighteenth-century novel.

SIR ISAAC NEWTON (1642–1727)

During this era, philosophy encompassed what we now call science. Newton was the most creative scientific thinker of the Enlightenment. It was he who discovered that all motions in nature, from the fall of an apple to the movements of planets, are based on the principle of gravity or, as it was then called, attraction. Although Newton wrote much of his scientific work in Latin, he used English with great clarity and precision.

Letter

Newton's *Letter Containing His Theory about Light and Colors* (1672) presents his method in plain, clear, descriptive narration, followed by a numbered list of the propositions to be concluded from his study. Newton's ideas, not always fully grasped by the public, nonetheless excited enthusiasm. He was cited as a prodigy of human reason, promising that all of nature's laws could eventually be discovered by human intelligence.

The difficult and complex ideas of Locke and other Restoration thinkers were neither fully understood nor widely studied, but readers of popular literature began to absorb simplified versions of these ideas in essays and other more accessible forms. Their liberal view of the individual's place in the world and of the possiblility for human progress was welcomed by an increasingly literate and urbane public.

The philosophical ideas of late seventeenth century are important because they caused people to revise their concepts of themselves and how they came to be what they are. These ideas are reflected in the poetry, prose, and drama of the period, and they continued to influence the protrayal of literary characters for a long time to come.

Selected Readings

Baird, Charles W. *John Bunyan: A Study in Narrative Technique*. Port Washington, NY: Kennikat, 1977.

Bryant, Arthur. *Samuel Pepys*. New York: Macmillan, 1933.

Cranston, M. W. *John Locke: A Biography*. New York: Longmans, 1957.

Greer, Germaine and others, eds. *Kissing the Rod: An Anthology of Seventeenth-Century Women's Verse*. New York: Farrar, 1988.

Latham, Robert and Linnet Latham, and others, eds. *A Pepys Anthology: Passages from the Diary of Samuel Pepys*. Berkeley: University of California, 1988.

Vieth, David M., ed. *The Complete Poems of John Wilmot, Earl of Rochester*. New Haven: Yale University Press, 1968.

Wilders, John. *Hudibras*. Oxford: Clarendon, 1967.

20

Restoration Literature (1660 to 1700): Development of the Drama

1642	Civil War; theaters closed
c. 1660	Two companies of actors chartered: the King's Players and the Duke's Players; new theaters built include galleries and private boxes for spectator seating
1660–1685	Reign of King Charles II
1663	Drury Lane Theatre built
1664	Etherege, *Love in a Tub*
1665	Moliere, *Tartuffe*
1666	Historic fire of London
c. 1667–1668	Etherege, *She Would if She Could*
1668	Dryden, *Essay of Dramatic Poesy*; Dryden named poet laureate
1670	Dryden, *The Conquest of Granada*
1671	Wycherley, *Love in a Wood*
1672–1674	Wycherley, *The Gentleman Dancing Master* and *The Country Wife*
1676	Etherege, *The Man of Mode*; Wycherley, *The Plain Dealer*
1677	Behn, *The Rover*
1678	Behn, *Sir Patient Fancy*

1679   End of censorship of the press; rise of Whig and Tory parties

1680   Comédie Francaise is established in Paris

1688   Behn, *Oroonoko*

1689–1702   Reign of William and Mary

1690   Dryden, *Don Sebastian* and *Amphitryon*

1691   Purcell's opera *King Arthur*

1693   Congreve, *The Old Bachelor* and *The Double Dealer*

1695   Congreve, *Love for Love*

1697   Congreve, *The Mourning Bride*

1698   Collier, *A Short View of the Immorality and Profaneness of the English Stage*; Cibber, *Love's Last Shift*

1700   Congreve, *The Way of the World*; Dryden, *The Secular Masque*; death of Dryden

After 1660 in Restoration England, the stage play had to be developed all over again. The theaters had been closed by the Puritans since 1642, more than a full generation earlier. Acting companies had disbanded. Even the tradition of writing drama for the theater had been interrupted.

In his Essay of Dramatic Poesy *(1668), John Dryden took up the problems facing the new playwrights. He created four characters who discuss the issues. Should they try to revive the Elizabethan style and imitate Shakespeare? Should they follow the classical models of drama and the rules laid down by Aristotle? Should they imitate the French neoclassicists? How could they write the most pleasing drama for the new English audience? The debate is inconclusive. But out of this essay and other critical discussions of the time came a number of experiments with various forms of drama.*

COMEDIES OF MANNERS

The most notable results of the experiments with new forms were heroic dramas and comedies of manners. Heroic plays were briefly fashionable, but their style was too extreme. Dryden's long and complex heroic drama, *The Conquest of Granada* (1669–1670), is the most fully developed play of this kind, full of ranting speeches, violence, and sudden plot reversals. But comedies of manners, which were satiric presentations of the falseness and artificiality of the aristocracy and its imitators, were popular until the end of the century. These comedies were written by aristocratic men who understood and could comically dissect and make fun of the follies of their social class. The best of these playwrights were Etherege, Wycherley, and Congreve.

Sir George Etherege (1635–1691)

Etherege was a courtier and a man of leisure. He wrote plays for pleasure. His three comedies of manners are *Love in a Tub*, *She Would if She Could*, and *The Man of Mode*. In each, Etherege aims at the realistic portrayal of the life style of his contemporaries. For that reason the plays' dialogue seems more important than their plot.

THE MAN OF MODE, OR SIR FOPLING FLUTTER

Etherege's last play, *The Man of Mode* (1676), was his most famous. Sir Fopling is a fool who imagines that a fine Parisian suit of clothes and a few French phrases will make him admired in London. His character is then a foil for the truly witty and more sensible men of the town, Dorimant and his friend Medley. Dorimant, said to be a portrait of the earl of Rochester, is a self-indulgent man about town who is casting off one mistress, Loveit, seducing a second, Belinda, and trying to marry a third, Harriet. He is a complex character, both predatory and attractive. He emerges as the hero because he wins, not because he deserves Harriet.

William Wycherley (1640–1716)

The four comedies of William Wycherley are rough and bitter in tone. Like Etherege, Wycherley had an aristocratic background, and he built on Etherege's example. His plays are *Love in a Wood*, *The Gentleman Dancing Master*, *The Country Wife*, and *The Plain Dealer*. However, in the latter two plays, Wycherley moves toward a more frank display of emotion, even to the point of violence. Impoverished in his later years, Wycherley was cynical about human motives.

THE COUNTRY WIFE

The sexual appetites of both the city rake and the country innocent can scarcely be controlled in the 1675 play *The Country Wife*. The social framework of marriage and moral convention is artificial and easily broken down. The central figure, Horner, is a rake who asks his physician to circulate the rumor that Horner has suffered a disease that has left him sexually impotent. Using this false report as a shield, Horner is able to have access to the wives of his friends. But as much as he sexually exploits them, they also are merely using him for physical pleasure. However, Margery, the innocent country wife, really loves Horner and almost spoils his plans by revealing the truth about him. In the end, Margery must go back to the country with her dull old husband, Pinchwife, but Horner is also seen to be isolated from society by his narrow preoccupation with sexual pleasure.

Meanwhile, Margery's sister-in-law Alithea has been courted and won by the sincere, ideal lover, Harcourt. He has won Alithea by believing in her virtue when Horner has caused a scandal against her. Thus Alithea and Harcourt represent the right way, and their marriage provides the comic ending.

Along with many lesser writers, Etherege and Wycherley developed a sophisticated audience and a set of theatrical conventions and stock characters that were later exploited by Congreve.

William Congreve (1670–1729)

Congreve's father, a younger son in a gentrified family, was stationed with the army in Ireland during the playwright's youth. As a student, the young Congreve attended the same schools as Jonathan Swift, though being of different ages they did not attend the same classes. In 1691 Congreve went to London to study law but was soon enticed from this field by the theater. He became acquainted with the aging Dryden at Will's Coffee House, where the literary talk was stimulating. Dryden encouraged Congreve and praised his early comedies, *The Old Bachelor* and *The Double Dealer* (both 1693).

THE WAY OF THE WORLD

The crowning point of Congreve's writing career, this play, written in 1700, was not at first a popular success, perhaps because the dialogue is so clever and the action so involved that it is difficult to understand on first viewing. This failure helped convince Congreve to retire from play writing.

The play epitomizes the Restoration comedy of manners, focusing on the problems of courtship among the wealthy and would-be wealthy. The plot, though highly contrived, is compatible with the intensely stylized dialogue that quickly identifies each character as either a true wit or a would-be wit. Those who only aspire to wit are disqualified from the verbal games and the romantic competition. To lack wit is to be an outsider, a loser.

Act I. The first act introduces the major male characters. The hero, Mirabell, whose name indicates that he "sees pretty women," is playing cards at a coffee house with Fainall, whose name means that he always pretends; he is a fake. Fainall will become the villain of the play. The two men discuss Mirabell's problems in courting the beautiful Millamant. These problems are caused by the hatred of Millamant's aunt, Lady Wishfort, who controls half of Millamant's dowry. Mirabell must find a way to convince Lady Wishfort to approve his marriage to Millamant and give her whole fortune to them when they wed. His secret plan is not yet revealed. First, the audience meets two silly would-be wits named Petulant and Witwoud. These two also are courting Millamant, but they are not serious rivals.

Act II. The second act, set in a London park, introduces the major female characters. Mrs. Fainall and Mrs. Marwood talk about how horrid men are. Actually, Mrs. Marwood is having an affair with Mrs. Fainall's husband, and Mrs. Fainall is the ex-mistress of Mirabell. When these men enter, Mrs. Fainall walks away with Mirabell, leaving Fainall to have a lover's quarrel with Mrs. Marwood. He is jealous that she might also be attracted to Mirabell. Then the others return, and soon Millamant appears, followed by Witwoud. When Mirabell finally gets to talk to Millamant alone, he scolds her for wasting time with fools and for being cool toward him. She merely laughs at Mirabell for being unfashionably serious and sincere. She knows that he loves her, and she also knows that his secret plan is to have his servant, Waitwell, impersonate his uncle, Sir Rowland, and in this disguise to court old Lady Wishfort. When Lady Wishfort has signed a marriage contract with Sir Rowland, Mirabell will reveal that he is only a servant and force Lady Wishfort to allow Mirabell to marry Millamant in exchange for releasing her from the contract with Sir Rowland/Waitwell.

Act III. In act III Lady Wishfort is at her house, preparing for a visit from the supposed Sir Rowland. As she frets about her appearance, Mrs. Marwood visits her and momentarily steps into Lady Wishfort's closet (an inner room) so that later, when Lady Wishfort has gone to dress, Mrs. Marwood overhears the secret plan being discussed by Mrs. Fainall and Foible, Lady Wishfort's maid. She contrives a counterplot to inform Lady Wishfort of Mirabell's plan and to thus make her so angry that she will give all of Millamant's money to Mrs. Fainall, who is her daughter. This would benefit Fainall, because a husband controls his wife's money. Thus it would benefit the man who is Mrs. Marwood's lover. After another short scene between the main lovers, Mirabell and Millamant, Sir Wilfull Witwoud arrives from the country. He is the nephew of Lady Wishfort and a half-brother to Witwoud; he represents the unfashionable but straightforward manners of the country, in contrast to Witwoud and Petulant's artificial and silly behavior. At the end of this act, Mrs. Marwood tells Fainall about his wife's previous affair with Mirabell. He becomes enraged and determines to join Mrs. Marwood in spoiling Mirabell's plan. Fainall hopes to get both his wife's and Millamant's money by threatening Lady Wishfort that he will divorce his wife, her daughter.

Act IV. At the beginning of act IV, Lady Wishfort rehearses for her meeting with Sir Rowland (Waitwell). Meanwhile, Millamant and Mirabell have a serious conversation about their anticipated marriage. Scene 5 is the famous "proviso" scene, where each of the lovers sets out the necessary conditions for a successful life together; each will respect the other's privacy and dignity. But Lady Wishfort has talked Sir Wilfull into paying court to Millamant in the hope that she will make a marriage with anyone other than Mirabell. Sir Wilfull's approach is very awkward and ineffective; he then gets drunk and quarrels with Petulant and Witwoud over who has the right to court Millamant. At the same time, Sir Rowland (Waitwell) courts Lady Wishfort successfully until a letter from Mrs. Marwood arrives, asserting that he is only a servant. Lady Wishfort is in doubt, so Sir Rowland offers to fetch a "black box" of documents concerning his estate.

Act V. In act V Foible, Lady Wishfort's maid and, incidentally, Waitwell's wife, tells Mrs. Fainall that Fainall is Mrs. Marwood's lover and that they are scheming against Mirabell and Millamant. Lady Wishfort then tells her daughter, Mrs. Fainall, of threats of divorce from Fainall. These threats frighten Lady Wishfort; she will do anything to avoid a scandal. Fainall comes in and presses his demands for money. Lady Wishfort gives in, but while Fainall is having a document prepared giving him control of the family money, Mirabell enters and offers to help Lady Wishfort out of her predicament if she will approve his marriage with Millamant. The desperate Lady Wishfort begs for Mirabell's help; he then produces a legal document, previously drawn up, that gives him control of Mrs. Fainall's fortune. Thus Fainall is foiled; in rage he draws his sword to strike his wife, but Sir Wilfull steps in and prevents any violence. In the final scene, Lady Wishfort is reconciled to Mirabell, the lovers are united, Fainall has gone off in a rage of defeat, and Sir Wilfull calls for a dance. The audience sees that, unlike the Fainall marriage, the marriage of Mirabell and Millamant will succeed because it is based on love, not merely on money.

These witty and highly stylized comedies of the Restoration required a very sophisticated and broad-minded audience. Toward the end of the century, as audiences became more middle class and began to include more women, playwrights came under pressure to modify the tone of their comedies, showing less immoral conduct and less indecent dialogue. Moreover, the brittle cynicism of these comedies was not compatible with a more progressive and optimistic view of human nature. The audience wanted to feel good after the play. They wanted not only to be amused but also to be reassured of the possiblility of goodness and social harmony.

Selected Readings

Dobree, Bonamy, ed. *Comedies by William Congreve.* New York: Oxford University Press, 1925.

Holland, Norman N. *First Modern Comedies: The Significance of Etheredge, Wycherley, and Congreve.* Bloomington: Indiana University Press, 1959.

Loftis, John, ed. *Restoration Drama: Modern Essays in Criticism.* New York: Oxford University Press, 1966.

Wilson, John Harold. *A Preface to Restoration Drama.* Boston: Houghton Mifflin, 1965.

21

Eighteenth-Century English Literature (1700 to 1785): Eighteenth Century

1701	The Act of Settlement passed by Parliament
1702	First daily newspaper, *The Daily Courant*, published
1702–1714	Reign of Queen Anne
1703	Defoe jailed for political pamphleteering
1704	Swift, *A Tale of a Tub* and *The Battle of the Books*
1704–1711	Defoe, editor of the *Weekly Review*
1707	The Act of Union unites England and Scotland; the union is called Great Britain
1709–1711	Addison and Steele, *The Tatler*, the beginning of the periodical essay
1710–1713	Swift, *Journal to Stella*
1710–1714	Swift aligns himself with Tories; writes political articles defending Tory ministry
1711	Pope, *Essay on Criticism*
1711–1712	Addison and Steele, *The Spectator* published
1712	Pope, first version of *The Rape of the Lock*
1713	Swift made dean of St. Patrick's Cathedral, Dublin
1713–1726	Pope translates Homer, edits Shakespeare
1714	Addison and Steele, *The Spectator* revived

1714–1727 George I, first of the Hanoverians, becomes monarch

1717 Last witchcraft trial in England

1719 Defoe, *Robinson Crusoe*

1721–1742 Robert Walpole serves as Britain's first real prime minister

1722 Defoe, *Journal of the Plague Year* and *Moll Flanders*

1726 Swift, *Gulliver's Travels*

1727–1760 Reign of George II

1728 Gay, *The Beggar's Opera*

1729 Swift, *A Modest Proposal*; Johann Sebastian Bach composes the *St. Matthew Passion*

1730 Thomson, *The Seasons*

1731 *Gentleman's Magazine* established

1733 Pope, *Essay on Man*

1735 Pope, *Epistle to Dr. Arbuthnot*

1737 Theatre Licensing Act

1740 Richardson writes novel *Pamela*, or *Virtue Rewarded*

1741 Fielding, *Joseph Andrews*

1742 Handel's *Messiah* first performed

1747 Collins, *Ode to Evening* and *Ode on a Distant Prospect of Eton College*

1747–1755 Johnson working on his dictionary

1748 Hume, *Inquiry Concerning Human Understanding*

1749 Fielding, *Tom Jones*; Johnson, *The Vanity of Human Wishes*

1751 Gray, *Elegy Written in a Country Churchyard*; vol. I of French *Encyclopedie*

1752 Gregorian Calendar adopted

1753 British Museum founded

1755 Johnson's *Dictionary of the English Language*

1756–1763 The Seven Years' War gives Great Britain a predominant position in both North America and India

1759 Johnson, *Rasselas*; Voltaire, *Candide*

1760–1767 Sterne, *Tristram Shandy*

1760–1820 Reign of George III

1762 Johnson receives pension from Crown

1764 Johnson and others establish the London "Literary Club"

1765   Johnson's edition of *Shakespeare*; Watt invents steam engine

1766   Goldsmith, *The Vicar of Wakefield*

1768   Spinning machine invented

1770   Goldsmith, *Deserted Village*

1773   Goldsmith, *She Stoops to Conquer*; *The Kenrick Dictionary*, the first to mark vowel sounds

1775   Sheridan, *The Rivals*

1776   Gibbon, *Decline and Fall of the Roman Empire*; Smith, *Wealth of Nations*

1777   Sheridan, *School for Scandal*

1779   Johnson, *Lives of the Poets*; Hume, *Natural History of Religion*

1781   Kant, *Critique of Pure Reason*

1783   Great Britain acknowledges American independence

1784   Death of Johnson

1791   Boswell, *Life of Johnson*

Although England was involved in several wars on the European continent during the eighteenth century, at home it was a period of relative peace, prosperity, and growth. The Whig party, which represented the growing middle-class viewpoint rather than the Royalist views, maintained and consolidated control of British political life except for a brief period toward the end of the reign of Queen Anne. She, a Protestant daughter of James I, was the last Stuart monarch. In 1714, because of the lack of a Stuart heir, the crown passed to a Hanoverian (German) cousin, George I, and was worn by his descendants for the remainder of the century. These Germanic rulers had little interest in English literature; patronage was almost dead. The powerful Whig Prime Minister Robert Walpole, brilliant but corrupt, was the butt of many satires during his administration (1721–1742), so there was little or no official encouragement of literature.

Literary sponsorship was taken up by a new group, the London publishers and booksellers, under whose influence printing and most writing became oriented toward commercial success. The reading public was growing. As the population expanded, the rate of literacy also increased, and the distribution and sale of printed works became better organized to serve the larger public. By midcentury, increasing industrialization brought about urbanization and social class mobility, with new opportunities of wealth and more leisure time for reading. Women became consumers of literature; circulating libraries were established in even modest-sized towns. The successful writer addressed his or, increasingly, her works to a broad, middle-class audience, using language and forms that did not assume that the reader had a classical education. The issues of proper conduct and good taste were explored; models for both were provided.

ANCIENTS AND MODERNS

During the first three decades of the century, however, partisan feelings were still intense. These feelings were paralleled by a literary division between disciples of the Ancients (who insisted that classical texts and forms should be studied and imitated) and the Moderns (who asserted the superiority of new learning in this advanced age). The great Tory satirists, Swift, Pope, and Gay, with some of their like-minded friends, formed a loose association, the Scriblerus Club, for the purpose of mocking the literary pretensions of the Moderns. They created a corporate persona, Martinus Scriblerus, to whom they attributed the authorship of various dull and pompous works. The club did not last long; it broke up when the Tories fell from power in 1714. The ideas generated among its members, however, provided the inspiration for several of the best satires of the next decade. Gradually, like the Whigs, the Moderns prevailed.

Sensibility

The highly complex, intellectual, and allusive satires of the age of Pope and Swift gave way to the literature of sensibility, of refinement of feeling. The ability to weep became a test of good character. The midcentury also saw a public reaction against wit as a literary criterion, and a hunger for sincere emotional expression inspired experiments with new poetic forms and a revival of interest in early folk literature.

Theater

The theater, however, languished, dominated by revivals of old plays and by vehicles for great actors. In 1737 Prime Minister Walpole had succeeded in getting Parliament to pass the Licensing Act, essentially a provision for precensorship of all new plays. Satiric comedy was thus thwarted. There was no outcry, for the public seemed to prefer spectacles and sentiment to serious drama.

LITERARY FORMS

During the early eighteenth century, satire pervaded all forms of literature. In narrative prose, the satiric travel book or tale served to mock current
events and ideas. (Satire is not a single form but rather an attitude of attack
or parody that can inhabit almost any established form of literature.)

The Novel

By the 1740s, however, a new form, the novel, came to dominance.
While some novels contained satiric elements, the novel's main function
was to develop images of real life, with authentic-seeming characters
working their way through the common problems of courtship, marriage
or worldly survival, succeeding in ways with which the reader could
identify and sympathize. The basic plot of the eighteenth-century novel
showed the hero or heroine finding a path through the maze of society's
restrictions and demands, hoping to keep his or her integrity along the
way. Brevity was not valued; the reader was assumed to have plenty of
time to linger over all the circumstantial details and to follow all the turns
of an extended plot. While some novels had a single narrator, like the
earlier epic poems, many others were told as a series of letters between
various correspondents (epistolary novels), yielding multiple points of
view and, usually, some lengthy redundancy.

Poetry

Very little lyric poetry was produced in the first quarter of the century,
a time when satiric wit rather than sincere feeling was central. But a reaction
developed, beginning with poets of nature who used the landscape as a
setting on which to project their emotions. These poets tended to find their
models among the medieval and Renaissance poets and in the folk tradition
of popular lyrics and ballads. Shakespeare's reputation rose while Dryden's
declined. The ballads, elegies, and odes these poets composed looked back
with nostalgia and melancholy at the long and, the poets thought, declining
history of England.

Drama

Lacking court patronage and an elite audience, the drama of the
eighteenth century flagged. Theaters remained open, but their staples were
the sentimental comedy as well as revivals and revisions of plays from the
previous century. In the 1730s, a thriving new satiric drama, epitomized by
Gay's *Beggar's Opera* and by the farces of Fielding, was squelched by the
Licensing Act. Interest in theater productions focused on the performance
by "great" actors who were admired for their abilities to move the audience
to terror or to tears. In the middle of the century, Goldsmith and Sheridan
attempted to revive the "laughing comedy," to recapture some of the satirical
spirit of the comedy of manners, but their efforts did not initiate a general
movement.

Periodical Essay

A new form that developed specifically for the new middle-class readership was the periodical essay. Periodicals and newspapers were not new, but those published during the Restoration contained essentially journalistic material, such as dispatches from European capitals, battle accounts, and biased reports of government activity written to support (or attack) political party interests. The new periodical essay avoided bad news in favor of entertaining discussions of fashions and urban life. Matters of dress, the theater, the street, domestic behavior, and family harmony were explored. This was the first time in English literary history that a publication was written for this particular audience, to cater to their desire for more refined status. Correspondents, real or fictional, sent in requests for help with the everyday problems of life. Good and bad taste in literature, the theater, and art were defined for readers who hoped to gain some polish and urbanity from the hints and recommendations of the essayists. The style of such publications was personal and intimate. The essayist developed a comfortable, fatherly persona, thereby cultivating a loyal readership. The prose was easy, simple, and lucid. Many of the qualities of the novel and its narrator were begun by periodical essayists; they wrote for the same audience.

During the early and middle eighteenth century, the literary life of England was more divided than it had been in any previous century. There were two mainstreams. In the first, respect for the examples and the rules established by ancient Greek and Roman writers dominated the tastes of the conservative elite. The educated upper class read works of wit and sophistication. Satire reached its highest development in this era. Satirists created complex, urbane, and intellectually demanding works in poetry, prose, and drama. This is the era of the heroic couplet, for example, one of the most technically difficult poetic media. The great Tory satirists, Swift, Pope, Gay, and Johnson, amazed and mocked their compatriots with subtle and outrageous depictions of a world gone mad or declining toward chaos. The terms neoclassical and Augustan refer to this stream of literature.

Meanwhile, a more liberal and optimistic literature was developing to appeal to the tastes and interests of the middle class. The growth of the printing and book-selling industries made literature a commodity as well as an art form. Responding to the market, writers adapted their works to a newly literate and newly leisured audience. Discarding or modifying classical forms, they sought to reflect the new emphasis on the spiritual and psychological lives of characters in a real rather than an ideal or heroic world. With faith in the essential goodness and equality of human beings, this literature found its heroes not in the powerful but in the men and women of feeling. New prose forms developed. The drama of this era was in prose,

*and the periodical essay and the novel made avid readers of those who
wanted to understand the manners and morals of the world they lived in.
Lyric poetry, neglected in the early part of the century, re-emerged among
poets who celebrated the landscape and the influence of nature and who
explored the life of the countryside sympathetically.*

**Selected
Readings**

Bredvold, Louis I., Alan D. McKillop, and Lois Whitney, eds. *Eighteenth-Century
Poetry and Prose*. New York: Ronald, 1973.

Butt, John. *The Augustan Age*. New York: Norton, 1965.

Hilson, J. C., M. M. Jones, and J. R. Watson, eds. *Augustan Worlds: New Essays
in Eighteenth-Century Literature*. New York: Barnes, 1978.

Persson, Agnes V. *Comic Characters in Restoration Drama*. The Hague: Mouton,
1975.

22

Eighteenth Century (1700 to 1785): Swift, Gay, Pope, Addison, and Steele

1702   First daily newspaper, *The Daily Courant,* published

1704   Swift, *A Tale of a Tub, The Battle of the Books*, and *The Mechanical Operation of the Spirit*

1709   Pope, *Pastorals*

1709–1711   Addison and Steele, *The Tatler*, the beginning of the periodical essay

1710   Swift, *A Description of a Morning*

1710–1713   Swift, *Journal to Stella*

1710–1714   Era of Scriblerus Club; Swift aligns himself with Tories; writes political articles defending Tory ministry, such as *The Conduct of the Allies*

1711   Pope, *Essay on Criticism*; Swift, *An Argument Against Abolishing Christianity in England*

1711–1712   Addison and Steele, *The Spectator* published

1712–1714   Pope, first version of *The Rape of the Lock*

1713   Addison, *Cato*; Swift made dean of St. Patrick's Cathedral, Dublin

1713–1726   Pope translates Homer, edits Shakespeare

1714   Addison and Steele, *The Spectator* revived

1716   Gay, *Trivia*, or *The Art of Walking the Streets of London*

1717   Pope's final version of *The Rape of the Lock*; Pope, *Epistle from Elosia to Abelard*

1719   Swift, *On Stella's Birthday*

1721–1742   Robert Walpole serves as Britain's first real prime minister

1722   Steele, *The Conscious Lovers*

1724–1725   Swift, *Drapier's Letters*

1726   Swift, *Gulliver's Travels*

1727–1760   Reign of George II

1728   Gay, *The Beggar's Opera*

1728–1743   Pope, *The Dunciad*

1729   Swift, *A Modest Proposal*

1732   Covent Garden Theatre built

1732–1747   Franklin, *Poor Richard's Almanack* published in the American colonies

1733–1734   Pope, *Essay on Man*

1734   Voltaire, *Letters Philosophiques*

1735   Pope, *Epistle to Dr. Arbuthnot*

1737   Theatre Licensing Act; confirms monopoly of patent theaters and censorship

1738   Swift, *On the Death of Dr. Swift*; Gay, *Fables*

1742   Handel, *Messiah* first performed

*T*he great Tory satirists, Swift, Gay, and Pope, and their Whig counter-parts, Addison and Steele, dominated the London literary scene during the first decades of the century. All were involved in partisan issues and used satiric prose or verse to influence public opinion. They all knew each other and were friends at first, but after 1710 both political differences and literary rivalries drove them into opposing camps.

JONATHAN SWIFT (1667–1745)

Although Swift was thirty-three years old at the beginning of the century, his writing career had not yet begun. He was an Anglo-Irish (born in Ireland of English parents) and had been educated in Ireland, but he had spent his early adulthood in England as secretary to the retired statesman Sir William Temple. After Temple's death in 1699, Swift sought a career as a clergyman in the Anglican church. His political sympathies had been with the Whigs, but increasingly Swift sided with the Tories because of their support for the established church. During the era of the Scriblerus Club (1710–1714), Swift was intimate with the most powerful men of the Tory government, Oxford and Bolingbroke. For them he was an effective propagandist and counselor. However, Queen Anne, offended by some of Swift's rough satire in *A Tale of a Tub*, discouraged attempts to reward him with a high post in the church. Therefore, when the Tories fell from power and the queen died, Swift returned to what he felt was exile in Dublin, becoming dean of St. Patrick's Cathedral.

Except for the occasional brief trip to England to visit his friends or to attend to publication of his works, Swift remained in Ireland until his death. He never married; as a lifelong sufferer from attacks of vertigo, Swift feared eventual madness. He had, however, what he called a "violent friendship" with Esther Johnson, a woman whom he had met when she was a girl in the Temple household and who came to live near him in Dublin in later years. She is the "Stella" of his poems. His letters to her have been published as *The Journal to Stella*. Swift's services to Ireland included a series of pamphlets, *The Drapier's Letters*, in which he advised and exhorted the Irish to assert economic independence, and his *Modest Proposal*, which he wrote to thwart some of the more outrageous exploitative policies of England.

One constant of Swift's technique in both prose and verse is the use of a persona, that is, of a narrator who is a character created by Swift rather than Swift himself. This speaker has weaknesses or blind spots that the reader comes to understand, so that there develops a significant difference between what the speaker/persona says and what the acute reader perceives to be the actual truth of the matter. Thus Gulliver is not Swift; Gulliver is more naive and ultimately unsound of mind. The only works in which Swift speaks in his own voice are the poems to Stella and the first part of *Verses on the Death of Dr. Swift*. Even in this last poem, he mocks himself by pretending to be a jealous and selfish person. Swift's skill lies in being able to imitate the verbal style of many different sorts of people, all of whom reveal their shortcomings in their own voices.

Steele's *Tatler* was the first to publish Swift's poems; *A Description of a Morning* and *A Description of a City Shower* (1710) are brief street scenes written in heroic couplets capturing moments in the lives of various passersby. Later, Swift composed a series of complimentary and affectionate poems for the birthdays of Esther Johnson, his "Stella."

Verses on the Death of Dr. Swift

Written in 1739, this was Swift's most ambitious poem. It is a study of his own reputation as a satirist and a justification of his career as a corrector of public morals. In tetrameter couplets, Swift describes what he imagines would be the reactions of his friends and acquaintances and of the reading public to the news of his death. He pictures ladies chatting about his illness and his legacies while they play cards. Finally, he pictures a discussion about himself in a London tavern, where an impartial speaker gives a fair and ultimately positive judgment of the value of Swift's work and of his honor as a man.

Tale of a Tub

This prose satire was first composed at the end of the previous century, but Swift revised it several times before its publication in 1704. The targets of his satiric attack are two: religious hypocrisy and the shallowness of modern philosophy. An allegorical narrative of the Christian church in the even-numbered chapters follows the progress of three brothers, Peter (the Roman Catholic church), Martin (the Church of England, inspired by Martin Luther), and Jack (the fanatical Dissenters, followers of John Calvin) and shows how each faction deviates in its own way from the essence of Christianity. The alternate chapters contain a series of digressions, the absurd musings of the supposed author, a dull and nonsensical modern thinker who becomes more and more engrossed in himself, even to the point of madness. The book does not conclude so much as disintegrate into crazy confusion.

The *Tale of a Tub* was published in the same volume with *The Battle of the Books*, a defense of ancient against modern learning.

Gulliver's Travels

This prose satire was the product of Swift's "exile" in Ireland, during which he looked back with revulsion on the social and political events of the first two decades of the century. The work is a political allegory reflecting on the corruption of English government under the Whigs. Published in 1726, it is written in the form of four travelogues, each mocking the outrageous lies and exaggerations that travelers are liable to tell. Swift's persona is the ordinary man, Gulliver, caught in a series of adventures that exhaust his capacity to understand himself or the world. After some puzzling front matter, in which the old man Gulliver chastises his readers for not having reformed themselves, there are four parts covering four different travels.

PART I

Gulliver goes to the land of Lilliput, where the folk are only about six inches tall. The two Lilliputian political parties, the High Heels and the Low Heels, represent the absurd differences between the Tory and Whig parties. Similarly, the Big Endians (the Roman Catholics) and the Little Endians (the Anglican church) are divided by the issue of which end of an egg to break before eating it. In capturing the fleet of the enemy Blefesoue (France), Gulliver tries to be a loyal Lilliputian, but he is undermined by enemies at court. His fate parallels the trouble of Swift's friends, Robert Harley, earl of Oxford, and Henry St. John, viscount Bolingbroke, and it also reflects some of Swift's own disappointment at suffering suspicion as a reward for his public service.

PART II

This section reverses the proportions; here Gulliver is tiny and his hosts gigantic. Likewise, Gulliver is a moral pygmy compared with the benevolent and wise king of Brobdingnag, which is portrayed as a utopia. At the heart of Book II is a dialogue between Gulliver and the king in which Gulliver finds that his exaggerated descriptions of the glories of England all backfire. The king is unconvinced that England is a model state because he understands human nature well enough to doubt the truth of Gulliver's assertions. Attempting to impress the king with the power and technology of England, Gulliver brags about the use of gunpowder, prompting the King's horror and disgust. Gulliver's pride suffers repeated assaults until he is accidentally lost by his owners, rescued, and then returned to England.

PART III

Part III describes Gulliver's varied adventures among people of ordinary size but of diverse intellectual excesses. Gulliver visits a floating island on which the inhabitants think only abstractly and are oblivious to common sense and affection. He visits the Academy of Logado, Swift's parody of the Royal Society, where nasty and pointless experiments in applied science are pursued by modern enthusiasts. He then travels to lands where some people never die and where the dead can be called back for conversations. The general objects of Swift's criticism in this book include a wide range of intellectual fads that he found absurd.

PART IV

Part IV portrays a dystopia, or the opposite of a utopia. Gulliver believes he has found a perfect place, because the evils of Houyhnhnm Land are concealed beneath a surface of uniform rationality and benevolence. Houyhnhnms are a race of intelligent horses who tell no lies and commit no sins. But they keep as slaves the race of Yahoos, creatures who display all the worst traits of humanity—lust, dirtiness, greed, gluttony, and rage. Repelled by the Yahoos, Gulliver rejects his own human nature and emulates Houyhnhnmhood. But he cannot be integrated into Houyhnhnm society; he is feared and rejected and finally sent away by a society unable to adjust to or tolerate a deviant, rational Yahoo. After returning to Europe, Gulliver remains unreconciled, hating humanity and longing for the false ideal of Houyhnhnmland.

Through the four parts of his travels, Gulliver's character has deteriorated from that of a mild and sensible ordinary Englishman of good intentions to that of a mad and irascible misanthrope. His perceptions of the world have become biased and distorted toward the negative. Gulliver reflects Swift's fear that the whole tendency of modern philosophy and science is to diminish the individual's moral awareness and to subvert traditional moral values.

A Modest Proposal

Written in 1729, this essay epitomizes the pamphlets Swift wrote in support of the Irish against economic exploitation by England. In it a mild and reasonable-sounding projector (proposer of public improvements) makes the ironic suggestion that the Irish, who are driven to poverty and despair by economic burdens, be encouraged to market their own infants as gourmet meats for the rich. The outrageous proposal, treated with dead-pan seriousness, contains an implicit and unrelenting condemnation of absentee landlords and irresponsible officials. Swift includes a list of practical suggestions for helping the poor, but the projector, his persona, rejects all these as unlikely to be tried. This is one of the best examples of sustained irony in English prose.

JOHN GAY (1685–1732)

Gay was the most beloved of the great Tory satirists. An orphan, he was continually seeking but never finding a secure position at court or in government to relieve himself of his fear of poverty. His poetic works were mainly burlesques based on formal models from classical literature. *Trivia*, or *The Art of Walking the Streets of London* (1716) is a mock-georgic describing the city scene in a manner similar to that in which the georgic describes country life. Gay also composed two collections of verse fables (1727 and 1738). As a member of the Scriblerus Club, Gay associated with Pope and Swift in their projects of parody and burlesque. Because of the stimulation of the club, Gay conceived his most famous and most financially rewarding work, the satire *The Beggar's Opera*.

The Beggar's Opera

This operatic parody written in 1728 grew out of Swift's suggestion that Gay write "a Newgate pastoral." (Newgate was the central prison of London.) Based on a series of parallels between high life and low life in London, it is a parody of the Italian opera, using familiar English tunes instead of lofty operatic arias. Gay also aimed to attack the well-known corruption of the Whig prime minister, Robert Walpole. Walpole is reflected in the characters of Peachum, the receiver of stolen goods, and Macheath, the highway robber. Peachum also suggests the famous real-life London fence, Jonathan Wild, who would betray or "impeach" those thieves who were no longer subservient or useful to himself. In the opera, Peachum's daughter

Polly is a silly girl whose head has been turned by reading too many romances. She is contrasted to the tougher Lucy Locket, the jailer's daughter, who helps Macheath escape. The rivalry of these "ladies" is an allusion to a rivalry between two opera singers of the time. The action consists of MacHeath's being captured, escaping, being captured again, and then being released. The mock-opera is set within a framework dialogue between the player (actor) and the poet-beggar (Gay) about the poor taste of London audiences. However, *The Beggar's Opera* was so popular with London audiences that it offended Walpole. Thus, Gay's sequel, *Polly*, was not permitted to be produced.

ALEXANDER POPE (1688–1744)

The two most decisive factors in the life of Pope were his Roman Catholicism at a time of fierce anti-Catholic feeling in England and his suffering from tuberculosis in childhood, which stunted his growth and caused him lifelong pain and disability. Pope attended no school and was largely self-educated at home, with guidance and encouragement from his father, among others. Pope's early ambition was to become what England had not yet produced, a really "correct" poet, that is, one whose poetry was polished and refined and met the classical standards of excellence. It is not surprising, therefore, that one of his earliest works was the *Essay on Criticism*.

Pope was a precocious poet and won praise for his early works, but he also provoked jealousy and began to make literary enemies. Addison and Steele, for example, had been among his early literary friends, but later, when the Tories were in power and Pope was closely associated with Swift and the powerful Tory ministers Oxford and Bolingbroke, the old crowd broke with Pope. Addison encouraged some of Pope's antagonists in their attempts to undermine Pope's reputation. In the Scriblerus Club, however, Pope found his closest political and poetical companions.

Pope's career as a poet is often divided into three periods. In the first (1706–1714) he made his reputation with both satiric and somewhat romantic poetry. During the middle years (1715–1728) he was mostly occupied with translating into English heroic couplets from Homer's *Iliad* and *Odyssey* and preparing an edition of Shakespeare's plays. All this activity brought him great financial success and independence, which culminated in the *Dunciad*. During the third period, Pope's last years (1729–1744), he was concerned with creating ethical, moral, and philosophical poetry. In his mature years, Pope reacted with disgust to the corruption of the Walpole-Whig government, and he felt that England was in a period of decline and decay. He saw himself as a champion for traditional humanist values and as the spokesman for a way of life now endangered by commercial wealth, literary dullness, and vulgarity. At his garden and villa retreat in suburban Twickenham, he not only composed poetry but also cultivated his garden and maintained an extensive correspondence with like-minded friends.

Essay on Criticism

Written in heroic couplets, this 1711 poem is called an essay because it discusses in an apparently informal style the problems of being a good critic. It was written as a response to attacks on wit as being superficial and held that wit and judgment are two essential qualities of mind. Pope restates and harmonizes the major concepts of neoclassical literary theory, celebrating the rules derived from the study of classical criticism and literature. Pope, however, says that these rules should not restrain the genius of a modern poet and allows for some exceptions.

PART I

Pope argues against pride. Since human limitations are part of the orderly plan of nature, the critic must know his own limitations and study to improve.

PART II

Next, Pope explores various kinds of false criticisms that arise from a partial view of poetry. Critics who are overly preoccupied with trifling errors, diction, metaphors, and numbers (meter) make false judgments, as do those who value only the works of either the Ancients or the Moderns.

PART III

Finally, Pope exhorts the critic to speak the truth but also to be fair to the poet and to act as a friend. This part contains a brief history of great critics, from Aristotle down to Pope's own advisor, William Walsh (1663–1721). The ideals of moderation and good taste that this poem advocates are found in all of Pope's later works.

The Rape of the Lock

This mock-heroic satire in heroic couplets pokes fun at fashionable society. The plot is based on an actual incident in Pope's social circle. Miss Anabella Fermor, a fashionable young lady, was angered by Lord Petre's cutting off of one of the ringlets of hair at the back of her neck. Pope ridicules the family feud that resulted by treating it ironically as if it were a serious assault, a true rape. The first version of the poem (1712) was short, containing only two cantos. A revision in 1714 expanded it to five cantos and added the sylphs, the supernatural beings who oversee the heroine's fate. Pope published the final version in 1717, adding the speech by Clarissa in Canto

V. Its treatment of a trivial occurrence in grand heroic style makes this poem a burlesque.

CANTO I

Belinda, a coquette, sleeps as the sylph Ariel explains his protective role and warns her of some vague danger. Belinda then awakes. Forgetting the warning, she prepares herself for the day's social encounters by arranging her hair and make-up at her dressing table (called her toilet). The preparations are treated mock-heroically as if they were a sacred ritual of preparation for battle.

CANTO II

Pope introduces Belinda's antagonist, the baron, who performs a parallel ritual, praying to get Belinda's lock of hair. Meanwhile Belinda goes to Hampton Court, one of Queen Anne's palaces, accompanied by Ariel and his band of sylphs. In a heroic speech, Ariel rallies the troops and assigns them to defensive positions about Belinda's head and body.

CANTO III

Most of this canto describes a card game (a mock battle) in which Belinda defeats the baron. The crisis occurs late in the canto, in lines 151 to 154, when the baron, using scissors borrowed from Clarissa, cuts off the lock while Belinda bends her head over a cup of coffee. Belinda screams, but the baron brags about his victory over her.

CANTO IV

Now the gnome Umbriel replaces Ariel as Belinda's guardian spirit, indicating that she has changed from being a coquette to being a prude. Umbriel visits the Cave of Spleen; Spleen is a goddess of sickness and melancholy. He receives a bag of winds to propel the angry outbursts and laments of Belinda. Returning to the scene of action, Umbriel finds Belinda prostrate in the arms of her friend and fellow prude Thalestris. Both women make exaggerated complaints about the enormity of the baron's "rape."

CANTO V

The final canto contains the mock battle scene; the weapons are scornful looks, cutting remarks, snapping fans, and a pinch of snuff with which Belinda makes the baron sneeze. She even draws out a bodkin or pin from her dress to threaten him, as if with a sword. At the conclusion of the battle and of the poem the lock has been lost in all the confusion, and Pope pays a poetic compliment to the heroine by asserting that her hairs have become a new constellation in the heavens.

The poem was an immediate success as a satire on manners; contemporary readers familiar with ancient epics enjoyed the many echoes and parallels of phrasing that Pope used to develop the poem.

The Essay on Man

This philosophical poem in four epistles or letters, written in heroic couplets during 1733 and 1734, undertakes to explain the place of humankind in the universe. Pope attempts to harmonize the views of various contemporary thinkers, especially those of his friend Bolingbroke, and to provide a comprehensive and reassuring view that the individual, despite inherent limitations, can use reason to become reconciled to life. Pope works not so much by logic as by wit and metaphor, raising issues in rhetorical questions and answering them by analogy. As a satire, the poem creates an implied dialogue between the poet/satirist and his opponent, Presumptuous Man. This opponent is a doubting malcontent, restless under the restraints of the human condition but proud of his own reasoning capacity. Pope uses the central image of the Chain of Being to represent the hierarchy of beings in the created universe and to indicate God's plan to make an orderly, structured world in which human beings must fill only their own appropriate ranks. Pope's ideas here are compatible with the deistic concept that the being and the nature of God are revealed by studying what He has created—Nature.

EPISTLE I

Pope asserts the absurdity of man's pride, given the limitations of place in the natural order. Man is only a part of the order of Nature; it was not made for him.

EPISTLE II

Pope considers man as a psychological entity, balanced between the demands of passion and the control of reason. Passion, which motivates us to action, can result in good or evil depending on how it is guided by reason. Man's position is always going to be uncomfortable.

EPISTLE III

This third epistle considers man as a social being; self-love expands to include others, and man is shown as capable of benevolent action and communal feeling.

EPISTLE IV

Pope catalogues the sources of human happiness. He concludes that the ultimate source of happiness is virtue. Although the poem stresses the limitations of human existence, it is generally optimistic about man's ability to find a right balance and to achieve goodness.

Pope first published this poem anonymously because he felt that it would not get a fair reading if his authorship were known. He had accumulated many literary enemies who would find faults with his philosophizing. He intended the poem as a foundation for a series of moral and philosophical poems on various more specifically focused topics.

Dunciad

Pope wrote two different versions of this satire during the fifteen years between 1728 and 1743, changing and adding to it as events suggested new materials and new targets of attack. Written in heroic couplets, the work's basic situation, borrowed from Homeric epics, is a series of heroic games played to celebrate the coronation of the new laureate of the goddess Dullness. The occasion for this satire was not only Pope's desire to get back at the many attacks on his own works by petty and mean-minded rivals but also the growth of literary London, fed by the publishing industry, in which Pope saw an increase in the number of second and even third-rate authors. These hack writers thrived, despite meager talents, because of the opportunities of the marketplace. Pope perceived in this the debasement of English culture.

BOOK I

In the first *Dunciad*, Lewis Theobald, a poet, critic, and Pope's rival as an editor of Shakespeare, is portrayed praying to the goddess Dullness. She takes him up into a tower to view the extent of her realm and makes him king of the Dunces. The images in this part are of creation gone awry, abortive offspring and monstrous births and ill-formed progeny. Dullness is shown as the corrupting rather than the nurturing mother of English society.

BOOK II

To celebrate the coronation of the king of the Dunces, games are being played among the various despicable printers, booksellers, poets, critics, and hack writers of Grub Street.

BOOK III

Pope recounts the past victories of Dullness and predicts that her power will one day conquer all England.

BOOK IV

The goddess Dullness, having moved from the lesser precincts to the west end of London, holds court. She is approached by a crowd of various petitioners, to whom she grants favors.

In 1743 Pope wrote a new Book IV and changed the victim of his satire from Theobald to Colley Cibber, an actor and theater manager of no poetic talent but who had, nonetheless, been made poet laureate to King George II. The tone of the new version of Book IV is darker. Chaos and Night are about to descend and take back the Earth, as the goddess Dullness sits enthroned with Cibber in her lap. Morality is being ceremoniously strangled, and Education is falling victim to political tyranny. Dullness makes a speech exhorting her devotees to go forth and conquer. In a reversal of a creation scene, the final passage presents a terrible vision of the return of the world to darkness and death.

Epistle to Dr. Arbuthnot	This 1735 poem is a dialogue in heroic couplets in which the mature Pope reflects on his career while his friend Dr. John Arbuthnot listens sympathetically and occasionally interrupts. Arbuthnot asks questions and warns Pope to avoid dangerous antagonists. Pope pictures himself as the last poet of integrity and courage in a world full of scribbling fools and jealous competitors. Pope presents a brief poetic autobiography, explaining how he became a poet by natural inclination and talent, how even his early attempts at verse provoked spiteful attacks, and how he has borne unflinchingly a lifelong series of enemies and flatterers, both equally distasteful. Pope asserts his own manliness, his independence from the mob and from any patronage. He then inserts portraits of some less manly and less generous characters, whom he verbally annihilates.

The first is Atticus, who represents Joseph Addison. He is portrayed as a false friend who pretends to praise one's work while encouraging others to attack and denigrate it. The second is Bufo, who represents any false patron who keeps poor poets dangling in hopes of being granted favors while he basks in their flattery. The third and most violent attack is on Sporus or Lord John Henry, a confidant of Queen Caroline. Sporus is described as an insect, a snake, a toad, "an amphibious thing." The epistle then concludes with Pope's self-portrait as manly, unswayed from his moral intentions by any unfair attacks, and a champion of virtue. He identifies his own father and Dr. Arbuthnot as men who embody the right way, in contrast to the creatures he has exposed.

JOSEPH ADDISON (1672–1719) AND RICHARD STEELE (1672–1729)

These two men are usually discussed together because, although each one wrote independently, their most influential products were the two series of periodical essays that they produced jointly. They were born the same year and attended the same schools, Charterhouse and then Oxford. Both were Whigs in politics, but while Addison traveled in Europe and prepared himself for a diplomatic career, Steele went into the army. Both men later held government positions, though Addison's positions were much more influential. Both were members of the Whig club of wits, the Kit-Cat Club. Finally, they both wrote plays. Addison's tragedy *Cato* (1713) glorified an ideal hero of patriotism. The play was received more as a political statement than as a literary work. Steele's sentimental comedy *The Conscious Lovers* (1722) is a prime example of the type of weeping comedy that appealed to the sympathy rather than the wit of the early eighteenth-century audience. However, as essayists, both Addison and Steele set a standard for wit and polish that endured for a century.

The New Mass Audience

Although educated gentlemen, Addison and Steele were interested in speaking to the new mass audience, the modern readers who were literate in English but who did not read the ancient languages or have the education that would enable them to recognize an allusion to Homer's *Iliad* or Virgil's *Aeneid* unless it were pointed out to them. Such readers needed guidance; they did not know what was well written, but they were eager to learn and grateful for the simple advice that the essayists were about to give them in gently mocking tones. These middle-class readers liked to feel a part of the mainstream of culture and to be reassured that with some moderate efforts they could learn to enjoy the best that life offered. They read *The Tatler* and *The Spectator* avidly, passed copies around among friends and family, and sent copies to their cousins in the country.

THE TATLER

In 1709 Steele started a thrice-weekly periodical called *The Tatler* (one who tattles or tells) under the pseudonym of Issac Bickerstaffe, a name previously used by Swift in a series of pamphlets mocking astrology. Steele's purpose was to reform manners, both in public and in domestic life. He set up a framework based on supposed "news" dispatches from various fashionable public places around London. From these locations he reported social observations about dress, the theater, drunkenness, and encounters in coffee houses and in the streets. He mocked scolding wives and pompous men. The tone of Steele's social criticism was blandly ironic rather than severe. After some weeks, Addison began to send some contributions from Ireland. They were also published under Bickerstaffe's name. Addison too aimed to improve the reader. *The Tatler* lasted until January 1711, when Steele gave it up. The anonymity of his authorship had been penetrated, and he felt that he could not effectively correct his readers' behavior once they knew who he was.

THE SPECTATOR

In March of 1711 Addison began a new periodical, a daily essay entitled *The Spectator*. This had the same general purpose as *The Tatler* but a somewhat different emphasis. This time the framework fiction was a club of men who represented various types and classes from English society: Sir Roger de Coverley, an old Tory squire who recalled the rakish days of the Restoration; Sir Andrew Freeport, a new man of commerce; Will Honeycomb, a middle-aged would-be ladies' man, and others. The activities and opinions of these characters broadened *The Spectator*'s range of topics, but increasingly Addison set aside the fiction of the club and took up more ambitious projects to improve literary tastes. By writing several series of essays that extended over several issues he was able to develop a single topic in more depth. For example, one of these series concerned an appreciation of Milton's *Paradise Lost*; another, *The Pleasures of the Imagination*, was an influential discussion of aesthetic theory. Richard Steele also contributed essays to *The Spectator*, but Addison's interests dominated. Addison's easy yet polished prose style became a model for English writers. *The Spectator* lasted until the end of 1712 and had a brief revival in 1714. Both *The Tatler* and *The Spectator* were later reprinted in bound volumes and continued to be read and imitated for many decades.

The first half of the eighteenth century, sometimes called the Age of Reason, is often thought of as essentially an age of prose. Such a name, however, ignores the poetic achievements of Pope and Swift and implies that literature of wit and irony is less valuable than literature of emotion. The satirists of this era saw clearly that emotion is a strong force in human nature; they did not ignore feeling but showed the dangers of following the promptings of feeling without the restraints of reason or judgment. They sought a balance between passion and reason and demonstrated how difficult this balance is to achieve or to maintain. Their favorite mode—irony—was useful in its capacity to say two things at once—to balance the overt statement against the implied meaning. Parallels and contrast structure the poetry and prose of this age as the writers sought to define the difficult and unstable middle way, which to them always appeared to be the best way.

Selected Readings

Erskine-Hill, Howard and Anne Smith, eds. *The Art of Alexander Pope*. New York: Barnes, 1979.

Gravil, Richard, ed. *Swift: Gulliver's Travels: A Casebook*. New York: Macmillan, 1974.

Greenberg, Robert A. and William Bowman Piper, eds. *The Writings of Jonathan Swift: Authoritative Texts, Backgrounds, Criticism*. New York: Norton, 1973.

Mack, Maynard. *Alexander Pope: A Life*. New York and New Haven: Norton and Yale University Press, 1985.

Quintana, Ricardo. *Swift: An Introduction*. New York: Oxford University Press, 1955.

Rogers, Pat. *An Introduction to Pope*. New York: Harper, 1975.

Rogers, Robert W. *The Major Satires of Alexander Pope*. Urbana: University of Illinois, 1955.

23

Eighteenth-Century English Literature (1700 to 1785): Johnson and Boswell

1733	Pope, *Essay on Man*
1735	Pope, *Epistle to Dr. Arbuthnot*
1737	Theatre Licensing Act
1738	Johnson, *London*
1740	Richardson writes novel *Pamela*, or *Virtue Rewarded*
1742	Handel's *Messiah* first performed
1744	Johnson, *Life of Richard Savage*
1748	Hume, *Inquiry Concerning Human Understanding*
1749	Johnson, *The Vanity of Human Wishes*; Fielding, *Tom Jones*
1750–1752	Johnson, *The Rambler* and *The Idler* essays
1751	Vol. I of French *Encyclopedie*
1753	British Museum founded
1755	Johnson's *Dictionary of the English Language*
1759	Johnson, *Rasselas*; Voltaire, *Candide*
1760–1820	Reign of George III
1762	Johnson receives pension from Crown

1763　Boswell meets Johnson

1764　Johnson and others establish the London Literary Club

1765　Johnson's edition of Shakespeare; Watt invents steam engine

1768　Spinning machine invented

1773　Johnson and Boswell tour Scotland; *The Kenrich Dictionary*, the first to mark vowel sounds

1775　Johnson, *Journey to the Western Islands of Scotland*; Sheridan, *The Rivals*

1776　Gibbon, *Decline and Fall of the Roman Empire*; Smith, *Wealth of Nations*; American Revolution, Continental Congress issues Declaration of Independence

1779　Johnson, *Lives of the Poets*; Hume, *Natural History of Religion*

1781　Kant, *Critique of Pure Reason*

1784　Death of Samuel Johnson

1791　Boswell, *Life of Johnson*

The middle of the eighteenth century is sometimes called the Age of Johnson, because Samuel Johnson dominated the literary scene personally and through his Literary Club. Johnson was the last great defender of conservative values, the Ancients, in literary criticism, but he was also aware of the changes taking place around him, of the growth of the novel and the revival of lyric poetry. Johnson's satire was less biting and more humane than that of the previous generation. He became a beloved character among his contemporaries, and his image was projected into the new age through the vast and detailed biography of Johnson written by his young friend, James Boswell.

SAMUEL JOHNSON (1709–1784)

Johnson's career illustrates the emergence of writing as a trade, although in talent and learning he surpassed the crowds of ordinary hack writers who subsisted in London during the mid-eighteenth century. Johnson was the son of a bookseller in the town of Litchfield, and he read avidly the offerings of his father's shop. Therefore, although the lack of funds cut short his attendance at Oxford, Johnson's background had given him an ample stock of learning on which he was able to draw for his many writing projects— poetry and plays, translations, political and legal tracts, criticism and biography, essays, tales, and eventually even a dictionary of the English language. Physically he was not attractive. Large and robust, he had suffered from scrofula in childhood and the disease left facial scars. He was almost blind in one eye and had a variety of nervous tics. It was said of him, however, that as soon as he began to speak, one forgot all these disfigurements and disabilities in the pleasure of his wit. He was a man of immense literary energy who repeatedly scolded himself for laziness and procrastination.

Having failed as a schoolmaster near Litchfield, Johnson traveled to London with David Garrick, one of his pupils, who later became a celebrated actor and theater manager. Johnson received writing assignments from the editor of *The Gentleman's Magazine* and entered into the professional writing world called "Grub Street." In Grub Street, the area of London where poor writers lived and worked, men hired out their talents at so much a page or, if for poetry, at so much a line of printed copy. Writing to order, they composed essays, biographies, histories, poems on special occasions, as well as translations or abridgments of the works of others. Plagiarism was common. These writers compiled, digested, and simplified material for pamphlets, periodicals, and books. Some writers were attached to one or the other of the major political parties, but others would write for whatever political position was paying.

Johnson had such a wide range of knowledge and such a keen intellect that he never resorted to the lowest kinds of hack writing, but he did write to order for pay. He could turn out a suitable dedication or preface to make a mediocre work more impressive. He wrote parliamentary speeches merely on the basis of knowing who the speakers were and what the issue was. He stopped writing political speeches, however, when he realized that his written versions were being mistaken for the speeches that had actually been given.

Dictionary of the English Language

In 1747 Johnson asked for and got booksellers' support for a project to compile the first systematic and comprehensive dictionary of the English language. This task cost him eight years of endless drudgery. The Dictionary, first published in 1755, earned him a royal pension in 1762.

Meanwhile, he was producing other work, including the periodical essays entitled *The Rambler* (1750–1752). After the Dictionary, he wrote a second series of essays for *The Idler* (1758–1760) and the philosophical tale *Rasselas* (1759).

Late in his life, Johnson befriended James Boswell, a young Scot who was to become his biographer. Johnson continued to produce writing in many forms. The works of his late years include *A Journey to the Western Islands of Scotland* (1775), which describes a trip he took with Boswell, and *The Lives of the Poets* (1779–1781), a biographical and critical survey of the major English poets since the Renaissance.

Johnson's Club   By this time Johnson had become London's most prominent literary celebrity and arbiter of taste. His group of friends, called simply the Club or the Literary Club, was an exclusive assemblage of the most important writers and thinkers of his era: the poet Oliver Goldsmith, the philosopher and lawyer Sir Edmund Burke, the painter Sir Joshua Reynolds, the actor and theater manager David Garrick, the playwright Richard Brinsley Sheridan, and others.

Johnson's Poetry   Johnson's verse was mainly of two kinds. He wrote two formal verse satires in heroic couplets based on the models of Juvenal, the great Roman satirist. One of these satires, *London* (1738), describes the dangers and decadence of the city. The second kind of poetry Johnson wrote is also satiric, but it tends to be light and playful and written for a specific occasion. An example is *A Short Song of Congratulation*. However, Johnson's moving poem *On the Death of Dr. Robert Levet* falls into neither of these categories.

THE VANITY OF HUMAN WISHES

In this formal verse satire written in 1749, Johnson expresses an idea central to much of his work. He believed that discontent and restlessness are a greater part of human existence than is satisfaction. Written in heroic couplets, the poem is generally considered one of Johnson's best and most powerful, but it is highly allusive and difficult. Imitating a satire by the Roman poet Juvenal, the poet voices his complaints in a series of images of corrupted individuals who fall from power into degradation.

Johnson's Prose   ### RASSELAS

This philosophical prose tale has some elements of romance, such as the abduction and rescue of a maiden, travels to exotic lands, and encounters with bizarre characters. But the subject matter really focuses on the everyday problems of life—marriage, family harmony, and work. The title character and his sister, Nekayah, are royalty. They escape from their confinement in the Happy Valley, a pleasurable but dull land, to seek the best "choice of life." Their guide is the wise poet Imlac (a self-portrait of Johnson), with whom they observe and discuss various scenes of urban and rural discontent. They see that each style of life at first seems attractive to the outsider but that further investigation shows its disadvantages. Generally, they conclude, any style of life becomes dull or frustrating just because of the repetition of the same activities. The individual always wants what he or she does not have, imagining that the change will bring satisfaction. The tale concludes ironically when each of the main characters makes a choice and at the same time realizes that he or she will necessarily become dissatisfied with the outcome of that choice. Johnson's prose style in *Rasselas*, as elsewhere, is highly formal, with sentences organized in balanced parallel or opposite phrases; for example, "Marriage has many pains, but celibacy has no pleasures."

THE LIVES OF THE POETS

This work was at first intended as a series of prefaces for a bookseller's edition of major English poets. Johnson, however, went beyond the original conception to develop lengthy essays of appreciation and criticism that merited being published on their own. Johnson gives a biographical study of each poet and follows it with an assessment of the strengths and weaknesses of the poet's major works. In the course of these essays, Johnson develops the technique of literary criticism. He introduces moral as well as aesthetic criteria into his judgments. In his discussion of the works of Abraham Cowley, Johnson gave the name "metaphysical" to the school of seventeenth-century poetry led by John Donne. Johnson is always concerned with a poem's effects on the reader's feelings and beliefs. He sometimes allows his personal dislikes (for instance, his dislike of pastoral poetry) to distort his evaluations. Thus he finds Milton's great pastoral elegy *Lycidas* to be dull and insincere. Nevertheless, Johnson set a new standard for English literary criticism.

JAMES BOSWELL (1740–1795)

The son of a devout and demanding Scottish judge, Boswell escaped to London with the impractical idea of getting an elite military commission. Instead he met Samuel Johnson, who became a surrogate father to him and the subject of Boswell's one great book, *The Life of Samuel Johnson*. Boswell was a constant recorder of his own activities, observations, and conversations. His innovation and strength as a biographer was the detailed, intimate, and apparently accurate accounts of conversations reconstructed from memory after a day or an evening spent with his subject. Boswell loved and sought out celebrities. He ingratiated himself to three of the most famous men of his age—Voltaire, Rousseau, and Johnson. His lifelong diary of his own experiences revealed not only the motivations for his actions but also his inner life of fantasy, his hopes and fears, his unstable self-image, and the games he played by adopting from time to time the personality of someone else. Thus Boswell left voluminous manuscripts in addition to the works published during his life. His journals and letters continued to be discovered, edited, and published during most of the twentieth century.

The Life of Samuel Johnson

When Boswell met him, Johnson was already fifty-four. Most of his works had been written, and he was already established as a great moral and literary authority. In fact, this is what attracted Boswell. For his account of Johnson's earlier life, therefore, Boswell had to rely on anecdotes and remembrances of Johnson himself and those who had known him. Boswell found a great deal of material and weighed it carefully before concluding what was factual. But the essence of his biography consists of the many encounters and conversations between Boswell and Johnson and the other members of the Club. Boswell even set up situations and "scenes" in order to provoke interesting comments and reactions from Johnson, which he, Boswell, then described. Boswell presents Johnson as a powerful mind, an almost heroic character. The passages that describe Johnson's peculiarities and rough manners only serve to emphasize, by contrast, his generous nature and precise insights. Samuel Johnson emerges as a bear of a man, eccentric and witty, but entirely humane. In its scope and detail, Boswell's *Life of Johnson* far surpassed any previous biographical study.

The mid-eighteenth century is a period of transition from the high wit and satire of earlier literature of the century to the sentiment of later literature. Johnson, although he seems to be a spokesman for the past age, also makes the transition. He welcomes the growth of the novel and encourages interest in new poetry. As a critic, he sorts out the valuable from the superficial and imposes a moral as well as an aesthetic standard of values. The image of Johnson, sharp-tongued but basically kind, was projected not only in his own works but also in the study of him made by his devoted admirer, Boswell.

Selected Readings

Bate, W. J. *The Achievement of Samuel Johnson*. New York: Oxford University Press, 1955.

Bloom, Harold, ed. *Dr. Samuel Johnson: Modern Critical Views*. New York: Chelsea House, 1989.

Hagstrum, Jean. *Samuel Johnson's Literary Criticism*. Minneapolis: University of Minnesota, 1952.

24

Eighteenth-Century English Literature (1700 to 1785): Lyric Poetry

1713	Finch, *Miscellany Poems on Several Occasions*
1721–1742	Robert Walpole serves as Britain's first real prime minister
1726	Thomson, *Winter*
1727–1760	Reign of George II
1728	Thomson, *Spring*
1730	Thomson, *The Seasons*, first version
1742	Handel's *Messiah* first performed
1746	Collins, *Odes on Several Descriptive and Allegorical Subjects*
1747	Collins, *Ode to Evening* and *Ode on a Distant Prospect of Eton College*
1748	Thomson, *The Castle of Indolence*
1751	Gray, *Elegy Written in a Country Churchyard*
1753	British Museum founded
1757	Gray, *The Progress of Poesy* and *The Bard*
1760–1820	Reign of George III
1763	Smart, *A Song to David*
1765	Percy, *Reliques of English Poetry*; Johnson's edition of Shakespeare

1766   Goldsmith, *The Vicar of Wakefield*

1770   Goldsmith, *Deserted Village*

1773   Goldsmith, *She Stoops to Conquer*

While satiric poetry written in couplets dominated in the early part of the eighteenth century, the middle part (1740–1780s) saw a reemergence of the lyric poem and the development of descriptive nature poetry. The new school of sensibility placed feeling instead of wit at the center of the poetic experience. Burlesque and parody were replaced by sentiment and by familiar or nostalgic images of the landscape. This was partly a reaction against the brittle and elitist tone of satire. Nature poetry is less exclusive, more available to the ordinary reader who lacks a classical education. Instead of striving to be clever or brilliant, this poetry was sincere and morally uplifting.

The lyric forms were revived; poets wrote elegies and odes. They looked back to medieval English and to Shakespeare and Spenser for inspiration. Interest in old popular ballads arose; an important collection, Reliques of English Poetry *(1765), was published by Thomas Percy. The term gothic, which had been a synonym for rude and coarse, became instead a term of praise, implying an antique, authentic or primitive quality; rough perhaps, but emotionally valid. Nature poetry was valued for its appeal to the heart and its ability to move the reader, to inspire a moral sensitivity such as one feels in the presence of impressive natural sights. Nighttime and graveyard settings were used to intensify poetic effects. Generally, the new poets of the midcentury sought ways to enlist the reader's feelings to support the right moral values.*

ANNE FINCH,
COUNTESS OF WINCHILSEA (1661–1720)

As a young woman and a maid of honor during the Restoration period, Anne Finch had been involved in the life of the royal court. She married a colonel, who later became the earl of Winchilsea. But at the time of the Glorious Revolution in 1688, Anne and her husband both lost their positions, so they retired to their country estate. In retirement, she began to write poetry, focusing on descriptions of the natural surroundings. In 1713 Lady Winchilsea published a collection of poems titled *Miscellany Poems on Several Occasions, Written by a Lady.* Although women did not write (except secretly), much less publish, poetry in the early eighteenth century, the countess asserts in the introduction to her work that women are capable of doing many things from which faulty education and social disapproval hold them back.

A Nocturnal Reverie

This meditative lyric poem in couplets shows many images of a quiet landscape at nightfall. The poet surveys the coming of darkness to the fields, flowers, and distant hills. She hears the sounds made by animals in nearby pastures. In such a setting, the mind grows calm and peaceful. The poet feels a simple joy of being in the presence of nature. This poem anticipates the tone and imagery of later eighteenth-century poetry by Collins and Gray.

JAMES THOMSON (1700–1748)

Thomson grew up among the rustic scenes of the Scottish border country. He was educated for the ministry, but he felt a poetic vocation and traveled to London in 1725.

The Seasons

Thomson was among the earliest of the nature poets of this century. *The Seasons*, his major poem, describes in blank verse the appearance of the English countryside at various times of year. Human action is incidental. The major movements described in the poem are the forces of wind, air, and water as the climatic changes take place. Thomson wrote the first part, *Winter*, in 1726. It was well received, and he continued to add other parts and to revise the poem until the final version, titled *The Seasons*, was published in 1744. As a Deist, Thomson saw nature as the essential revelation of God.

Thomson's ode *Rule Britannia* survives as a patriotic British song that is still sung today.

THOMAS GRAY (1716–1771)

Gray was a scholarly poet, spending almost all of his life, except for a tour of Europe, at Cambridge University. He studied not only the Greek and Roman classics but also the surviving examples of Welsh and Norse poetry. He is known for two great philosophical poems, both of which express a melancholy sense of the limitation of life and the inevitability of human misery.

Ode on a Distant Prospect of Eton College

Gray's first ode was written in 1747. It presents the poet looking down across the hills toward Eton College (a prep school rather than an American type college) and reflecting on the happiness of the bóys there who will before long discover that life holds more trouble and suffering than they can now comprehend. He concludes that they are better off not anticipating the trials of adult life. It is better to be ignorant.

Elegy Written in a Country Churchyard

Gray's second major ode is more well known. This elegy, written in 1751, places the speaker before a vista that includes the burial grounds of a small country church. Within a larger landscape, Gray describes the churchyard at evening time and moralizes on the fates of the simple folk buried there. They had lived obscure and simple lives, without heroism or glory, but they also avoided any great evil. The poet identifies with these folk and ends the poem by creating his own epitaph for that time when he will be buried among them.

WILLIAM COLLINS (1721–1759)

Collins was interested in poetic theory and in the revival of folk forms of poetry, although he imitated classical forms as well. His best-known poem is an unrhymed ode based on the structure of an ode by Horace as translated by Milton.

Ode to Evening

The ode presents a very beautiful pastoral address by the poet to the evening star as it emerges above a rustic scene. The poem is replete with elves and nymphs. It briefly describes the landscape as it will appear in other seasons, when the poet may take refuge in some mountain hut. While the syntax is complex, the images of nature are clear and seem already familiar. The poem is admired for its melodious sounds.

CHRISTOPHER SMART (1722–1771)

In his own time Smart was known more for his madness than for his poetry. A brilliant student at Cambridge, Smart took prizes for poetry several times. After he came to London to seek literary employment, he fell into a state of religious obsession and was likely to kneel to pray at any moment in any public place. Samuel Johnson defended him as harmless, but Smart was confined to an asylum and after his release was confined again. During this time, he broke into a new and energetic poetic style, based on prayer and on the events and characters of the Old Testament. He died while confined in a debtor's prison.

| **A Song to David** | This complex poem written in 1763 works out a pattern of repetitions in groups of three, seven or nine, their multiples or combinations. The impression created is of enthusiastic forward movement, a rush to reach the climactic state of awe or adoration. David is portrayed as king of Israel and more essentially as the singer of God's praises. In that exalted role, he is pictured as celebrating the glory of creation. The cumulative effects of many repetitions seem to end in a state of ecstasy, the poet praising David who is praising God. |

OLIVER GOLDSMITH (1730–1774)

Goldsmith is another of the many eighteenth-century English writers who was born and educated in Ireland. He was a medical doctor but never a successful one. He became a hack writer, producing periodical essays and satires. Goldsmith was often purposeless and usually indigent. He was befriended by Samuel Johnson and invited into the Club, where Boswell found him an absurd figure because of his awkward attempts to be the center of attention. However, Goldsmith produced notable works in three major genre—a sentimental novel, *The Vicar of Wakefield* (1766), two comic plays, *The Good Natured Man* (1768) and *She Stoops to Conquer* (1773), and his most famous poem, written in 1770, *The Deserted Village*.

| **The Deserted Village** | In this poem, Goldsmith uses the heroic couplet, a form generally ignored by other poets of his generation. More than a descriptive and nostalgic re-creation of village life, the poem is also an attack on the new commercial forces that were buying up the land and forcing the peasants out of their ancestral homes. |

> Ill fares the land, to hastening ills a prey,
>
> Where wealth accumulates, and men decay.

The poem contrasts images of village characters such as the good parson, the schoolmaster, simple maidens, and vigorous farmers with images of decay and vice associated with the encroachment of unfeeling land owners. The village folk are driven to the city or go abroad to the New World. Goldsmith conveys his feelings that the displaced villagers will perish of exposure to the dangers and corruption that never touched them in their old village. Luxury is the personified villain, and Goldsmith sees even Poetry herself fleeing England.

These eighteenth-century lyric poets provide a background for the great outpouring of lyric poetry in the early part of the next century, the romantic age. Although the next generation of poets would reject their poetic precursors as stilted and lifeless, the focus on the poet in the landscape was already established and provided a foundation from which to work.

The eighteenth-century lyric poets also revived the lyric forms, particularly the ode and the elegy. They established the link between individual feeling and the moral sense that guides one to the right way. The landscape and the poet are both infused with religious feeling, which finds its outlet in the expressions of the poet, the images of the natural world that he creates and that arouse sympathy in the reader.

Selected Readings

Butt, John and Geoffrey Carnall. *The Mid-Eighteenth Century.* Oxford: Clarendon Press, 1979.

Grant, Douglas. *James Thomson, Poet of "The Seasons."* London: Cresset, 1951.

25

Eighteenth Century (1700 to 1785): Drama and the Novel

1702	First daily newspaper, *The Daily Courant*, published
1702–1714	Reign of Queen Anne
1703	Defoe jailed for political pamphleteering
1704–1711	Defoe, editor and founder of the *Weekly Review*, with the patronage of Harley, leader of the moderate Tories
1706	Defoe, *The Apparition of Mrs. Veal*
1707	The Act of Union unites England and Scotland; the union is called Great Britain
1710–1714	Swift aligns himself with Tories; writes political articles defending Tory ministry
1713	Swift made dean of St. Patrick's Cathedral, Dublin
1714	Addison and Steele, *The Spectator* revived
1714–1727	George I, first of the Hanoverians, becomes monarch
1717	Last witchcraft trial in England
1719	Defoe, *Robinson Crusoe*
1721–1742	Robert Walpole serves as Britain's first real prime minister
1722	Defoe, *Journal of the Plague Year* and *Moll Flanders*
1724	Defoe, *Roxana* and *Jack Sheppard*

1724–1726	Defoe, *Tour Thro' the Whole Island of Great Britain* in three volumes
1726	Swift, *Gulliver's Travels*
1727	Defoe, *The History of Apparitions*
1727–1760	Reign of George II
1729	Swift, *A Modest Proposal*
1730	Fielding, *Tom Thumb*, dramatic burlesque play
1731	*Gentleman's Magazine* established
1736–1737	Fielding, *Pasquin* and *The Historical Register for the Year 1736*
1737	Theatre Licensing Act; confirms monopoly of patent theaters and censorship
c. 1739	Richardson writes book of specimen letters
1740	Richardson writes novel *Pamela*, or *Virtue Rewarded*
1741	Fielding, *Joseph Andrews*
1743	Fielding, *Miscellanies*
1747–1748	Richardson, *Clarissa*
1747–1755	Johnson working on *Dictionary of the English Language*
1749	Fielding, *Tom Jones*
1751	Gray, *Elegy Written in a Country Churchyard*; Vol. 1 of French *Encyclopedie*
1753–1754	Richardson, *Sir Charles Grandison*
1759	Johnson, *Rasselas*; Voltaire, *Candide*
1760–1767	Sterne, *Tristram Shandy*; Books One and Two were published first in New York Colony
1760–1820	Reign of George III
1764	Walpole, *The Castle of Otranto*
1765	Watt invents steam engine
1768	Sterne, *A Sentimental Journey*
1770	Goldsmith, *Deserted Village*
1775	Sheridan, *The Rivals*
1776	Sheridan buys Garrick's share of Drury Lane Theatre and assumes managership
1777	Sheridan, *The School for Scandal*
1779	Sheridan, *The Critic*

*P*opular literature aimed at a middle-class audience burgeoned during the eighteenth century. The middle class had always enjoyed literature that was exciting and sensational but ultimately reassuring to their own image of the world. Villains are corrupt aristocrats; heroes are men and women of feeling who submit to the restraints of society. The most successful popular writers were those who could provide novelty and excitement without violating middle-class expectations. Thus the plays became more bland while the acting and productions became more elaborate and impressive. In prose, the lengthy novels depicting a series of surprising adventures and near-disasters tended to end with the hero's discovery that he is a gentleman after all, not an outcast from society. These popular forms reassured the middle class that its values were correct and that they would lead to success and proper rewards. At the same time, the comforting message was delivered in an entertaining way, through the media of theater and fictional narrative. Examples of correct manners provided models for the audience's behavior.

EIGHTEENTH-CENTURY DRAMA

The theater in eighteenth-century England generally flourished as a commercial enterprise. Theater managers promoted popular interest in spectacular productions, and great actors developed loyal followers. As a literary expression, however, the drama had few bright spots.

Sentimental Plays

After the decline of the brilliant Restoration comedy of manners, sentimental drama, aimed at appealing to middle-class audiences, came to dominate the stage. Such plays relied on the "sudden change of heart" in the rake-hero to give the audience an emotional thrill. Colley Cibber's play *The Careless Husband* (1705) is an early example of the type. One of the most sentimental of these plays is Richard Steele's *The Conscious Lovers* (1722), a play intended to make the audience weep in sympathy with its hero and heroine. Thus the dramas were not very distinct in tone from the pathetic tragedy of George Lillo, *The London Merchant*, or *The History of George Barnwell*, where the audience wallows in sympathy as the hero goes to his death.

Satiric Plays

The theater of wit survived in satiric comedies such as Gay's *Beggar's Opera* and in the satirical farces of Henry Fielding, such as *The Tragedy of Tom Thumb* (1731). In the midcentury, Oliver Goldsmith deplored the lack of what he called "laughing comedy" and wrote his own nonsentimental offering, *She Stoops to Conquer* (1773), which was not at first well received.

But Sheridan was more successful in following the direction that Goldsmith had laid out.

Oliver Goldsmith (1730–1774)

Already discussed as a lyric poet, as a member of Samuel Johnson's Literary Club, and as a hack writer who nevertheless expressed concern about the declining state of literature in England during his era, Goldsmith wrote in 1773 a critical essay titled *Essay on the Theatre*, or *A Comparison between Laughing and Sentimental Comedy*. In this essay Goldsmith cited Aristotle and called the modern sentimental comedy a "bastard tragedy" because it focused on the calamities of middle-class life rather than on its follies. He sought a return to the sort of comedy that causes laughter, not weeping. The same year, Goldsmith wrote a successful play that fulfilled his own prescription for good comedy.

SHE STOOPS TO CONQUER, OR THE MISTAKES OF A NIGHT

This play is set in the country among unfashionable people, a family of country gentry who live in a big, old-fashioned, rambling house. The children in the Hardcastle family are Kate, Mr. Hardcastle's pretty daughter by a previous marriage, and the over-indulged booby Tony Lumpkin, Mrs. Hardcastle's son by a previous marriage. Mrs. Hardcastle is promoting a marriage between her step-daughter and her son, but Kate is too clever to be wasted on such a fellow. The plot is very complex.

Act I. In act I young Marlow, son of an old friend of Mr. Hardcastle, has been sent down to the country to court Kate, but he is too bashful. He is always shy with women of his own social class, although he is not so with servants and other lower-class girls. Marlow and his friend Hastings, who loves Kate's cousin Constance, lose their way. Tony directs them to the Hardcastle house but tells them that it is an inn so that the two young visitors will make fools of themselves.

Act II. Act II begins as Marlow and Hastings enter the Hardcastle home, thinking that it is an inn. They treat their host as an innkeeper and complain about their reception. They demand to know the supper menu and quarrel with what is offered. Mr. Hardcastle is astounded, having expected a shy young man. Meanwhile Hastings finds Constance, and they agree to keep Marlow ignorant of where he really is to prevent an attack of shyness. Marlow meets Kate, who hides her face in a huge bonnet and engages in an insipid sentimental dialogue with him. She plans to "cure" him of his shyness by acting the role of a servant. Tony, who does not want to marry Constance, reaches an agreement to help Hastings elope with her, thus getting her out of the way.

Act III. In the beginning of act III, Mr. Hardcastle and his daughter, Kate, talk about Marlow; Hardcastle sees the youth as rude and bold, while Kate knows he is shy. Meanwhile, Tony has stolen Constance's dowry, consisting of jewels, from Mrs. Hardcastle's room and given them to Hastings in anticipation of the elopement. Mrs. Hardcastle discovers the loss because Constance had asked her for the jewels. Kate, pretending to be the barmaid, flirts with Marlow. His behavior becomes very forward, but they are interrupted by Mr. Hardcastle, who is once again shocked at Marlow's boldness and threatens Kate that he will throw Marlow out. Kate asks him to delay one hour.

Act IV. Act IV reveals a mix-up with the jewels. Tony, who stole them for Constance, gave them to Hastings, who gave them for safekeeping to Marlow, who thought they would be safer in the care of the innkeeper's wife, so he gave them back to Mrs. Hardcastle. Thus the elopement is delayed. Marlow boasts of his success with the pretty barmaid (Kate), but he is confronted by Mr. Hardcastle, who demands that he leave the house. Marlow is confused. Kate sets him straight about the house, telling him that it is a family home and not an inn, but she claims to be merely a poor relation of the family. Embarrassed and conscience-stricken, Marlow wants to flee, but when Kate weeps at his leaving, he melts. His reserve is conquered. Now Hastings and Constance have new problems. They have decided to elope without the jewels, but their plan is uncovered because Mrs. Hardcastle has read the note from Hastings to Tony concerning the getaway. (Tony can't read, so he showed the note to his mother.) Mrs. Hardcastle is outraged and prepares to take Constance deeper into the country to stay with the odious Aunt Petigree. Marlow argues with Hastings about the trick of letting him believe he was at an inn, but Tony says he has a plan. They must wait two hours.

Act V. In act V Old Sir Charles Marlow, the hero's father, arrives; his son's error is explained and laughed at by Mr. Hardcastle. But the relationship of their children is a puzzle; Kate says that Marlow loves her, but Marlow says he scarcely knows "Miss Hardcastle," not realizing that the sweet girl who identified herself as a poor relation was really she. Meanwhile, at the back of the garden, Tony, who has been driving Constance and Mrs. Hastings around in circles for two hours, has now dumped them in a pond, pretending an accident. Mrs. Hardcastle is terrified, and the exhausted Constance resolves that she will ask outright to marry Hastings, appealing to Mr. Hardcastle. Back inside the house, Kate has arranged a dialogue with Marlow, with their two fathers listening behind a screen. At first Marlow tries to reject Kate because he thinks she is poor, but his love is too great. When he speaks his feelings sincerely, the fathers emerge from hiding and bless the marriage. Constance and Hastings come in and ask for mercy; their marriage is also approved, to the general joy of everyone.

The ending is a conventional comic resolution; the two young men deserve and get the girls and their dowries. Tony is free and his mother is reconciled. Kate has "stooped" by pretending to be lower-class and poor, but she has conquered by winning a sincere declaration of love from

Marlow. The play is full of verbal wit, but unlike the Restoration comedies of manners, this comedy is wholesome and innocent, with no immoral situations or indecent dialogue.

Richard Brinsley Sheridan (1751–1816)

The son of an Irish actor and theater manager, Sheridan had a very early success as a comic playwright. He became the manager and part owner of London's Drury Lane Theatre. Later Sheridan's first play, *The Rivals* (1775), was a remarkable success, largely because of the comic character, Mrs. Malaprop, whose fractured use of the English language made her name a standard term for misuse of vocabulary. Sheridan was an important Whig member of Parliament, celebrated for his oratorical skills. He was also a member, like Goldsmith, of Samuel Johnson's Club.

THE SCHOOL FOR SCANDAL

This witty 1777 comedy contrasts two brothers, Joseph Surface, a hypocrite who mouths dull sentiments while trying to seduce his friend's wife; and his brother, Charles Surface, an apparent neer-do-well who actually has a generous heart. In a second plot, Lady Teazle, the young bride of a middle-aged husband, studies the fashion of gossiping and almost loses her marriage through a flirtation with Charles Surface. In the famous screen scene, in act IV, scene 3, both plots come together. Lady Teazle hides behind a screen in Charles Surface's apartment when her husband, Peter Teazle, comes to ask Charles's advice about his wife. Moved by her husband's sincere concern for her, she resolves not to have an affair with Charles. Then, when the screen accidentally falls, revealing her presence, she refuses to lie to her husband but makes an unfashionable speech of repentance. Though the play promotes goodness of heart, its primary appeal lies in the satirical wit of its mockery of manners.

THE EIGHTEENTH-CENTURY NOVEL

During the same time that poetry was developing a new emotional tone, another form, that of extended prose fiction, was becoming the most popular literary form. The roots of the novel lay in forms not usually considered literature: periodical essays, letters and diaries, news reports, criminal confessions, and the spiritual autobiographies of Dissenters. In all these subliterary forms, the focus is on the day-to-day experiences of ordinary people in realistic situations. With these roots the novel was clearly distinguished from the romance tale, in which idealized or allegorical characters undertake surprising and fantastic adventures. From its beginning, the novel displayed the textures of family and social relationships and of the material world in which these characters existed. The reader was urged to trust in the authenticity of the story. One of the conventions of the early novel is a preface in which a supposed editor, really the author, tells how the manuscript was found and vouches for the truth of the events recorded. Such claims had two functions: they evaded the still common puritanical objections to fiction as mere lies and they helped the reader identify with the situations and characters.

READERS OF THE NOVEL

An important influence on the novel's development was its audience, for a group of new readers was developing for whom this form was adapted. Literacy was spreading in England from the upper classes to the lower. As the middle class solidified their economic position, they had more leisure for reading and more money to spend on books. Women especially began to read more as household drudgery began to yield to middle-class comfort. Even servants and apprentices began to have more than minimal literacy as urban centers grew and rural ignorance was replaced by town experiences. Circulating libraries were founded in provincial towns so that a person of modest means could have access to a great number of books for a small fee. This new readership meant that the author had a lucrative new field of opportunity. The form of the novel could be legitimately entertaining, not learned or weighted with classical allusion but depicting instead recognizable scenes and incidents. No one needed an elite education to relish a novel. On the contrary, authors appealed to the desire of ordinary readers for models of fashionable behavior and correct social attitudes, a need also addressed by the periodical essay.

THEMES OF THE NOVEL

The basic theme of the eighteenth-century novel was the central character's search for a rightful and comfortable place in society. Frequently the plot involved finding one's true parentage or making the right marriage—two great determiners of social class in eighteenth-century England.

Since the novel's early contention was that it contained a true account of actual events, the narration was frequently realized in authentic-seeming forms such as confessions, diaries or letters, again all reflections of the novel's roots in these forms. The early novelist Defoe used the personal confession, an account in the character's own voice of his or her own experiences. Richardson was able to achieve a more complex effect by creating letters supposedly written by several characters in which each tells his or her own version of events. Henry Fielding, more rooted in classical literature, made for himself a role as the all-wise narrator in imitation of epic narrations. Combinations of and variations on these techniques became widely used; each style had the advantage of intimacy with or distance from the psychological state of the individual character. The point of view from which the story was told helped determine its impact. That is, the character telling his or her own recent experience can plausibly give a much more minute and emotional account than a judicious but remote narrator who can only set out to narrate in his or her own terms the various circumstances of a range of other characters.

Daniel Defoe (1660–1731)

It is debatable who was the first English novelist, but most literary historians have settled on Defoe. Defoe came from a family of shopkeepers and religious Dissenters, and many critics see the commercial and moral values of that class reflected in his fiction. Defoe also worked as a political journalist and pamphleteer; he was an enterprising, though not always successful, businessman, and he described in his *An Essay Upon Projects* (1697) solutions for a number of practical social problems.

Defoe came to novel writing late in life. At fifty-nine he read a first-hand account by a seaman who had been stranded alone on a desert island. Defoe turned this true account into the captivating tale called *Robinson Crusoe*. After the popular and financial success of this book, Defoe wrote a sequel. He then proceeded, using the same pattern of first-person narration, to write the lives of a series of other interesting and typically low-life characters caught in practical difficulties. They all must use ingenuity and personal resourcefulness to work their ways out of their predicaments. The hallmark of a Defoe hero or heroine is adaptability to the necessities of a demanding world.

ROBINSON CRUSOE

This almost mythic story of survival, written in 1719, is presented as the real words of an actual man, an entrepreneur who, alone on an island after a devastating shipwreck, set up a household and a form of economy, making himself master of his domain and managing to defend himself from attack. Crusoe also provides comforts and abundance by his own ingenuity and well-planned labor. His isolation is seen as punishment for both spiritual arrogance and restlessness. He is eventually rewarded by finding a companion and servant, Friday, and later by returning to civilization and prosperity. The how-to-survive practicality of the plot is balanced against the spiritual progress of Crusoe from despair and abandonment through the test of courage and ingenuity on the island to a final fulfillment and reward.

MOLL FLANDERS

Written in 1722, this first-person narration presents itself as the confessional reminiscences of a female rake. Moll's test of survival takes place on the streets of London and other English cities. Born in Newgate prison but aspiring to be a gentlewoman, Moll is seduced by her first lover. She becomes disillusioned and manipulative and finds only temporary prosperity and respectability through a series of marriages, each one somehow flawed or cut short. At middle age, Moll resorts to thievery because she fears poverty; she becomes skilled at picking pockets and at talking her way out of tight spots. This part of the novel becomes a manual of advice on protecting oneself against theft. Eventually caught and put back in Newgate, Moll experiences a spiritual crisis, despair, and repentance to find faith, salvation, and joy. In her old age, comfortable and apparently reformed, Moll confesses her shady past to the reader in tones varying from abhorrence to smug satisfaction. The interpretative problem of this novel is how seriously to take Moll's claim to be reformed.

ROXANNE, OR THE FORTUNATE MISTRESS

The title of this novel (1724) was meant ironically; it could not be considered "fortunate" to be a mistress. Wifehood was the only accepted role for a woman. The central character, however, speaks from the point of view of one who was married very young to a foolish husband. He dies within a few years, leaving her destitute and burdened with infant children. Forced by necessity, she abandons the children and drifts into the life of a courtesan, that is, the mistress of a series of increasingly rich and influential men. Early in the novel, Roxanne has a dialogue with one of her lovers, who wants to marry her. She discusses at length why she will never marry again, analyzing the many disadvantages to women in marriage. Wives become mere "passive creatures," she says, victims of the tyranny or weakness of the husband. Her career reaches its peak when she is patronized by a royal prince. But as she succeeds and becomes financially secure, her reputation is endangered. Fearing public exposure, Roxanne has her own daughter murdered. The final scenes show Roxanne suffering from guilt and fear, even as she has achieved worldly success and triumph.

Samuel Richardson (1689–1761)

Richardson rose from apprentice printer to owner of his own business, having prudently married his employer's daughter. As a youth, Richardson was precociously involved with young women and their affairs of the heart. He lent his services to help them write love letters and gave them advice about how to conduct themselves with suitors. As an adult, he was a copious writer of letters, as are all his main characters. Richardson did not plan to become a novelist. He was engaged in a project to compile a handbook of model letters for use by inexperienced and unpolished folk who wanted to correspond with dignity. As he wrote, Richardson began to weave in a narrative connection. Setting aside his original project, he followed his narrative impulse to create in 1740 the epistolary novel *Pamela*.

PAMELA, OR VIRTUE REWARDED

The heroine is an upper servant in the household of a wealthy country family. Her mistress has trained her in some of the feminine accomplishments, such as writing, singing, dancing, and the way of dressing that characterizes upper-class girls. After the death of her mistress, Pamela finds herself the object of the attention of her mistress's son (Mr. B.), who finds her all the more attractive because she persistently and cleverly resists his sexual advances. Pamela writes an intimate and sensational account of her fears and escapades to her poor parents. Frustrated, Mr. B. has Pamela abducted and confined in one of his other houses, where Pamela makes several unsuccessful attempts to get away. Finally, Mr. B. realizes that he is hopelessly in love with Pamela. He decides, in spite of her lower-class origins, to marry her and to make a lady of her by finishing the social training his mother had begun. The suspense and titillation of the novel made it vastly popular with all classes of readers, but most especially with women. Some critics, however, saw more opportunism than virtue in Pamela's strategy of preserving her virginity until she was safely married.

CLARISSA

Richardson's best and most influential novel was published in several volumes (1747 to 1748). It also concerns a virtuous girl besieged by an abductor. Raised in a newly wealthy and upwardly mobile family, Clarissa struggles against an odious arranged marriage. Desperate, she is tricked into an elopement by her antagonist, Lovelace, an aristocratic rake. (Richardson, who deplored the morals of the aristocracy, used the novel to expose the problem.) Clarissa is witty and refined, more than a match for Lovelace, except in his deceptions. He loves tricks and disguises, forgeries and the use of secret agents. Ultimately, finding that Clarissa cannot be seduced, he rapes her, but even that outrage does not subdue her sense of self and her devotion to divine law. Clarissa wins a moral victory and social vindication as she dies, the victim of a broken heart. The letters through which this long story is developed come from a variety of correspondents, each one expressing a different and partial view of the central situation. Although the novel's moral message is clear, readers are enmeshed in a fabric of cross-currents and nuances, of sympathy and suspense. It was an immensely popular work. Readers of the early volumes (there were seven in all) wrote to Richardson discussing what should happen to Clarissa and pleading with him to save her life.

Henry Fielding (1707–1754)

Unlike his predecessors in the novel, Fielding came from the gentry and had a gentleman's education at Eton in classical literature. Because he did not inherit wealth, he studied law and later became a London magistrate. As a young man, Fielding sought a career as a playwright, producing a series of farces and political satires for the stage between 1728 and 1737. His last play attacked political corruption and satirized Prime Minister Walpole so effectively that it provoked the passage of the Licensing Act, a censorship law. Forced then to turn to other literary forms, Fielding produced a parody of Richardson's *Pamela* called *Shamela*, in which the heroine is pictured as a lewd and manipulative fake. Still reacting to Richardson's novel, Fielding again parodied *Pamela* in the opening chapter of *Joseph Andrews*. But this time he went on to develop a full-length fiction with its own theme of charity. It has an episodic structure rather loosely derived from the classical epic. Fielding called this fiction a "comic epic in prose." Concentrating now on the novel as a legitimate form, Fielding produced his masterpiece, *Tom Jones*, in 1749. But by then his health was failing, and his work at the magistrate's court was taking its toll. Fielding died on a trip to Lisbon in search of better health.

THE HISTORY OF TOM JONES, A FOUNDLING

This voluminous novel, written in 1749, contains eighteen books and presents forty-four distinct characters in an extended, complex plot. "Tom Jones" was Fielding's greatest work in both scope and artistic achievement. The hero, a foundling, is given an ordinary name, Tom, to suggest that he represents every young man's attempt to achieve an identity and social role. The narrator, who points out Tom's faults as well as his good points, holds him up as typical rather than ideal. Fielding puts Tom through a series of skirmishes, misadventures, and near-disasters to test his mettle. Tom makes mistakes, but most of these result from his generosity and high spirits. During the novel he has to learn prudence and to suffer apparent defeat before he can be made deserving of his beloved, the beautiful Sophia. She is an example of female courage and perception. Sophia is loyal to Tom through all his errors because she responds to his basic good nature. The narrator, always in control of this story, makes a game of concealing and revealing to the reader just as much as we ought to know to enjoy the fun of suspense and the pleasure of surprise. The panoramic and intricately complex plot foreshadows the large structure of the Victorian novel in the next century.

Lawrence Sterne (1713–1768)

The great eccentric author of the eighteenth-century novel was a provincial clergyman who began as a satiric pamphleteer involved in local church politics. Heavily influenced by the psychology of Locke, Sterne emerged from the obscurity of Yorkshire to become a celebrity of literary London and to play the role in real life that he had laid out as narrator of his books.

THE LIFE AND OPINIONS OF TRISTRAM SHANDY, GENT.

Published in multiple volumes between 1759–1767, "Tristram Shandy" pretends to be an attempt at autobiography by the central figure, Tristram. But the narrator finds himself caught in a web of digressions, tangential explorations, and incidental anecdotes, all held together by their chance association in his mind. Thus he never progresses beyond his childhood, having required two volumes to proceed from the moment of his conception to his birth. The novel implies that, as isolated human beings, it is never possible for us completely to explain or to understand each other. The major characters, called My Father, My Mother, and My Uncle Toby, are each caught up in individual mental preoccupations and habits, so that while affection may exist between them, true communication is continually thwarted. My Father, in particular, is a man of theory and a planner of projects. His grand schemes are never understood by others and always come to nothing. Sterne continued to publish additional volumes of "Tristram Shandy" as long as he lived, and it is a debatable question whether or not the novel concludes with Volume Nine.

Horace Walpole (1717–1797)

Son of the great Whig prime minister Sir Robert Walpole, Horace was less involved in politics than in literature and criticism. He was a friend of the poet Thomas Gray. The two men toured Europe together, and later Walpole published Gray's *Odes* at his private press at Strawberry Hill, his country seat. Walpole wrote a great deal of criticism and commentary on the arts, and he was a voluminous letter writer. His best-known work, however, is his contribution to the development of the gothic novel, a reaction against what he found to be the dull and boorish qualities of the novels of Richardson, Fielding and Sterne.

THE CASTLE OF OTRANTO

This mysterious romance written in 1764 centers around the frightening fulfillment of an ancient prophecy. Walpole establishes the atmosphere when, at the beginning of the novel, a huge helmet drops out of nowhere into the courtyard of the castle, killing the son of the usurper of the castle and leading to the eventual restoration of the true heir. Supernatural and nightmarish phenomena abound; the intent is to produce a pleasurable terror in the reader. The novel is very brief by eighteenth-century standards, hardly more than a tale. But Walpole introduced a new stream in the development of prose fiction. His followers included Anne Radcliffe, whose *Mysteries of Udolpho* (1794) epitomizes the form.

*T*he drama and the novel were both popular middle-class forms that aimed at improving the tastes and sensibilities of large audiences. The novel grew to be the most widely read literary genre and held that position throughout the *following century. Its wide scope, including both pathos and humor, and its identifiable characters in suspenseful plots made novel reading a pasttime of choice, a primary recreation of the English public.*

Selected Readings

Battestin, Martin C., ed. *Twentieth Century Interpretations of Tom Jones: A Collection of Critical Essays.* Englewood Cliffs, NJ: Prentice, 1968.

Blewett, David. *Defoe's Art of Fiction—Robinson Crusoe, Moll Flanders, Colonel Jack and Roxana.* Toronto: University of Toronto, 1979.

McMillin, Scott, ed. *Restoration and Eighteenth Century Comedy.* New York: Norton, 1973.

Shinagel, Michael, ed. *Robinson Crusoe/Daniel Defoe: An Authoritative Text, Backgrounds and Sources, Criticism.* New York: Norton, 1975.

Sutherland, James. *Daniel Defoe: A Critical Study.* Cambridge, MA: Harvard University Press, 1971.

Wilson, John Harold, ed. *Six Eighteenth Century Plays.* Boston: Houghton Mifflin, 1963.

26

Literary Names and Terms: Literary Forms

TABLE OF FORMS

Narrative	**Lyric**	**Dramatic**
narrator speaks:	*poet speaks:*	*characters speak:*
epic	song	mystery plays
fable	ode	morality plays
tale	elegy	comedies
ballad	ballad	
satire	satire	satire
fabliau	complaints	histories
romance	sonnets	tragedies
novel		comedies of manners
short story		heroic plays
		dramatic monologues

Each literary genre and subgenre falls into one of three major categories: narrative, lyric, and dramatic. In each case the major generic form is determined by the person or persons speaking the words that make up the literary work.

NARRATIVE FORMS

Narratives are written in both poetry and prose. In a narrative, the person speaking describes the thoughts and actions of other characters.

Narrative Speaker

Narrators can comment on the characters and their behavior or on the events surrounding them. The narrator stands *between* the characters in the story and the reader, interpreting and revealing as he or she sees fit but not participating in or affecting the events being narrated.

Narrative Strategy

The narrator thus controls what the reader knows, when the reader knows it, and to some extent how the reader feels about it. The narrator's personality influences the reader's perception of story events. If the narrator seems to be distorting the story, the reader may conclude that the narrator is not always to be trusted to give the most appropriate emphasis or the correct interpretation of events. If this occurs, the narrator is said to be "unreliable." He or she thus takes on some of the qualities of a character but still occupies the position of narrator in relationship to the other characters and to the reader.

LYRIC FORMS

Although prose may contain lyrical-sounding passages, almost all lyrics are in verse.

Lyric Speaker

In a lyric, the person speaking seems to be the poet. The lyrical speaker tells of his or her own actions, thoughts, and feelings in such a way as to seem to be talking to him- or herself, to some unknown other person who may be present or absent or directly to the reader. In a formal lyric such as an ode, the speaker may be addressing the public in general or some large segment of it. Whatever the audience, the speaker is primarily creating a feeling. He or she may relate brief stories or bits of conversation (dialogue), but the speaker's own feelings are the focus of the poem.

As the speaker of a lyric, the poet may project a version of self that does not exactly represent his or her whole self or perhaps reflects that self only as it was a given moment in the past. To the extent that the poet creates a somewhat separate personality for the speaker, the poem moves away from being a lyric and becomes more like a dramatic monologue.

Lyric Strategy   Because it presents a feeling, the lyric is ordinarily written in the present tense. The essence of a lyric poem is "I feel"—that is, first person, present tense. The lyric poet creates images and metaphors that suggest the feelings rather than stating flatly what they are.

DRAMATIC FORMS

In dramatic literature, the only speakers are the characters. One or more of the characters may represent the attitudes or values of the playwright, but the playwright does not appear on stage.

Dramatic Speaker   Each speaker or character in a drama sees the situation from his or her own point of view and engages in dialogue with the other characters, each character expressing his or her own thoughts and feelings.

Dramatic Strategy   The reader of the play or its audience must comprehend and evaluate each character's statements and actions as a part of the whole work and then come to an understanding of the meaning of the play. The conflict of values acted out by the characters needs to be resolved by the end of the play, or else the audience feels puzzled and unsatisfied. Usually, the playwright guides the audience by showing that the characters who represent the "right way" are those who succeed in the end, but this is not always so. In a tragedy, the hero may be destroyed even though his values are the most praiseworthy.

27

Literary Names and Terms: Glossary

Allegory   In an allegorical form of narrative, the characters, places, and actions represent abstract ideas at the same time that they operate as parts of the story. In an allegory, characters may, for instance, stand for the good or bad traits of humankind, places may represent the status or the goals of the characters, actions may represent right or wrong choices. For example, in an allegorical story, a road may stand for the way, right or wrong, that a character proceeds on during his or her journey through life. The goal of that journey may be represented as a splendid castle, a city of light or a beautiful garden. In allegories, the names of the characters may indicate what traits or abstractions are being represented by the character. If, for instance, a character is called Mankind or Everyman, the character stands for the universal condition of human beings in relationship to the moral forces at work in the narrative. If, as in *Hamlet*, the character's name is Fortinbras, which means strong arm, then it is likely that he represents physical strength. Calling a character Sir Politic Would-be as in Ben Jonson's *Volpone* indicates that the character represents a person who wishes to be thought of as shrewd and well informed in political matters.

In the working out of an allegorical narrative, the shifting relationships among the characters are intended to show the reader how these qualities or traits function in relationship to each other. The final victory of the characters who stand for "the best way" or the "right" qualities produces the meaning of the narrative.

In interpreting an allegory, however, it is usually best to assume that not all the traits of every character are translatable into abstractions. Certain details may be included merely to advance the story or to make it more exciting. Some major allegorical works in English literature before 1785 include *Everyman*, *The Faerie Queene*, *Volpone*, and *Gulliver's Travels*.

Alliteration   Two or more words are said to alliterate if they have the same initial sound. "Lovely lilies lying along a lonely lane" alliterates on the *L* sound; five of the words start with *L*. Notice also that the word *along*, while it does not start with *L*, has that letter as the first sound of its stressed syllable; therefore, it is also part of the alliterative pattern. In Old English poetry, alliteration is the primary sound pattern. Sounds used to create alliteration are ordinarily consonants, but in Old English poetry, initial vowel sounds are also used to alliterate.

The use of alliteration is a way of giving emphasis, but it can also be used merely to create a pleasant, singing effect. Further, it may have been used by the scop as a memory aid to assist in delivering the oral literature. *The Vision of Piers Plowman* takes place "on a May morning on Malvern Hills."

Sometimes alliteration is also used in prose, especially formal prose, to emphasize parallel phrases or corresponding ideas; for example, "He was trained and taught and tediously raised." Sometimes alliteration and rhyme are used together in the same poem to reinforce each other, as in the ballad of *The Wife of Usher's Well*.

Allusion   When a writer refers indirectly to some well-known person or event, expecting the reader or audience to recognize the reference although it has not been specifically named, that writer is making an allusion. To mention, for example, "the fall of our first father" is a way of bringing to the reader's mind the story of Adam and his expulsion from the Garden of Eden without digressing into a complete retelling of Adam's story. The author expects the reader to catch the reference and to understand its relevance to the present text. Of course, allusion requires that both the writer and the reader are familiar with the same body of literature and information; otherwise the allusion does not work. The reference will not be recognized and the additional meaning will be lost. In a Christian culture, for example, allusions to the Bible will be frequent, but allusions to Islam's Koran will be almost nonexistent.

Topical allusions, those that refer to a recent and local event, cause a literary work to become dated and difficult to read by a new generation of readers. It thus becomes the work of scholars and editors to seek out the sources and meanings of the allusions and to add them, in the form of notes, to literature of a past era or different culture.

One of the most allusive poets in English was John Milton, whose wide reading and vast knowledge of the literatures of various cultures and religions made even the early readers of *Paradise Lost* feel the need of explanatory notes.

Anatomy   The literary term *anatomy* was borrowed from early medical science and indicates an investigation by dissection and/or complete and exhaustive analysis of a subject—its causes and effects and all the known opinions on and studies of it, all systematically arranged. The writer of an anatomy seeks to be, or at least claims to be, more comprehensive than an essayist; the anatomist surveys everything that was ever written, in ancient or modern literature, on the particular topic of his or her work. The best known anatomy in English literature is *The Anatomy of Melancholy* by Robert Burton. While it has some of the characteristics of an intellectual treatise, the anatomy also can be personal in tone or it can be slanted to support a particular attitude about the subject.

Anglo-Saxon   Anglo-Saxon is the name of the Germanic tribes who invaded Britain during the Middle Ages. It is also the name of their language, which was spoken throughout most of what is now called England until the Norman invasion and conquest of 1066. It is the language of *Beowulf* and of other early medieval poems and prose. Anglo-Saxon is also called Old English to distinguish it from Middle English (the language of Chaucer) and modern English (the language used since the Renaissance). Although Anglo-Saxon is the root of the modern English language, it is so totally different in vocabulary and grammar that most modern readers need translations of works written in it.

Anglo-Saxon is heavily inflected, which means that the forms of the words change in systematic ways to indicate their grammatical functions within the sentence. A noun's ending, for instance, will depend on whether it is used as a subject or an object in the sentence.

Aside   When characters in a play speak, the audience assumes that they are talking to one another and that each character hears what the others say. However, sometimes characters speak an "aside," which means that the remark is directed not to the other characters but to the audience. The playwright will usually indicate that the remark is an "aside" in the stage directions or by somehow separating it from the character's ordinary dialogue. In an aside, the character is understood to be expressing his or her real feelings or the actual truth as he or she sees it, while within the context of the play the character may be making false or misleading statements to other characters. The author uses the aside to reveal, for example, hidden motives or secret plans that help the audience understand characters' motives and enable it to anticipate the action of the play. Asides were extensively used by playwrights of the Elizabethan and Jacobean ages.

Autobiography   An autobiography is a personal narrative about the author's own life. The writer presents his or her own life story as he or she sees it and recollects it. An autobiography differs from a diary, which is written daily or almost daily over a long time, because in an autobiography, the writer has the benefit of hindsight and can show how certain early events or conditions led up to latter events. The autobiographer thus presents his or her life as a unified whole and traces one or more themes through its development.

The autobiographical form is sometimes borrowed for novels. In a fictional autobiography, the author pretends that the narrator is telling his or her own story. Early novels, such as Daniel Defoe's *Robinson Crusoe* and *Moll Flanders* are fictional autobiographies.

Ballad   A ballad is a song that tells a story. This poetic form is both narrative and lyric. The narrative ballad usually focuses on some single striking incident or event, often the violent crisis of a sequence of actions not fully explained. The characters of the narrative ballad are usually described sketchily in conventional formulaic phrases; their motivations are implied rather than stated. The story of the ballad may be developed through dialogue between the central characters. Love, treachery, betrayal, and death are common themes of ballads. In love ballads, rejection and infidelity are found more often than sincerity and truth.

Folk ballads were transmitted orally in the early stages of their development. As they were repeated, minor variations were introduced. The less dramatic stanzas often were forgotten, so that various versions of a ballad sometimes came into existence. Later, when the ballads were written down, it was not possible to retrieve the "original" version or even to say which version was the original one. When folk ballads were first being collected in print in the eighteenth century, the collectors and editors also introduced some changes. Nevertheless, these old story-songs retain their vitality. Many are still sung.

Beast Fable   A fable is a brief narrative that illustrates a legendary story or a moral. If the characters are animals with human characteristics, the story is called a beast fable. The animals allegorically represent various human traits or weaknesses. Thus, a fox is often used to illustrate slyness or trickery; a lamb often represents innocence or meekness, and a pig usually stands for greed or gluttony. Beast fables are found in many cultures. The famous beast fables of Aesop, an ancient Greek, have been popular since their creation. In the best beast fables, human qualities or motivations are blended with details of actual animal behavior so that the character is both beastlike and human at the same time. For example, the cock Chauntecleer from Chaucer's *The Canterbury Tales* is described as an actual fowl with gorgeous plumage, but his pride and vanity are recognizably human characteristics.

Biography   Biography is the narrative account of a person's life. The term implies that the writer has investigated the person's life and that the authenticity of the events recounted can be vouched for. The biographer may have consulted written records, letters, diaries, journals, and even account books and may also have gathered anecdotes or gossip. However, as a biographer, he or she is obliged to have weighed the relative accuracy of all such materials and exercised judgment about what to include. Thus a biography is more historical than literary. It can also be considered a literary work if it is well written, and if the biographer brings to the subject sufficient imagination, sympathy, and perception, and if the biographer has developed a theme or idea that the life illustrates.

Biography was a late development in the history of English literature. Dryden invented the term during the Restoration period. The most monumental and standard-setting biography in English is James Boswell's *The Life of Samuel Johnson.*

Blank Verse   A poem written in iambic pentameter (a line of five iambic feet) with no rhyme is said to be written in blank verse. This form, rarely found in lyric poetry, is used most commonly in narrative, dramatic or philosophical poetry because the relatively long and open line it provides gives the poet freedom and flexibility to imitate speech or to discuss ideas at length. Because blank verse does not rhyme, Renaissance dramatists were able to use it to create effective dialogue that could be either lofty or natural-sounding.

Blank verse was introduced in English by Henry Howard, the earl of Surrey, in the sixteenth century; he used it to translate epic poetry. Because Marlowe adapted blank verse to the drama, Ben Jonson referred to it as "Marlowe's mighty line." It was the dominant line used by Shakespeare in his plays. In the seventeenth century, Milton used blank verse in his great epic poem, *Paradise Lost.*

A wide variety of effects can be achieved in blank verse by making the lines either end-stopped or run on. Also, a pause within the line (a caesura) can be placed at the end of any one of the five poetic feet. The poem's pace and smoothness can thus be adjusted to suit the subject matter and mood. This flexibility accounts for the past and present popularity of blank verse.

Burlesque   When the subject of a literary or dramatic work is deliberately and grossly ridiculed, the resulting work is called a burlesque. In a burlesque, lofty matters may be presented in a low, vulgar or silly way, or trivial matters may be given a mock-serious treatment. The lack of harmony between the subject matter and the way it is presented becomes a source of comedy or satire. Burlesque can be the broad mockery of a literary form or style, such as grand opera or sentimental plays. If one particular work, such as a play or a poem, is being made fun of, the effort is called a parody. In *The Beggar's Opera*, for example, John Gay burlesques Italian opera in general by having the characters sing out their feelings to the tunes of common London street songs. Burlesque is often noisy and rowdy in order to lower the dignity of high art forms; thus the name has been loosely applied to some stage entertainments that are merely loud and vulgar but do not intend to make any satiric point.

Caesura

A *caesura* is a stop or a pause within a line of poetry. The pause may be indicated by punctuation or simply by the natural grouping of words that would occur if the line were spoken. For example, the first line of a couplet in Alexander Pope's *An Essay on Criticism* has a caesura marked by a comma:

> True ease in writing comes from art, not chance,

> As those move easiest who have learned to dance.

Although it is not indicated by punctuatuion, the pause after the word *easiest* in the second line is also a *caesura* because the rhythm of the line seems to hesitate at that point.

Canto

A *canto* is a section of a long narrative poem. It is similar to a chapter in a prose narrative. Cantos are usually numbered, as in Spenser's epic poem *The Faerie Queene*.

Carpe Diem

The Latin phrase *carpe diem* translates as "seize the day." It is taken from the Roman poet Horace. In the lyric poetry of the English Renaissance and the poetry of the early seventeenth century, poets frequently express the idea that the pleasures of the present moment should be indulged in without restraint because the future is uncertain and similar pleasures may not come again. In love poetry, the carpe diem theme was a standard part of the argument of seduction. The lover points out to his lady that youth and beauty do not last, and he urges her to enjoy the pleasures of love while she is still at the peak of her charm and while they both have the vigor and capacity to make love well. The most famous *carpe diem* statement in English poetry may be Robert Herrick's lyric *To Virgins to Make Much of Time*, which begins with the well-known line, "Gather ye rosebuds while ye may." The poet suggests that the beauty of virgins is like the beauty of the rose because it too is fragile and temporary. Thus, virgins should take advantage of their beauty to find and enjoy lovers before it is too late.

Cavalier

The term *Cavalier* applies to both a political position and a poetic style. The courtly poets who supported King Charles I against the rising tide of Puritanism during the 1620s and 1630s tended to write in a similar poetic style. They wrote mainly light and smooth lyric poems. They sought ease and melody, in contrast to their contemporaries the "metaphysical" poets, who were more intellectual and also more abrupt and difficult. The Cavalier poets were also called "Sons of Ben" to indicate that they followed the example and poetic standards set by Ben Jonson. Most of them were courtiers and aristocrats rather than professional men of letters. The best known Cavalier poets include Robert Herrick, Thomas Carew, John Suckling, and Richard Lovelace. Gallant and witty men, they did not produce a great volume of poetry.

Chivalry

During the Middle Ages, the aristocracy in England and other European countries was organized into a system of mutual protection, service, and obligation based on the honor of each individual knight. The knight vowed obedience to his king, loyalty to his fellow knights, and faithful love to a single maiden, whose protector and champion he became. The knight followed, or tried to follow, a lofty code of conduct.

As a literary character, the knight was the hero of the medieval romance. Although actual knights were often less than ideal, the chivalrous knight of romance sought glory in self-sacrifice and heroic risk-taking against any odds. He was a devout Christian, chaste and humble before God and a defender of Christianity against pagans. On the other hand, the knight would undertake seemingly impossible tasks in service to his chosen lady. He would go on long journeys and wait years for the fulfillment of his desires. The code of chivalry blended Christian morality with military honor to provide a comprehensive set of standards for action. The knights of King Arthur's Round Table, as described in Malory's *Morte Darthur*, illustrate the life of chivalry.

Comedy

In the most general sense, any literary work that ends happily for its major characters is a comedy. More specifically, the term *comedy* applies to a kind of play that makes fun of human weaknesses and follies. Comedy shows the less-than-ideal aspects of human nature and makes them the objects of laughter. Often the characters of a comedy are of low social rank, rustic fellows or simple folk. Aristocratic comedy riducules the middle class.

Comedy of Humors

This form of comedy bases its characterizations on the theory of humors, which states that every individual's personality has a single dominant trait or bias that inclines the character to behave always in the same way regardless of circumstances. Thus a character in this type of comedy often behaves inappropriately and even ridiculously. For example, the miser hides his gold even from himself; he continues to hoard treasure but fails to attend to any other needs or responsibilities, thus ruining his life. Humor characters were used in Renaissance comedies, but it was Ben Jonson who made them the center of his comedies, including the play *Every Man in His Humour* (1598). A humor character's name usually describes his or her humor or inclination. For example, Sir Politic Would-be in Jonson's *Volpone* likes to be well informed about political secrets and pretends to have inside knowledge of the actions of great men.

Comedy of Manners   Plays whose main object was to criticize manners dominated the stage during the Restoration period. In a comedy of manners, the courtship customs, social behavior, and superficial values of a fashionable and style-dominated set of characters are shown to be artificial and false. Hypocrisy and pretense are exposed to ridicule. Characters for whom the play ends happily have somehow risen above the general level of affectation and found a way to express their feelings sincerely or to maintain genuine honor rather than merely holding on to reputation or avoiding scandal. The appeal of a comedy of manners lies often in the quick wit of the dialogue, or repartee. Despite the artificiality of the characters' charm or glamor, they are nevertheless appealing. Like the romantic comedy, a comedy of manners usually ends in the marriage of those characters who represent the right way.

During the Restoration period (1660–1700), the English stage produced a number of excellent comedies of manners. They were written to appeal to an elite, sophisticated audience of courtly and upper-class spectators who came to see their own attitudes and manners, slightly exaggerated, displayed on the stage. Although the playwrights who produced these comedies might have intended to correct the faults of the audience, they also tended to glamorize their behavior by presenting it in heightened and refined form. The epitome of the Restoration comedy of manners is perhaps William Congreve's best play, *The Way of the World* (1700). The comedy of manners was briefly revived in the mid-eighteenth century by Oliver Goldsmith and Richard Brinsley Sheridan and again in the late nineteenth century by Oscar Wilde.

Conceit   Found mainly in Renaissance and seventeenth-century poetry, a conceit is a figure of speech that draws a rather far-fetched and strained comparison between two things. A conceit is enjoyed not because it is obvious or natural but because it is ingenious and shows how cleverly the poet is able to sustain various details of the comparison. In a short lyric poem such as a sonnet, the working out of a single extended conceit may comprise the whole structure of the poem. There are two special kinds of conceits in English poetry. One, the Petrarchan conceit, which was used by the sonneteers of the Renaissance, compares the lover to some object such as a storm-tossed ship or a baffled warrior. The other, the metaphysical conceit used by John Donne and his followers, compares some unlikely object such as a drawing compass or a biting flea with the situation of the lovers in the poems. When applied to modern poetry the term *conceit* usually refers to an especially important and witty extended analogy.

Convention   A writer who uses the forms, devices, and techniques that were used by earlier writers within a certain genre is following the conventions of the genre. The advantage of a writer's adhering to literary conventions is that his or her readers or audience will be familiar with the conventions and will therefore understand the new work more readily and react to it in somewhat predictable ways. The audience of the Elizabethan theater, for example, were familiar with the convention of the aside, in which a character sharing his or her private thoughts with the audience is understood to be unheard by other characters. When Milton uses the conventional invocation of the Muses at the beginning of his epic poem *Paradise Lost*, he is following a classic precedent. However, he does not call on the same Muses that the ancients did because he is writing a Christian poem. Conventions provide familiar signposts to experienced readers, helping them recognize the structure and strategies of the literary work and enabling them to put it into a context of other works of the same kind.

Copia

Copia is a characteristic of some prose styles, especially in the late sixteenth and early seventeenth centuries. The term comes from the Latin phrase *copia verborum*, which literally means "plenty of words." The writer with a copious style does not try to be simple or economical; he or she piles up words, including many synonyms and variations. Preachers also used copia in pulpit oratory to overwhelm the listeners with multiple allusions and examples that advanced a point. Unlike mere wordiness, copia is a planned effect, aimed at convincing the reader of a truth through the sheer abundance of evidence and illustration. Robert Burton's *Anatomy of Melancholy* employs copia in its mass of materials of all kinds.

Coquette

A female stock character, the *coquette* avoids falling in love herself but flirts and teases so as to make men fall in love with her. She typically keeps several young men dangling, encouraging each suitor enough so that he does not give up hope of winning her favor, but never actually yielding to any lover's pleas or committing herself to any frank declaration of her own feelings. The coquette must necessarily be very pretty to attract a variety of suitors and at least somewhat clever to keep them under control. In comedies of manners, the coquette may find herself finally abandoned by all her lovers, who give up in disgust. Or, the heroine may behave like a coquette to some foolish suitors but reveal sincere affection for one suitor, whom she wins at the end of the play. The most famous coquette in English poetry is Belinda in Alexander Pope's *The Rape of the Lock*. The false and unkind behavior of the coquette makes her a standard object of attack in satires of various genres.

Couplet

Two lines of poetry that end with the same rhyme sound comprise a couplet. Ordinarily, both lines of a couplet are the same length. That is, they have the same numbers of metrical feet and the same meter. The most common couplet in English is made up of two rhyming lines of iambic pentameter with the sentence or sentences within the couplet having a complete grammatical structure—that is, not running forward into the first line of the next couplet. Such couplets are called heroic couplets because they were used in the heroic literature of the seventeenth century, particularly in the heroic drama. This form of couplet was also widely used in satiric literature of the eighteenth century. Here is an example from Alexander Pope:

True ease in writing comes from art, not chance,

As those move easiest who have learned to dance. (ll.363–364)

These lines from *An Essay on Criticism* contain one complete thought, stated as a general truth in the first line and repeated as a simile in the second. Couplets are also found as concluding lines in other forms, such as the last two lines of an English sonnet or the last two lines of a scene of a play written in blank verse.

Courtesy Book   A type of treatise, often in the form of a dialogue, was written in the Renaissance to explore the necessary qualities and appropriate behavior of an ideal courtier. The role of the courtier was not only to defend but also to advise the king. Therefore, he should seek to perfect himself in political wisdom and especially in moral virtue. This virtue would be reflected in all his actions and give his manners a polish and refinement, making him both gentle and honorable. The most famous courtesy book, which influenced the composition of all later ones, was *Il Cortegiano (The Courtier)* by the Italian Baldassare Castiglione. It was translated into English by Sir Thomas Hoby in 1561, and several imitations were published during the following decades. The general idea of the courtesy book—the education of the courtly young man—is also associated with Edmund Spenser's epic, *The Faerie Queene*, which is not a courtesy book in form. The form has also been applied loosely to eighteenth-century novels that teach refined manners, such as Fanny Burney's *Evelina*.

Courtly Love   In the Middle Ages, the relationships of men and women were governed, in literature at least, by a code of conduct and set of ideals called courtly love. Based on ideas found in writings of the Latin poet Ovid, the courtly love ideal was a part of the knight's life of chivalry. Courtly romances followed a conventional pattern: lovers fell in love completely, at first sight; they felt absolutely overwhelmed by emotion so that they became restless, sick, pale, and distracted; they sigh, weep or complain about their state, feeling weak and helpless from the effects of love and from despairing of ever being worthy to be loved in return. If the lady recognizes the courtly lover, he is joyous and inspired with hope; he undertakes to perform some difficult or dangerous task to prove his worthiness. Meanwhile, he keeps his love a secret and protects the lady's name and reputation, defending it with his life, if necessary. Thus, courtly love combines an idealization of the lady with sensuous, even illicit, pleasure. The courtly lover is, above all, absolutely faithful despite all obstacles and delays. The origin of many ideas about courtly love in

England was the twelfth-century treatise *The Art of Love* by the Italian Andreas Capellanus.

Didactic   This adjective can be applied to any literary work whose purpose is to teach a lesson or illustrate a moral. The message of a didactic work is usually unambiguous. Unlike fables, which may be ironic, didactic stories provide clear examples of the wrong way and/or the right way to act or think. Didactic works tend to rank rather low artistically because they do not deal imaginatively with the complexities of human behavior. However, since every effective piece of literature expresses some values, it is not possible to say what is or is not didactic in any absolute sense. Rather, the term *didactic* is applied to those poems, stories, and plays that teach a lesson in an obvious or heavy-handed way. The term has negative connotations of narrowness of view or dullness of presentation.

Doggerel   A form of verse that is below the level of poetry, doggerel is crude, jogging, and trite. It is full of cliches and tired phrases. Doggerel is sometimes used for satiric purposes, to make fun of ideas or to mock sentiments by putting them into low, undignified form. Written for comic effect, doggerel uses obvious rhymes, but sometimes the rhythm or meter is grossly out of order, creating false emphasis and awkward phrasing. One fixed form of doggerel is the limerick, but almost any verse form, if exaggerated and poorly executed, can become doggerel. Samuel Butler's *Hudibras* uses doggerel to mock the political opponents of the royalist cause during the English Civil War.

Dystopia   This is a kind of satire that describes a bad society. It is the opposite of a utopia, which describes a good or ideal society. In a dystopia, faulty doctrines or flawed concepts of human nature determine the power structure and distort the relationships among people. Characters may mistakenly admire the orderly dystopia at first, but more experience reveals that it somehow violates basic concepts of fairness or individual integrity. One of the most famous dystopias of English literature is found in Book IV of Jonathan Swift's *Gulliver's Travels*, in which Gulliver admires the society of horses, only to be rejected by it as an intolerable deviant.

Eclogue   This form of lyric poem is a type of pastoral poetry in which idealized shepherds are the speakers. The shepherds may converse in alternating stanzas, or one shepherd may sing a song to the other. The stanza forms are varied. The purpose of such poetry is to create a smooth and beautiful effect. The English eclogue is mainly exemplified by Edmund Spenser's *Shepheardes Calender*.

Elegy   A type of lyric poem, the elegy expresses serious or mournful feelings. It is usually a meditation on death. Many elegies are written to mourn the death of a particular person. For example, John Milton's poem *Lycidas* is an elegy on the death of his school friend Edward King. This poem contains some conventional elements of a pastoral elegy: the questioning of fate, the procession of mourners, the strewing of flowers, and the final consolation. Other elegies are more general meditations on the meaning of death, its inevitability, and the sense of loss associated with it. One of the most famous of such elegies is Thomas Gray's *Elegy Written in a Country Churchyard*, in which the poet contemplates the graves of the common folk and honors the dignity of their simple lives and obscure deaths. The elegiac poem sustains a mournful mood.

Elizabethan   This adjective is applied to the literature produced in England during the reign of Queen Elizabeth I from 1558 to 1602. This period may be considered the height of the Renaissance in England. A period of great national growth and prosperity, the Elizabethan age saw the flowering of both lyric poetry (the sonnets) and dramatic poetry (that of Shakespeare and his contemporaries). Allusions to the queen herself were abundant, as in Spenser's *The Faerie Queene*.

Emblem   An emblem is a simple, symbolic picture printed above a poem and corresponding to some idea or image in the poem. A heart, a rose, a ship or a tree might be used to focus the reader's attention on some concept developed in the poem. An emblem might also be accompanied by a brief motto, the meaning of which is explored in the poem. Collections of poems with printed emblems and mottoes were created during the seventeenth century; they were called emblem books. The best-known of these was compiled by Frances Quarles. Simply called *Emblems*, it was published in 1635.

Empiricism   In the early development of scientific thought, the English philosophers Francis Bacon and John Locke both advocated an examination of actual objects and events. This approach contrasted with that of the rationalist philosopher Descartes, who started with abstractions and made deductions from them. The empiricists believed that a broad and systematic examination of nature would reveal natural laws, the principles by which the universe operates. In his *Essay Concerning Human Understanding* (1690), Locke examines and explains his own mental processes and asks the reader to verify his conclusions by looking into his or her own mind.

End-stopped Line   When the end of a grammatical unit of expression—a clause, a phrase or a sentence—coincides with the end of a line of poetry, that line is said to be end-stopped. Reading aloud, one would pause slightly at the end of such a line, even if no punctuation is given. This line from Milton is end-stopped:

Better to reign in Hell than serve in Heaven.

For lines that are not end-stopped, the term is "enjambement."

Enjambement   Enjambement results when a line of poetry does not contain a complete meaning, and the reader must proceed to the next line to grasp the sense. Here is an example from Milton:

> Here at least
>
> We shall be free: th'Almighty hath not built
>
> Here for his envy. . . .

Enlightenment   A philosophical movement commonly called the Enlightenment developed during the seventeenth and early eighteenth centuries in England and western Europe. This name refers to its basic premise that many beliefs of the past had been dark, that is, mere superstitions or false systems of thought based on faulty authority. The new philosophers tried to free their minds of all established and traditional explanations of humanity and nature, getting down to essential, directly observable or self-evident propositions. They laid the foundations for the modern scientific method and at the same time tended to undermine religious faith by seeking rational explanations for all phenomena. However, many individual Enlightenment thinkers retained faith in God even as they came into conflict with church authorities who feared the effects of their new ideas. France was the center of Enlightenment thinking, but its influence was felt in all the major European cities. The father of French rationalist thinking was Rene Descartes, whose *Discourse on Method* (1637) shows the necessity for radical doubt of all received opinions. In his treatise *Novum Organum* (1620) the English essayist Francis Bacon analyzed the various "idols" or false ideas that distort thinking. He advocated direct observation of nature as the source of truth. Building on these foundations, Enlightenment philosophers undertook to reexamine the laws of nature and the foundations of human nature. Their studies led them to political theory, mathematics, physics, psychology, astronomy, and new theories of education, as well as many other fields. The new ideas generated in the Enlightenment are often cited as one cause of the social unrest that culminated at the end of the eighteenth century in the French Revolution. While Enlightenment thinkers were not revolutionaries, their writings tended to undermine traditional sources of authority and to stress the essential equality of human beings.

Envoy   Sometimes spelled *envoi*, this term has the root meaning of "to send." It refers to a final stanza that "sends" or directs a poem to a specific person. However, sometimes the term merely indicates a conclusion or a repetition of a refrain found earlier in the poem.

Epic   A long, narrative poem, the epic was considered the highest form of literature in classical and Renaissance critical theory. Expressing the values and the legendary history of a culture or national group, the epic focuses on the deeds of a central hero who embodies those qualities most admired and worthy of imitation. The narrator of the epic poem comments on the hero's actions, maintaining a tone of objectivity but also pointing out certain truths about human experience illustrated by the hero's fate. The style of an epic poem is serious, lofty, and dignified. Characters make lengthy speeches, often including long lists, called catalogs, of the names of warriors, ships or armor. Some other conventions of the epic poem are: the poet calls upon a Muse or deity for help or inspiration in telling the epic story; the action begins in the middle of things (*in medias res*) and the earlier episodes are added later; supernatural beings oversee and sometimes direct events that either help or hinder the hero's progress; extended metaphors (epic similes) and allusions extend the range of reference of the epic to include other actions or situations from other literary sources. The epic hero is usually both physically strong and courageous; he is also clever and wise and a good speaker and skillful leader of other men. He represents an ideal version of manhood, which frequently has begun to decline by the time the epic poet speaks.

Epics are classified as either folk or literary. Folk epics are derived from the compilation and organization by one poet of a wide range of legendary tales of heroic or fantastic deeds. The major English folk epic is *Beowulf*. In a literary epic, the poet may deal with traditional materials, but he creates a more original and individual composition based on his own unified poetic idea. Two of the finest English literary epics are Edmund Spenser's *The Faerie Queene* and John Milton's *Paradise Lost*. Other works that use some of the conventions of epics are also referred to as "epic." For example, Henry Fielding calls his novel *Joseph Andrews* a "comic epic in prose."

Epic Simile   The kind of simile or figurative comparison found in most epic poems is more extended and more fully developed than other similes. In making such a simile, the epic poet seems to interrupt the flow of the action in order not only to describe, by comparison, the present setting, character or incident but also to present the content of the simile, the thing compared, for its own sake. That is, the epic simile may temporarily take the reader into a realm that is only loosely parallel to that of the poem. In imitation of the style of Homer, John Milton uses the epic simile to create complex effects. For example, at the end of Book I of *Paradise Lost*, he compares the swarm of demons approaching Pandemonium with a swarm of bees pouring out of a hive, buzzing around spring flowers and conferring about "state affairs." This simile both gives a visual impression of the bees' swarming and suggests that the nature of Satan's followers is insect-like in that it is busy but trivial.

Epistle   Most simply, an epistle is a letter. A literary epistle is a dignified and serious letter in poetic form. Frequently it is written on some issue of state or to convey advice to a group or person. Alexander Pope, in imitation of the Latin poet Horace, called many of his verse compositions epistles. He addressed each one to some important person who represented the values or the moral position he advocated in the poetic epistle. However, Pope also used the term *epistle* loosely; his *Epistle to Dr. Arbuthnot* is a satiric dialogue that honors Pope's friend Dr. Arbuthnot as an ideal friend.

Epistolary Novel   In the later seventeenth and the eighteenth centuries, many novels were presented in the form of collections of letters supposedly written by the characters of the novel. In these letters the characters described to each other the events of their lives and explained their feelings about these events. Thus the novel had no objective narrator; the reader had only the characters' own versions of events. The letters gave an air of authenticity to the fiction; frequently an "editor" claimed in a preface that these letters were the records of actual people that had been found or mysteriously left to be discovered and printed. Such a preface was, of course, part of the total fiction. The advantage of an epistolary novel is that it allows the characters to present spontaneous and private thoughts about events soon after they happen or even while they are going on. The character can be presented as being interrupted in the midst of writing a letter by the events of the story and can be supposed to return to the letter immediately afterward to report what has occurred. Also, the same event can be described from the points of view of several characters. Characters can comment about other characters and can anticipate what might happen next. In the absence of a reliable narrator, however, the reader is left to sort out the "truth" of the story from among competing accounts.

The most famous and influential epistolary novel in English is Samuel Richardson's *Clarissa Harlowe* (1748), a novel of abduction and rape in which the heroine confides her fears and distress to her friend and correspondent while the abductor details his schemes in letters to his fellow rake. The use of the epistolary form of novel declined in the nineteenth century; some of its qualities of intimacy and psychological subtlety are found in the modern stream-of-consciousness technique.

Essay   An essay is a short prose work loosely organized around a unifying topic but admitting many variations in form and digressions in content. The essay gives the personal thoughts, notions, recollections, and anecdotes of the essayist in an informal or conversational style. The father of the essay is the French writer Montaigne, whose *Essais* were published between 1580 and 1595. The word *essay* means to try or to attempt, indicating that the essay was not a finished treatise but was more tentative, a sketch or preliminary thought. In England in the eighteenth century, series of essays were published in daily, weekly or thrice-weekly periodicals. The best known of these periodical essays were Addison and Steele's *The Tatler* and *The Spectator*.

Exemplum   An *exemplum* is a story or tale that is used to illustrate a moral point. It gives an example of the right or the wrong way. *Exempla* (the plural form) were a popular form in the medieval period, often being used in sermons and gathered into anthologies. Although intended to give moral guidance, good exempla are also marked by the human interest and amusing detail of an anecdote told for its own sake. Chaucer's Pardoner's Tale is an exemplum exposing the destructive power of greed.

Fabliau   A French medieval form, the *fabliau* is a story tale in verse, usually concerning the ordinary activities of middle or lower-class characters. Its tone is the opposite of courtly; it is frequently vulgar or obscene and almost always humorous. Chaucer wrote *fabliaux* (the plural form). The Miller's Tale in *The Canterbury Tales* is an ingenious and complexly plotted fabliau.

Farce   A farce is a short play that provokes laughter by means of physical humor such as slaps and falls or low-level verbal games that are sometimes merely pointless repetitions. Plot is minimal, situations are absurd, and characters are stock types. Elements of farce are sometimes included in comedy; the low characters of a subplot may engage in farcical actions, as the drunkards in Shakespeare's *The Tempest*, who beat the subhuman character Caliban.

Fit   The Anglo-Saxon word for a part or division of a poem is *fit*. The term corresponds to Canto or chapter, in Italian. In *Beowulf*, each major division of the epic is numbered as a separate *fit*.

Foil   In drama, a foil is a character who contrasts with the central character. The foil character highlights the hero's traits by being different or opposite. Thus in *Hamlet* the character Fortinbras is an aggressive young prince who will fight at the slightest excuse, unlike Prince Hamlet himself, who is hesitant and intellectual.

Folio   In early book printing, the size of the book page was determined by the number of times the standard printed sheet from the press was folded. For a large book, the paper sheet was printed so as to be folded in half only once, creating two leaves or four pages. The first standard editions of Shakespeare's plays were printed in such large books so that the term is associated with these early, authoritative editions.

Foot   A foot is a standard unit of meter or rhythm in a poetic line. In the line, a pattern of accented and unaccented syllables (or stressed and unstressed syllables) is divided into a number of similar units, each called a foot. In English, the most commonly used foot is the iamb, which consists of two syllables, the first unaccented and the second accented. The words *forget* and *begin* make iambic feet, as does the phrase "to grieve." Five such feet in one line makes iambic pentameter, the most frequently used line in narrative and dramatic poetry. Here is a line of five iambic feet:

Is this the face that launched a thousand ships?

Other types of feet commonly found in English poetry are these:

Trochee: two syllables, accent on the first—*reason*

Spondee: two syllables, both accented—*May day*

Anapest: three syllables, accent on the last—*for a while*

Dactyl: three syllables, accent on the first—*heavenly*

It is usual for a poet to vary meter by substituting an occasional foot of a different kind into lines written primarily in one foot. Another common variation is to omit the unaccented syllable at the beginning or ending of a line of poetry, leaving a foot of just one syllable.

Formal Verse Satire

This is a form of satiric poem, developed in Latin by the satirists Horace and Juvenal, in which the satirist speaks directly of the follies and evil conduct of the people in his city, describing their bad actions in strong terms, and in a sarcastic tone. The satirist usually locates himself in some open, public place, such as the street or the marketplace, where he can make observations on the passing fools and knaves. The satirist may seem to be addressing another person, called the adversarius, who may provoke even more intense disgust and condemnation in the satirist by taking a more moderate position. Formal verse satire is not highly structured; it does not develop a plot or follow a logical pattern. Rather, it is loosely unified by a central theme and contains multiple examples of one kind of corruption or human weakness. Formal verse satire may be witty, but its predominant mood is not comical. Its apparent intention is to make the reader scornful of the kinds of actions satirized. Formal verse satires were written by John Donne; John Wilmot, the earl of Rochester; and Samuel Johnson, whose poem *The Vanity of Human Wishes* is an imitation of a formal verse satire of Juvenal.

Gentilesse

In late medieval literature, an ideal of manners and good conduct became known as *gentilesse*. It did not depend on the high social rank of the individual; it consisted of courteous speech and gentle and kind behavior to all persons, no matter what their rank. Gentilesse is closely allied to the broad concept of charity in medieval Christianity. It emphasizes not elegance, but generosity of spirit. In Chaucer's *The Canterbury Tales*, the ugly wife in The Wife of Bath's Tale gives a lecture to her unkind husband on the virtue of gentilesse.

Georgic

Geo means the earth. A georgic poem is one that deals with the cultivation of the earth, that is, with farming and the life of the farm. The Latin poet Virgil first used the term to describe his writing on such topics. While describing some technical aspect of farm work, the georgic poem also celebrates the seasons and the style of life that farming creates.

Gothic   Gothic style is a medieval style named after the Goths, a Germanic tribe that prevailed in Europe between the ancient classical era and the Renaissance. The word describes the architectural style of the medieval cathedral, with its tall and narrow spaces, pointed arches, and elaborate stained glass windows. In a literary context, Gothic may have negative connotations, implying a crude and old-fashioned style, as seen by later, neoclassical critics. In the era of Alexander Pope and Joseph Addison, Gothic style was considered irregular and barbaric, without essential discipline, unity or restraint. Toward the end of the eighteenth century, the Gothic novel was one that neglected realism is favor of suspense, horror, and mysterious incidents. Anne Radcliffe's novel *The Mysteries of Udolpho* (1794) is a prominent example of this type of fiction. In the romantic era that followed, *Gothic* became a term of praise, suggesting what was free, wild, primitive, and unspoiled by too much civilization.

Gothic Novel   A form developed and made popular in the late eighteenth century, the Gothic novel does not observe the conventional realism of the mainstream English novel but borrows some of the techniques and devices of the medieval romance. It exploits the supernatural and the grotesque. It contains highly improbable incidents set in remote and threatening locales such as ancient, isolated castles. The characters of a Gothic novel tend to be stock figures; the emphasis is on mysterious situations and shocking events rather than on subtlety of characterization. The famous Gothic novel by Anne Radcliffe, *The Mysteries of Udolpho*, was satirized by Jane Austin in *Northanger Abby*, a mock-Gothic novel.

Hack Writer   A hack writer is one who writes to order, producing pages of fiction, poetry or essays on demand at a fixed rate of pay per page or, if poetry, per line. The term arose in the early eighteenth century when publishing became an industry and books became a commodity sold to a mass market. Many hack writers survived by doing translations, abridgements or reviews of more complex original works by others. Most hack writers remained poor and obscure; they were standard objects of satiric scorn. Samuel Johnson emerged from the hack-writing trade to become a recognized literary talent and authority. Nevertheless, he made it clear that he wrote mainly because he was being paid to do so.

Hagiography   A hagiography is an account of the life of a saint, detailing the saint's good deeds, sufferings, and miracles. By extension, any biography of an individual that presents him or her as much better than ordinary or as unbelievably good can be called a hagiography. This broader use of the term implies some skepticism.

Hero   A hero is the central character of a literary work, whose choices or actions determine the outcome of events. (If such a character is female, she may be called a heroine.) In classical dramatic theory, the tragic hero must be a person of high rank, and he must suffer from a flaw or weakness that causes his downfall. However, the term is also used more broadly to apply to any main character whose fortunes and struggles are central to the plot of a fiction or drama. In heroic literature, such as the epic, romance or heroic play, the hero exemplifies admirable conduct; courage and self-sacrifice are among his prominent traits. He represents an ideal, the best that human capacities can accomplish. But in more realistic genre, the novel, for instance, the hero is shown as developing from a state of immature and mistaken behavior to a better, wiser, and more capable condition. His heroism consists partly in discarding childish or inadequate ways; he is rewarded by being received as a full member of established society. In romantic literature of the late eighteenth and early nineteenth century, the hero is a sensitive person, a man of feeling, perhaps a poet. The idea of a hero thus changes according to the dominating values of the society in which he is created and for which he stands as an example of the right way.

Heroic Couplet   A heroic couplet is composed of two lines of iambic pentameter, both lines being end-stopped. It is called thus because the form was first extensively used in the Restoration period for the composition of heroic plays. However, the most famous English poems written in heroic couplets are satires, especially the mock-heroic poems by Alexander Pope. Here is an example from *The Rape of the Lock* describing the heroine Belinda:

> Favors to none, to all she smiles extends;
>
> Oft she rejects, but never once offends. Il. 12. 13

This couplet shows the balance and antithesis that are characteristic of many heroic couplets. The first line balances the two opposite objects of Belinda's attention: "all" get smiles, but "none" get favors. The same subject and verb—"she extends"—govern both objects. Similarly, in the second line of the couplet, the ideas of rejecting and offending are balanced against each other by the words *oft* (often) and *never*. Notice also that the second line tends to restate in different words the idea of the first line so that the whole couplet becomes a separate and closed unit of thought, compressed and complete, even though it exists in the general flow of the narration. While not all heroic couplets are so intricately structured, the most memorable and pointed statements of the work will tend to have this epigrammatical style.

Heroine   *See* **Hero.**

History   History is the narrative account of events of the past arranged in roughly chronological order and purporting to be true rather than fictional. But this term in a literary context has other implications. In the Renaissance, the history play was based on English national chronicles and tended to glorify England by representing worthy deeds. Such plays included the outstanding events of the reign of the king for whom the play was named; for example, Shakespeare's *Henry IV*. In the eighteenth century the term *history* was sometimes made part of the title of a novel, indicating the realism and authenticity of the narrative. Henry Fielding's *History of Tom Jones* is an example.

Humanism   Humanism was a broad artistic and philosophical movement that was a major aspect of the Renaissance. Starting in Italy in the fourteenth century and developing in England in the late fifteenth century, humanism was a reaction against the spiritual, ascetic, and other-worldly emphasis of medieval thought. European humanists studied the languages and the literatures of ancient Greece and Rome, wherein they found an emphasis on the earthly life of human beings rather than the medieval assumption that life on earth is merely a trial and preparation for life after death. Humanists celebrated the dignity of the individual and a person's capacity to learn and to enjoy a full moral life governed by reason. They sought to combine the dignity and restraint of classical culture with Christian idealism. In Europe humanism was epitomized by Desiderius Erasmus, a Dutch philosopher who became the friend of the English humanist Sir Thomas More, whose *Utopia* is a humanist vision of an ideal society. The humanists were educators and concerned themselves with developing a new system of study, including the classics, to teach the sons of noble families those values and attitudes necessary to make them wise counselors to the king. Since humanism was an international movement, humanists used the Latin language as a medium of communication, but they also advocated the development of literature in the vernacular languages of each country. Many humanist scholars translated classical and humanist texts to spread the influence of the ideas found therein.

Humors   The theory of humors (or humours) was a widely held theory of human personality or temperament based on ancient medical ideas. From the time of the Greek physician Galen, human beings were thought to have within their bodies four basic fluids corresponding to the four elements of the universe: air, water, earth, and fire. These fluids were mixed in various proportions in each individual, and the dominant fluid, or humor, in one's body determined the inclination or bias of one's temperament, according to the following scheme:

Dominant Humor	Elements	Temperament
blood	air—hot and moist	sanguine (hopeful)
yellow bile	fire—hot and dry	choleric (angry)
phlegm	water—cold and moist	phlegmatic (dull)
black bile	earth—cold and dry	melancholy

This was a medical theory as well as a system to explain differences in personality. A good balance among the humors resulted in good health and an even temperament. Extreme imbalances could cause disease and mental peculiarity, even madness.

References to this theory of humors are common in medieval and Renaissance literature. Hamlet is an obvious sufferer of melancholy, for example. The idea that a character should show one consistent inclination of personality was used by Ben Jonson as the basis for creating a type of character. In his comedies, Jonson created rigid and predictable characters, each of whom is always focused on a single idea or desire. These humor characters appear in *Every Man in His Humour* and *Volpone*.

Iambic Pentameter   A poetic line of five iambic feet, this is the most common verse line of English narrative and dramatic poetry. It is used in some lyric poetry as well, such as the Renaissance sonnet. The reason for the popularity of this line is said to be that it most nearly approximates the rhythm of prose speech. *See examples under* **Foot**. *See also* **Meter**.

Kenning   Used in Anglo-Saxon poetry, the kenning is a formulaic figure of speech in which a descriptive compound term is substituted for a noun. In *Beowulf*, for example, the ocean is called the "whale-road," and a battle is called a "sword storm." Each kenning comprises a half-line of verse.

Lay   This term, also spelled *lai*, was applied to certain short narrative poems originating in France in the twelfth century. If they were based on the Celtic lore of France, they were called Breton lais. Poems rewritten in this form appeared in England in the fourteenth century. Chaucer's The Franklin's Tale is a lay, as is the anonymous *Sir Orfeo*. Later poets use the term to refer to short historical or legendary poems related to the ballad.

Libertine   A stock character of the comedy of manners, the libertine is a young man who lives for pleasure, who is guided not by a moral code but by his appetites or desires. The libertine tends to have a cynical attitude toward human nature; he sees conventional moral restraints as hypocritical, as disguises that others adopt to conceal their natures. A manipulator of others, he will sometimes temporarily adopt a moralistic disguise in order to accomplish some deception, especially to promote his own interests. In Restoration comedies of manners, the libertine is frequently presented as an attractive and witty young man who has a series of affairs with aristocratic ladies but who is now attempting to negotiate the seduction of one particular lady who has a more demanding sense of her own honor. If the libertine is the hero of the comedy, he will eventually abandon his loose ways to win the love of this lady. But not all libertine characters are reformed. In William Wycherley's play *The Country Wife*, for example, the libertine Horner sacrifices his own honor so that he can seduce the wives of his friends. At the end of the play, his friend Harcourt marries the heroine, but Horner is left single and condemned to an empty life of mere fornication without love. His libertine philosophy isolates him from all normal ties of affection and loyalty.

There are a few female libertine characters in Restoration comedy. These women tend to be punished for their loose behavior by loss of reputation. Sometimes they are married off to some foolish or cowardly suitor who is obviously not a reward.

Litotes   A characteristic of Anglo-Saxon poetry, litotes is a form of under-statement cast in negative terms for an ironic effect. In *Beowulf*, instead of saying that the men were afraid to sleep in the mead hall, the poet says that it was "not hard to find one who slept elsewhere." The listener is assumed to pick up the implication of fear. More simply, if a speaker were to say of an overweight person that he had "not missed many meals lately," he would be using litotes implying gluttony.

Lyric   One of the major forms of poetry, the lyric is a poem of emotion, expressing directly the feelings of the speaker. The term *lyric* comes from the ancient custom of accompanying a song with the music of a lyre. A lyric poem may contain some narrative elements, some brief story or incident related to the feeling, but the primary emphasis is on conveying that feeling by image, metaphors, and modulations of tone. Lyric poems are written in a wide variety of verse forms. Some of the major kinds of lyrics are sonnets, songs, odes, and elegies.

Machinery   This term is used to refer loosely to supernatural beings, such as fairies and angels, gods and goddesses, who are added to a drama or a poem for ornament and to add spectacle or elaborate effects. The term derives from the fact that supernatural beings were introduced onto the stage seated on thrones or artificial clouds that were lowered onto the stage by means of ropes and pulleys. That is, they entered by machine. The term for the means of entry was transferred to the beings who entered. In his *Rape of the Lock*, Pope refers to the airy spirits as machinery even though this is not a play and no stage is in question. The term *machinery* also implies that these creatures are added to, not essential to, the main action of the poem.

Malapropism   One character in *The Rivals*, a play by Richard Brinsley Sheridan, is Mrs. Malaprop, a woman who consistently misuses vocabulary. She mixes up words to humorous and surprising effect. For example, she says of a courteous young man, "He is the very pine-apple of politeness." She means the pinnacle, of course, but the image of a pineapple makes a surprisingly fitting comment on the appearance of the young fellow. Malaprop comes from the French expression *mal a-propos*, which means "inappropriate."

Masque   A courtly form of drama, the masque developed during the late medieval period out of dances, processions, and games in which the participants disguised themselves. English masques flourished in the Elizabethan era and later at the courts of King James I and King Charles I. A fully developed masque used music, song, and dance to present an allegory. The characters represented pagan gods and goddesses, stock figures such as shepherds or fairies or abstractions such as time or fortune. Elaborate costumes and scenery were part of the masque, making it more a visual than a literary presentation. In court masques, members of the aristocracy might play some of the roles, and at the climax the gentlemen and ladies of the audience were invited to join in the dance. Some masques also included an anti-masque, a song and dance by ugly or grotesque figures expressing ludicrous or vulgar ideas in contrast to the masque itself. Masques were often written and performed for special occasions such as a coronation, a wedding or the anniversary of some great event.

Metaphor   This is a general term for figures of speech that compare two essentially unlike things. One or more qualities of the thing described (called the tenor) are said to be like qualities of the thing that makes the metaphor (the vehicle). For example, when Shakespeare in *Sonnet 73* compares his age to the season when few leaves are left on the trees, he says that old age, like autumn, is cold and spare, close to the end of life. The qualities of autumn are transferred metaphorically to the last stage of human life. If the comparison is made explicit by the use of a term such as *like* or *as*, the metaphor is called a simile. When a lover says that his mistress is like a flower (a common simile), he suggests that the qualities of beauty, freshness, and fragility that are found in a flower are also traits of the lady he loves. Metaphors are used intensively in poetry because of their emotional suggestiveness.

For special kinds of extended metaphor, see **Allegory, Conceit**, and **Epic Simile.**

Metaphysical   This term names a group of poets of the early seventeenth century, but these poets did not use the term to describe themselves. It was applied to them in the next century by the poet and critic Samuel Johnson. In philosophy, metaphysics deals with what is beyond (meta) the physical, that is, with the incorporeal, supernatural or transcendental. In a general sense, many philosophical poems can be called metaphysical, but in literary discussions, the term usually indicates those poets of the seventeenth century, John Donne and his followers, who challenged the conventions of the Renaissance lyric and wrote poems that questioned and probed the meaning of human existence and the individual's place in the universe and his or her relationship to God. Metaphysical poetry is intellectually challenging and often difficult and startling in its ideas. The metaphysical conceit, an extended metaphor, uses unconventional comparisons to provoke thought.

The metaphysical poets were not much read in the two centuries following their flourishing, but they were rediscovered in the early twentieth century.

Meter   The basic sound pattern in English poetry is created by repetition and alternation of stress and unstressed syllables (or accented and unaccented syllables). The overall pattern of a poem is called its meter (measure). In a poetic line, the pattern of stressed and unstressed syllables is divided into units of nearly the same length and arrangement of stresses; each such unit is called a foot or, in Anglo-Saxon poetry, a half-line. For example, in the line from Spenser's *The Fairie Queene*,

A gentle Knight was pricking on the plaine,

stresses fall on the second, fourth, sixth, eighth, and tenth syllables, so the meter is very regular and the line has five feet, each foot containing one unstressed followed by one stressed syllable. (The eighth syllable, "on," is perhaps not much stressed, but it is more so than the syllables just before and just after.) The meter of a line is named according to the number of feet. These are the usual names:

Meter	Number of Feet
monometer (seldom used)	one foot
dimeter	two feet
trimeter	three feet
tetrameter	four feet
pentameter	five feet
hexameter	six feet
heptameter	seven feet

Various kinds of feet can be used to make up the poetic line, but one kind tends to predominate. (*See* **Foot.** for a list of the different kinds of poetic feet.)

In English poetry, the shorter lines, trimeter and tetrameter, are found mostly in lyrics, while the longer lines, pentameter and hexameter, are used in dramatic, narrative and philosophical poetry. (*See* **Blank Verse.**) Anglo-Saxon poetry did not have such regular meter. Each half-line of the poem contained two stressed syllables and a variable number and arrangement of unstressed syllables.

Microcosm   A microcosm is literally a little world. In Renaissance thought, individuals were sometimes referred to as microcosms because they were believed to contain within themselves the four elements of nature—air, earth, fire, and water—as well as a spirit. Thus the human being epitomized the created world. In this respect, the individual was contrasted to the macrocosm, or great world, which consists of all of nature, including the heavenly bodies. This concept of the human being stresses that he or she is the ultimate creation, the best and most complex work of God. John Donne aludes to the microcosm in his *Holy Sonnet*, which begins

> I am a little world made cunningly
>
> Of elements, and an angelic sprite.

Here, *sprite* means spirit, or soul.

Middle English

Middle English was the language spoken in England from the early twelfth through the late fifteenth century. The language replaced Anglo-Saxon by the development of a combined Germanic and French vocabulary and the simplification of the Anglo-Saxon system of inflections. Middle English was the language of Chaucer, but it existed in several different regional dialects, most of which are more difficult for the modern reader than Chaucer's London dialect. After Caxton introduced printing in England in 1485, the London dialect began to dominate throughout England, and Modern English, the language of Shakespeare, began to take root.

Miracle Play

See **Mystery Play.**

Mock-Epic

A mock-epic is a satirical poem that uses the structure and style of an epic poem but deals with nonheroic or antiheroic materials. The term *mock-heroic* refers to the style or to the whole poem. In a mock-epic, the hero may be a low character, representing what is base, foolish or trivial, perhaps to show how far from ideal the culture has become. The conventions of the epic are parodied so that, for example, one reads a catalog of knaves instead of a catalog of heroes, as in *The Dunciad* of Alexander Pope. The epic similes make comparisons with things that are silly or vulgar rather than lofty. The purpose of a mock-epic is usually to make fun of the nonheroic subjects of the poem, to show by contrast to heroic norms how dull, superficial or degenerate these characters are. The mock-epic style was used by Chaucer in The Nun's Priest's Tale in which he made a hero of the barnyard fowl Chauntecleer. The most famous mock-epic is Pope's *The Rape of the Lock*, which uses a pretty but not too intelligent young woman as its hero and satirizes the manners and values of upper-class society of the early eighteenth century.

Morality Play

In about the fourteenth century, a kind of allegorical drama in verse developed to explore the means by which the soul might be saved. In a morality play, the central character represents the ordinary person or humankind in general. The other characters are personifications of the central character's qualities, the forces of goodness prompting salvation, and the forces of evil tending to lead individuals to damnation. The conflict takes place among these allegorical characters; the central figure is eventually saved, but the action is a protracted struggle representing the Christian concept of the trials and temptations of earthly existence that must precede salvation. Morality plays were written anonymously. Many of them contained scenes of comedy or farce. The stock character representing the Vice was a source of rough humor. The best example of the morality play in England was *Everyman*, written about 1500.

Mystery Play   Plays based on characters and incidents from the Christian Bible were performed during the late medieval period. Written in verse, these plays were performed for the public during religious holidays. Mystery plays originated within the church as simple representations of moments in the life, death, and resurrection of Christ. Eventually, more plays were added, depicting major events of the Old Testament, from scenes of Adam and Eve in the garden of Eden through the life of Abraham, Noah and the flood, and the prophets. As the plays became popular and began to include more secular elements, even some farce, they were expelled from the church and were performed by members of the various town guilds, which were associations of merchants and craftsmen. Fully developed cycles of mystery plays included the history of Christianity from the Creation to the death and Resurrection of Christ. They were performed on platforms mounted on wagons, called pageants, which could be moved to various locations within the town. Mystery plays, also called *miracle plays*, continued to be performed in prosperous towns until the early sixteenth century. The major cycles that remain are from the towns of Chester, Coventry, Wakefield, and York. The plays of Wakefield, also called the Townley plays, are very fully developed. The famous *The Second Shepherd's Play* is from this cycle.

Narrator   The narrator is the person who seems to be telling a story. This person can stand in various relationships to the author and to the characters of the story. In the simplest arrangement, the narrator may be identified with the author; such a narrator is not a character in the story but knows all about the characters and can describe their actions and even their thoughts. This narrator is omniscient (all-knowing). On the other hand, a narrator who is presented as one of the characters in the story can plausibly know only what is observable from his or her own point of view. This type of narrator has limited perceptions, but he or she may be very acute or somewhat biased and limited. If such a narrator is naive or mistaken, telling of situations that he or she seems not fully to understand, the narrator is said to be unreliable, and the reader may draw meanings from the story that the narrator appears to have missed or avoided.

In first-person narration, the narrator refers to her- or himself as "I" and recounts the story from a limited point of view. In third-person narration, there is no "I"; the telling is done impersonally, and all characters are "he" or "she," distinct from the narrator.

Nature
This broad term is difficult to define because its meaning changes as the concept of art and its purpose change. Nature always has positive connotations; it is the thing that art, including literature, is about, the basic subject that all literary works are supposed to explore, albeit in a limited way. In classical literary theory, literature imitates nature. In this conception, nature is the universal and unchanging way that things are in the world. Human nature especially is the subject, and since basic truths about human life and characters are assumed to be the same for all times and all places, a play or poem of ancient Greece or Rome will have relevance for modern life as well. Readers can judge the quality or value of a literary work by holding it up to the standard of nature, that is, to what they know about life from their own learning and experience. Nature is contrasted to art.

However, nature has other meanings as well. Sometimes it refers to the material world. In such cases what is human is contrasted to the realm of nature, the physical world. Nature is also contrasted to the spiritual realm, the supernatural. The laws of nature are orderly restrictions, but the supernatural can break those laws, creating visions, ghosts, and miracles.

In the late eighteenth century, a concept of nature arose that tended to fuse the physical and the spiritual definitions of nature. To the poets of that era nature embodied the uncultivated or rural world, the mountains, rocks, trees, flowers, and birds. But to these poets nature also contained spiritual force, so that the individual in a natural setting received impulses toward goodness by sympathetic association with nature.

Generally, then, nature is a value term, used to name whatever the writer values most highly and tries to present in the works he or she creates. The adjective "natural" is a general term of praise suggesting simplicity, sincerity, and truth.

Novel
The novel is a long prose narrative that traces the development of a main character or a group of characters through a series of events, situations or actions that may or may not be told in chronological order. Unlike a romance, a novel tries to give the impression of recreating real life, the ordinary day-to-day existence of believable people. Thus the novelist tends not to use highly improbable events or idealized characters. The novel emerged in the early eighteenth century and is not essentially a development of earlier romances or Renaissance narratives. The novel's roots lie in subliterary forms such as diaries, spiritual autobiographies, confessions, letters, and journalistic accounts of actual events. In the 1740s the novel became popular among the middle class as both a guide and an entertainment. It was particularly read and written by women, because reading a novel did not require a university education (women did not attend universities). However, the novel's appeal was very broad, and in the nineteenth

century novels became the predominant form of literature in England. *See* **Epistolary Novel, Gothic Novel.**

Numbers

This obsolete term means, narrowly, meter in poetry or, more generally, poetry itself conceived of as meterical language. The study of meterical patterns was also called numbers from the late Renaissance until the mid-eighteenth century.

Occasional Poetry

The term *occasional* refers to poems written to celebrate or commemorate a special occasion such as a coronation, a birthday, a marriage, a great victory or the anniversary of some significant historical moment. The *Epithalamion*, Edmund Spenser's poem celebrating his own marriage, is an occasional poem. The poet laureate was expected to provide occasional poems for his king.

Ode

The ode is an extended and lofty lyric poem expressing emotions about a significant occasion or a person to whom the ode is dedicated. As a dignified and inspiring work, the ode contains images of grandeur, creating a feeling of awe in the audience. The ode is derived from a Greek form of lyric that was part of the Greek play, a lyric passage separating the episodes of the drama and expressing the feelings of the chorus. Thus, unlike most lyric forms, the ode tends to be public and general, expressing the feelings of all rather than private or personal emotions.

Greek odes were separated into stanzas marked as the strophe, the antistrophe, and the epode, indicating different movements of emotions. These stanza terms are less common in English odes. The major types of odes written in English are: the Pindaric ode (named for the Greek poet Pindar), the Horatian ode (after the Latin poet Horace), and the irregular ode developed by the English poet Abraham Cowley. Briefly, the Pindaric ode uses varied stanza forms, while the Horatian ode keeps the same stanza form throughout. The irregular ode varies even more than the Pindaric; every stanza may use a unique form. John Dryden wrote many odes, among them the *Song for Saint Cecilia's Day* celebrating music; it is an irregular ode.

Old English

This is another name for the Anglo-Saxon language. It is the Germanic language spoken in England before the Norman Conquest (1066).

Omniscient Narrator

A story told by a narrator who knows all about everything, including the inner thoughts of the characters, has an omniscient narrator. Use of such a narrative point of view gives great flexibility; the narrator can shift easily in time and place and can arrange the events of the story to fit any strategy of revelation. The epic poem usually has an omniscient narrator.

Oral-formulaic

This poetic style results from the transmission of folk poetic materials from speaker to listener without the aid of written records. Such poetry tends to contain standard descriptive phrases and conventional images that are remembered from frequent repetition. The "formulas" are the phrases that are readily available to the oral poet from among a large stock of set phrases; they may be varied slightly to suit the particular context, but their use makes spontaneous composition easier and also helps the audience by presenting them with already familiar expressions that need no effort to comprehend. For example, in the folk ballad, a character who says "make my bed soon" (the formula) indicates that he or she feels the approach of death. Because the same formula occurs in various poems, the listener who is familiar with the folk tradition readily recognizes the meaning of the formulaic phrase.

Ottava Rima   This stanza form consists of eight lines of iambic pentameter with a rhyme pattern of a b a b a b c c. This is an Italian form, as its name indicates. It was used by various English Renaissance poets who experimented with stanza forms.

Paradox   A paradox is a statement that seems to contain its own contradiction. It seems that a paradox cannot logically be true, yet the poet asserts the paradox as an essentially true statement. John Donne, for example, asserts in several poems that he and his lady, two people, are also simultaneously one person. The metaphysical poets as a group were unafraid of paradox, using it to state mysterious truths.

Parody   Parody is a technique used in satire. In it, the writer closely imitates some of the conventional elements and the actual wording of a known and familiar literary work in order to mock that work or to make a ludicrous application of the style of the work to other, less dignified subject matter. The humor of the parody lies in the disparity between the serious style of the original and its application to trivial or low material. One of the most parodied speeches from Shakespeare's plays, for example, is the famous soliloquy from *Hamlet* that begins, "To be or not to be, that is the question." One such silly parody begins: "Toupee or not toupee, that is the question." Another: "To sneeze, or not to sneeze, that is congestion." Shakespeare himself writes parody when in *King Henry IV*, Part I he has Falstaff speak in the moralistic phrases of the Puritans, imitating their style. Christopher Marlowe's popular lyric poem *The Passionate Shepherd to His Love* is parodied by the poem of Sir Walter Raleigh called *The Nymph's Reply to the Shepherd*. Raleigh uses the same stanza form and parallels the images used by Marlowe in each stanza, but Raleigh's parody takes a more realistic or cynical view of love.

Pastoral   *Pastor* in Latin means a shepherd. Therefore, any literary work that has shepherds as its main characters can be called pastoral. In this broad sense, *pastoral* is an adjective modifying another literary form, as a pastoral drama, a pastoral elegy or a pastoral romance. The main characters in a pastoral are conventional rather than realistic shepherds. They speak in cultivated diction and sing elegant, even courtly, songs. The effect is highly artificial.

In a more specific sense, a pastoral is a kind of poem written in ancient Greece and Rome in which a shepherd speaks or, frequently, two shepherds engage in a dialogue. The customary subjects of pastorals were love complaints and elegies for the dead. The form of the pastoral was imitated in England during the Renaissance, especially by Edmund Spenser in *The Shepheardes Calender*. Also, John Milton employs the pastoral elegy in his poem *Lycidas*.

One idea common to all types of pastorals is the goodness of a simple and rustic life, in contrast to the evils of the sophisticated life of the court or the great city. The pastoral idealizes rural life as simple and pure, free of ambition and corruption. It is antiheroic, celebrating humble life.

Patronage

Before the full development of the printing and book-selling industry in the eighteenth century, writers who were not financially independent needed the gifts or support of wealthy patrons. These were men, and occasionally women, who were interested enough in literature to help support promising or established writers. Some patrons took the writer into their households as tutors or secretaries, allowing the writers to pursue their creative work with the security of a permanent post. In return, the writer often dedicated many of his works to his patron, writing prefaces of dedication in praise of the patron's good taste and generosity. Only playwrights could earn substantial amounts of money independent of patronage, since plays were immediate sources of income for the acting companies who paid the playwright or gave him a percentage of the proceeds. The patronage system died out when a large reading public and a well-organized printing industry made the sale of printed books lucrative enough to support writers by buying their manuscripts, hiring them as hack writers, and paying them royalties. Royal patronage lasted long after other forms of patronage had declined. Samuel Johnson received a royal pension for his Dictionary after it was completed. The poet laureateship is the current remainder of the patronage system.

Pentameter

A five-foot line. *See* **Meter.**

Periodical Essay

In the eighteenth century, before the development of the modern magazine or journal, individual prose essays were published in series under a unifying title. Two of the best-known early series were by Richard Steele and Joseph Addison: *The Tatler* (1709–1711) and *The Spectator* (1711–1712 and 1714). These men and a few of their friends wrote essays on topics of current interest: matters of taste, fashion, manners, the arts, and public life. Their general purpose was to instruct readers who were largely middle class, and to improve their manners while at the same time amuse them with mild satire. The essays were printed several times a week; each essay was a separate publication. As the century progressed, the easy prose style of the periodical essay became a model for general prose writing. Collections of periodical essays were reprinted as books and became a staple of private libraries.

Persona
The speaker of a literary work has a more or less well-developed personality or style. If the speaker's personality becomes a character clearly unlike the author's personality, this character is called the *persona*. The term literally means a mask. The author is conceived of as putting on the mask of another self for the purpose of the story he or she is telling. The concept of the persona is vital to discussions of the work of Jonathan Swift, who uses this technique in almost all his major works. In his famous *A Modest Proposal*, he pretends to be a dull and morally insensitive person who does not realize that the project he is proposing, to eat poor Irish children, is outrageous and totally repugnant. The real author Swift, of course, was not such a moral monster; he is adopting the persona as a means of making his point about the extreme poverty of the Irish peasants. Any narrator who projects another self into the story can be said to create a persona.

Personification
This is a figure of speech in which something that is not a person—for example, the sea, a sheep or a season—is presented as having human emotions or human responses to situations. The thing personified may be an object, an animal or a concept. Poets who use personification are suggesting that nature is in harmony with or participates in people's mental lives. Trees that weep, windows that yawn or rocks that stand guard are obvious personifications. In pastoral poetry, the whole landscape is full of sympathetic, personified objects and forces. In allegorical forms such as the morality play and the masque, the characters are personifications of concepts or ideas.

Poetic Justice
The dramatist who arranges matters so that at the end of a play the good characters, those whom we admire and sympathize with, are rewarded and made happy, while the bad characters, the villains, are punished, has created poetic justice. In dramatic criticism of the Restoration and eighteenth century, some conservative critics insisted that poetic justice was necessary to a moral play. Thomas Rymer took this position in opposition to the more liberal dramatic theory of John Dryden. In the best poetic justice, characters come to suffer punishments that are not only fitting and appropriate in proportion to their crimes but that also come about logically and inevitably as the indirect or long-range results of the character's own actions. Thus, Polonius in Shakespeare's *Hamlet* is appropriately stabbed while hiding behind a curtain to spy on Hamlet. Polonius's habit of spying catches up with him. Good poetic justice is neither far-fetched nor the result of mere coincidence.

Prosody
Despite the sound of its name, prosody has nothing to do with prose. It is the study of versification, a general term for all principles of meter, rhyme, and stanza form. All the various patterns of sound in a poem constitute its prosody. The term also names the rules and models that provide guidance and set up standards of making poetry.

Prude   A female stock character, the prude is found in satires and comedies of manners. She pretends to be very virtuous, chaste, and pious. She acts as if she were shocked by any gossip about the loose or immoral behavior of others, especially other women. But underneath, the prude is just as eager to enjoy illicit love as the women she criticizes. She is a hypocrite who faults others for doing what she does secretly, or what she would do if she could. Some prudes are portrayed as having become prudish in middle age after a more licentious youth. Clarissa is the prude in Alexander Pope's *The Rape of the Lock*. She makes a long speech about despising beauty and preferring good nature, but none of the other characters pays any attention to it.

Quatrain   A quatrain is a stanza consisting of four lines. The most common rhyme pattern for a quatrain is a b a b. This is found, for example, in Thomas Gray's famous *Elegy Written in a Country Churchyard*. Poets of course use other rhyme patterns as well. The English sonnet is composed of four quatrains and a couplet.

Rake   A stock character in comedies of the Restoration and eighteenth century, the rake is a young male (occasionally a female) character who displays a libertine or self-indulgent attitude toward life. His main purpose is immediate pleasure; he does not feel moral restraints on his actions. The rake is frequently a seducer of women, a gambler, and a heavy drinker. The rake schemes to get what he wants and enjoys deceiving naive people. In Restoration satiric comedy, the ultimate rake is Horner in William Wycherley's *The Country Wife*. Horner pretends to be sexually impotent in order to have easier access to the wives of jealous husbands. In the early novel *Clarissa* by Samuel Richardson, the heroine is abducted by the clever rake Lovelace. The rake is typically both attractive and evil; he has wit and charm, but he uses these qualities to trap others.

Romance   A romance is a kind of long fictional narrative that is more imaginative than realistic. The term derives from the fact that early narratives of this sort were composed in French, a language derived from the Latin language spoken by the inhabitants of the ancient Roman Empire. Medieval romances were mostly written in verse, although some late romances used prose. They were fantastic stories about the adventures of princes, knights, and their ladies. Lighter and more fanciful than the epic, the romance shows characters who are motivated by love and lofty notions of honor and who move in a landscape of castles and towers, caves and dungeons. Their adventures are shaped by chance; a loosely organized series of episodes brings the hero to his goal, the completion of his task or the fulfillment of his vow. The ultimate medieval romance in English is *Sir Gawain and the Green Knight*.

The term *romance* was also used in the eighteenth century to distinguish between two types of long prose narrative. In contrast to the novel, which proposed to describe real people in authentic or realistic settings and plots, the prose romance was less bound by the constraints of realism and could include ghosts, magical events, and remote, exotic settings. Emphasis in such a romance was on ingenuity of plot and on suspense rather than on character development or examination of manners. The Gothic novel was one kind of romance.

Other forms of literature that use the same imaginative approach and show similar characters motivated by love are often called romantic; for example, romantic comedy or romantic epic. Romantic poetry, however, derives from a different set of ideas and practices that developed from new poetic theories in the early nineteenth century.

Satire   A satire is a literary work that criticizes or attacks the values or behavior of its characters. Satires can be written in a wide range of genres. Satires work by showing in clear or exaggerated detail the foolish or wicked ways in which society or one social group conducts its affairs. In so doing, satire often causes laughter. It is witty or humorous because it shows the disparity between the characters' pretensions and their real attitudes or actions.

In direct satire, the speaker is the satirist, describing with scorn and sarcasm the debased world in which he or she lives. Formal verse satire, a genre developed in Rome by Juvenal and Horace, places the satirist in a position aloof from the society described, commenting on it with the hope of awakening the people to their wrong-headed ways. The Juvenalian satires were rough and bitter, containing obscene and disgusting detail. The satires of Horace were milder and more humane. He mocks the excesses of society, but he can also mock himself because he realizes that human nature is inclined to be weak and easily corrupted. The terms *Juvenalian* and *Horatian* are used to classify more modern satires according to the violence or mildness of their style.

In England, satires of various kinds have been written since the medieval period. Much of Chaucer's work is satiric. Satire is also found in the comedies of the Renaissance, especially in Ben Jonson's plays. But the satire flourished especially during the late seventeenth and early eighteenth century, when satiric prose, poetry, plays, and novels as well as mock-heroic literature dominated the literary scene. The great English satirists were John Dryden, Jonathan Swift, Alexander Pope, and Samuel Johnson.

Sensibility   During the first half of the eighteenth century, even while the great satirists of England were at their height, a countermovement began to develop that stressed the human quality that came to be called sensibility. Instead of wit and restraint, literature of sensibility promoted the values of the human heart. Based on the idea that human nature is essentially good, this literature was aimed at promoting and refining right ways of behavior by arousing feelings of sympathy and benevolence. Humankind was seen as basically unselfish; if one acted selfishly, it was because of faulty education or the pressures of a corrupt society. The writers of the school of sensibility—poets, prose writers, and dramatists—preferred the country to the city, the simple life to glamour of high life. Morality was seen as related to good taste. If the individual's tastes were properly cultivated by exposure to nature and to those works of art that promoted wholesome emotional responses, then that individual would spontaneously act for the good of others and feel great emotional pleasure in good actions. The chief spokesman of the school of sensibility in England was Anthony Ashley Cooper, the third earl of Shaftesbury (1671–1713), whose philosophical essays were published in 1711 under the title *Characteristics of Men, Manners, Opinions, Times*. These essays strongly influenced the development of middle-class literature for the rest of the century.

Sentimental Comedy

In the early decades of the eighteenth century, the theater audiences became less elite and more middle class. In response to the changing tastes of the audience, dramatists began to write comedies that exploited emotion rather than wit as their central appeal. Characters were caught in situations that required them to be generous, self-sacrificing, and sensitive to the feelings of others. Heroes were marked by their exquisite feelings rather than by their courage or cleverness. The play's villains were redeemed by having final-act changes of heart, by being reformed through feeling. They even cried. The most famous sentimental comedy in England was Richard Steele's *The Conscious Lovers*. Written in 1722, this play is in the mainstream of development of the school of sensibility.

Simile

A simile is a kind of metaphor that compares two things that are basically unlike but that have one or more traits in common. In this figure of speech, the word *like* or *as* makes the comparison explicit. When the poet Robert Burns says, "My love is like a red, red rose," he suggests the freshness, beauty, and delicacy of his beloved. A lady and a flower can have these traits in common, even though they are really very different from each other. *See* **Metaphor.**

Soliloquy

A convention of the English Renaissance drama, the soliloquy is a speech made by a character who is on stage alone. The character is not talking to someone else; he or she is expressing private thoughts. This convention allows the playwright to let the audience know what is in the mind of the character, such as conflicts and fears or schemes that could not plausibly be told by the character in dialogue. Sometimes the character is not really alone but merely believes that he or she is. The audience accustomed to the soliloquy convention will understand that no other character is supposed to hear the soliloquy. In Shakespeare's *Hamlet*, for example, the famous "to be or not to be" soliloquy is spoken by Hamlet when Ophelia is also on stage. She remains in the background until he notices her; then the soliloquy ends. Whatever the character says in soliloquy is the truth. That is, the character speaks sincerely, without deception or evasion. This convention allows for complex and subtle character development by contrasting what the character says in soliloquy with what he or she says to other characters.

An isolated soliloquy, that is, one that is not part of a play but written as a separate poem, is called a dramatic monologue. However, a dramatic monologue may be addressed to some other person.

Sonnet   A fixed form of lyric poem, the sonnet has fourteen lines of iambic pentameter. Several kinds of sonnet are distinguished by different rhyme patterns. The Italian sonnet has two parts: an octave (eight lines) rhyming a b b a a b b a, and a sestet (six lines) rhyming c d e c d e or c d c d c d. The English sonnet is arranged differently. The Spenserian sonnet has three quatrains (four lines) rhyming a b a b b c b c c d c d and a final couplet rhyming e e. The Shakespearian sonnet also uses three quatrains, but the rhyme sounds are different in each one: a b a b c d c d e f e f. The couplet follows, g g. Both Spenser's and Shakespeare's sonnets are called English sonnets to distinguish them from Italian sonnets. The English sonnet tends to emphasize the climactic ending of the couplet while the Italian sonnet, with its two-part structure, emphasizes the contrast or contradiction from the octave to the sestet.

The sonnet was originally a vehicle for love poetry. Renaissance poets wrote long series or cycles of love sonnets tracing the development of their love relationships with a single idealized woman. In the seventeenth century, however, sonnet form began to be used for a wider range of subjects, including religious and political statements. *See* Development of the Sonnet.

Symbols   Although words are symbols in that they stand for the things, concepts, or relationships they name, in a work of literature a symbol is something that not only exists as itself but also suggests other ideas or refers to other situations. For example, in Book I of Spenser's *The Faerie Queene*, the red cross on the knight's shield is understood not only to be a decoration or pattern painted on the shield but also to represent the idea of holiness, of Christian virtue and faith. A symbol such as the cross is widely understood and carries a similar significance in many different contexts. Other symbols are more specific to a single literary work. In Pope's *The Rape of the Lock*, the lock of hair represents the heroine's chastity and reputation for innocence. Locks of hair may have other meanings in other contexts, or they may have only literal meaning and not be symbolic at all.

Topographical Poem

A topographical poem is one written to describe, and usually to praise, a particular place. The poet views a landscape and creates images of its visual features and also suggests the feeling of the place, its quality of dignity or restfulness. Thus while the topographical poem is lyrical, it also has a philosophical aspect. Ben Jonson's poem *To Penshurst* describes the estate of the Sidney family as an ideal of English country life. Other important topographical poems include *Cooper's Hill* by John Denham and *Windsor Forest* by Alexander Pope.

Tragedy

One of the major forms of drama, a tragedy is a serious play that shows the central character, the hero or heroine, striving against overwhelming forces to carry out a significant action. The efforts of the hero ultimately destroy him; however, the action he has undertaken will make the moral status of his state or community better in some way or rid it of an evil. The essence of a tragedy is not that it is sad; passive victims are sad. Tragedy has more inspiring elements; it shows the dignity of human nature in making moral decisions and bearing the consequences.

The form and purpose of tragedy were first explained by the Greek philosopher Aristotle in his *Poetics*. His discussion of tragedy has influenced all later discussions. He defined tragedy as the representation of an action, thus emphasizing the plot. He said that the plot must show a hero, a person of more than common status and abilities, who is brought down from his high status to one of misery. The hero has a flaw in his character, so that he contributes to his own defeat. The purpose of the tragedy is to arouse two emotions—pity and fear—and to cleanse the audience of these emotions, a process known as catharsis. Aristotle's definition of a tragedy was based on the study of plays written in ancient Greece. Later writers have generally followed his main ideas but have introduced many variations in the tragic formula. The great age of English tragedy, the Elizabethan period, produced tragedies of more complex plots with kings, princes, and military leaders as tragic heroes. In Jacobean tragedy of the early seventeenth century, tragedies were more concerned with domestic situations such as jealousy and rivalries in love that lead to tricks, disguises, and intrigue. In the Restoration, Dryden reflected the complicated plotting of earlier English tragedies; he tried to write a tragic play according to the rules derived from Aristotle. However, he did not succeed in reviving the English taste for tragedy. Heroic and sentimental dramas almost completely replaced tragedy.

Tragicomedy

A tragicomedy is a serious play that is tragic in tone but in which the hero is not destroyed by the action. The plot is arranged so that a tragic outcome is possible; the characters are threatened with disaster, but something happens to avert the worst. The play ends, if not joyfully, at least with the accomplishment of the hero's central purpose. Tragicomedies were developed in the early seventeenth century principally by a team of playwrights, Francis Beaumont and John Fletcher. They emphasized spectacle and artificial situations, making a type of play that was highly unrealistic and full of unlikely tricks and that exploited the heightened emotions of the characters for theatrical effects. Tragicomedy was attacked as an illegitimate form by critics later in the same century; they pointed out that it violated basic rules of drama.

Unities, Dramatic   Certain rules of dramatic structure were developed by Italian and French Renaissance critics. They used Aristotle's *Poetics* as their fundamental source but elaborated on and refined Aristotle's theories about how a play should be organized. These critics evolved a consensus of rules. The most important rules required that a playwright maintain unity of time, unity of place, and unity of action.

Unity of time means that the entire action of a play should take place within a single day. The audience should not be expected to believe that the actors can represent the same characters at periods of time separated by months or years. The play should open close to the moment of crisis; facts about earlier events should be told in the dialogue.

Unity of place follows logically from unity of time. If the action takes place in a single day, the characters cannot plausibly travel to distant places during that day. A single city was the limit. Ideally, the entire action will occur in the same location, for example, in front of the Royal Palace.

Unity of action means that a single main plot is developed, with no subplots or digressions into nonessential situations. There should be no moments of comedy to violate the dominant tragic tone of the play. Concentration and intensity of effect were the purposes of observing the unities. These rules were not strictly observed by English playwrights; by contrast, they were carefully followed by the major French dramatists of the seventeenth century, Corneille and Racine.

Utopia   A utopia is a good place. In literature, it is a fictional narrative or description of an ideal society supposed to exist in some remote location. The term was used by Thomas More as the title of his philosophical story (1516) about a communal society established for the fulfillment of ideals of human justice, sharing of goods in common, and cultivation of harmony. Since then, the term *utopia* has been applied to any such fictional society that sets up an ideal set of social arrangements; it applies as well to the fiction in which the ideal is described. A negative utopia, one describing a bad or corrupt place, is called a dystopia.

Weird   Weird is the Anglo-Saxon concept of fate or destiny. In Anglo-Saxon poetry, the poet or the character may attribute the outcome of events to this unexplainable force that rules the lives of individuals. The hero may try to determine his own destiny, but ultimately Weird governs all; eventually his fate catches up with him. The connotation is usually negative, that is, Weird is a disastrous outcome.

Wergild   In Anglo-Saxon society, if a man was killed, his family or kinsmen were obligated to take revenge against the killer. However, in some circumstances, the killer or his family could avoid the revenge by paying a price, called the wergild (man-price) to the victim's family. The price was adjusted according to the rank of the victim. The money was not so much payment for the dead man's life as it was a tribute to the surviving relatives to show that they had not neglected their duty and merely allowed the death to go unnoticed.

Wit   The term *wit* can refer either to the intellectual quality of the author or to the witty quality found in the literary work. Derived from the Anglo-Saxon word for knowledge, wit is always associated with mental quickness and acute perception. The wit of the metaphysical poets, for example, was shown in their clever and ingenious conceits and extended metaphors. The association of wit with laughter came later. Wit is sharper, quicker, and more biting than humor and lacks its good-natured, clowning quality.

28

Literary Names and Terms: People and Places

OLD ENGLISH 410–1100

Alfred "the Great" (849–899)

King of Wessex (871–899), he fought against the Danes. After his victory in 878 he forced Guthrum, the Danish king, to leave Wessex and to accept a division of the country between them. He made his kingdom secure, partly by a network of forts and a fleet of vessels. Alfred attracted scholars to his court. To ensure the spread of the vernacular as a literary language he set the scholars to translating Latin texts into English, and he himself translated several works.

Birthnoth, Earl of

Also known as the earl of Essex, he was the commander of the English defense militia in the Battle of Maldon (991).

Charlemagne, Holy Roman Emperor (742–814)

King of the Franks from 768 and emperor from 800, he launched a vast expansion of his rule, conquering Germany, Bavaria, and Saxony, bringing Christianity to the people. At the request of the pope he took his army over the Alps into Italy, where he conquered Lombardy and established his son as king. His first expedition into Spain ended in failure and in the death of his commander, Roland (the hero of the romantic legend, *Chanson de Roland*). By 800 Charlemagne was the supreme power in western Europe. Although Charlemagne read little and never learned to write, he encouraged the foundation of monastic and episcopal schools. From his court at Aix he stimulated the revival of arts and letters known as the Carolingian Renaissance.

Cynewulf

A ninth century Anglo-Saxon poet, his name is mentioned a few times in the Exeter Book. He may be the author of *The Wanderer* and *The Wife's Complaint*. It is possible that he was a minstrel at the court of one of the Northumbrian kings. Although there is little certain knowledge about him, he left about 2,600 lines of verse.

Danegeld

The term refers to tribute paid to Vikings in return for peace. Danegeld was first levied nationally by Aethelred II (991–1012). The Normans turned Danegeld into a regular tax, not paid on royal property and subject to increasing exemptions under Henry I.

Danelagh

In 878 Alfred and his army defeated the invading Danes; half the Danes left England and the rest agreed to the Peace of Wedmore, which required them to confine themselves to northeastern England in what came to be called the Danelagh or Danelaw. This region adopted Danish customs and laws that made a lasting impression on English culture.

Exeter Book

A manuscript that contains the largest surviving collection of Anglo-Saxon poetry. It was transcribed about the tenth century and given to the Exeter Cathedral.

Geats

The Geats were people of southern Sweden. Some scholars identified them with the Jutes; to modern scholars they were the Getae, who are believed to have lived in late classical and early medieval times in southern Scandinavia.

Mead hall

In *Beowulf*, King Hrothgar builds a communal hall where he and his warriors can feast and drink together. Their drink is mead, a fermented drink based on honey. The mead hall was an important location of public ceremony, and its violation by the monster Grendel was an important strike at the heart of the clan of Hrothgar.

Northumbria/ Northumbrian Renaissance

An ancient kingdom of the Anglo-Saxons, Northumbria was located in the areas between the Humber and the Firth of Forth. It was formed when the two kingdoms of Bernicia and Diera united early in the seventh century. Inspired by the return of Christianity and of the clergy, during the late seventh and early eighth century a flourishing society developed there that came to represent the high point of Anglo-Saxon culture. The Northumbrian monastic culture produced scholars such as Bede, poets such as Caedmon and Cynewulf, and great illuminated manuscript books such as the *Lindisfarne Gospels* (c. 698).

Ruthwell Cross	This is an eighteen-foot high free-standing cross at Ruthwell in Dumfriesshire, Scotland, on which passages from the poem *Dream of the Rood* were carved in the runic letters of the Anglo-Saxons.

Scop	A scop was a member of the king's court who functioned as both historian and entertainer. Using the heroic legends of his people's past, the scop composed and sang poetic and inspiring narratives that glorified courageous deeds and taught the values of bravery, loyalty, and generosity. His role was important because he was a transmitter of culture and, to the individual hero, a recorder of personal fame and glory. The scop who originally composed the epic poem of *Beowulf*, for example, assured that hero of immortality in poetry.

Weland	The weland was the supernatural "workman" or "blacksmith," a Norse legendary character similar to Vulcan of classical mythology.

LATE MEDIEVAL PERIOD 1066–1485

à Becket, Thomas (c. 1118–1170)	The archbishop of Canterbury, Becket had been a friend of King Henry II and his chancellor for eight years before the king appointed him archbishop in 1162. Within a year of his appointment, he and the king quarreled over royal interference in the Church. Thomas à Becket was murdered in the cathedral in 1170. His tomb at Canterbury became a popular pilgrimage site, and miracles were reported to have occured there. Chaucer chose a pilgrimage to Becket's tomb as the setting for *The Canterbury Tales*.

Caxton, William (c. 1422–1491)	A merchant at Bruges, he learned printing in Cologne in about 1474. He published the *Recuyell of the Historyes of Troye*, which he had translated from the French. This is the first known book to have been printed in the English language. Returning to England in 1476, Caxton established the first English print shop at Westminster. In all, he published nearly 100 volumes. The bulk of his publishing was of his own translations from French, Flemish, and Latin. He published the English poetry of Gower, Chaucer, and Chaucer's followers. Caxton published his edition of *The Canterbury Tales* in 1478, and he was the first to print Sir Thomas Malory's *Morte Darthur* in 1485.

Gaunt, John of (1340–1399)	This was the fourth son of Edward III, and the father of Henry IV; he increasingly controlled the government as his father grew senile, and he retained power during the reign of his brother, Richard II. On his death, John's son Henry seized the throne. John of Gaunt was Chaucer's great patron, and Chaucer held positions both at Gaunt's home and through his patronage.

Gower, John (c. 1330–1408)

An older London contemporary of Chaucer, Gower wrote such poems as *Vox Clamantis* and *Confessio Amantis*. Most important, in *Confessio Amantis*, written in old English, Gower wrote stories in the Chaucerian manner. The two men were friends, and Chaucer sent Gower his translation of Petrarch's sonnet *Troilus and Criseyde* for "correction."

Magna Carta

The Magna Carta was in 1215 little more than a treaty between the king and his barons, but in the long term it provided England with a near approximation of a written constitution. The Charter of Liberties carried constitutional implications limiting the arbitrary exercise of royal power by precisely defining royal rights and by prescribing the proper exercise of government. The Charter made law courts generally open to free men and prevented the king from manipulating the law to his advantage.

Peasants' Revolt (1381)

Led by Wat Tyler and a priest named John Ball, the revolt spread from Kent to London. The immediate cause of the rebellion was the heavy and unequal burden of poll taxes and the cruel conduct of the tax collectors. Also, the crowds were somewhat swayed by the equalitarian moral teachings of poor clergymen and perhaps also by the teachings and radical interpretation of the Gospels by John Wycliff, a radical theologian of Oxford. Records of the period indicate that quotations from Langland's *The Vision of Piers Plowman* were used in the revolution. With the help of urban rebels, the crowds ransacked London, murdering the archbishop of Sudbury and the treasurer. Young Richard II and the mayor of London negotiated with the rebels, granting their demands. Walford killed Wat Tyler while defending Richard. Richard calmed the rebels, who then dispersed peacefully.

RENAISSANCE 1485–1603

Burbage, Richard (1567–1619)

Son of one of the founders of the Chamberlain's Men, which was the acting company to which Shakespeare belonged, Richard Burbage undertook the building of the Globe Theatre for that company. He was also one of the company's major actors, playing important roles in many of Shakespeare's plays. Although cast lists have not survived, scholars believe that Shakespeare wrote such roles as Richard III, Hamlet, Lear, and Othello for Richard Burbage.

Castiglione, Baldassare (1478–1529)

Castiglione was an Italian diplomat, courtier, and writer whose major work was *Il Cortegiano*, published in 1528.

Erasmus, Desiderius (c. 1466–1536)

Erasmus was a Dutch scholar and humanist philosopher who, in 1509, went to England to teach, first at Oxford and then at Cambridge. He encouraged the study of the classics, including Greek, Hebrew, and the Latin of Cicero. His works include *In Praise of Folly* (1509).

Gosson, Stephen (1554–1624)

In 1579 Gosson wrote *The School of Abuse*, which was an attack on the arts from the Puritan viewpoint. Sir Philip Sidney reacted to Gosson's work by writing the only major Elizabethan essay of literary criticism, *Defense of Poesie*, published posthumously in 1595.

Herbert, Mary, Countess of Pembroke (1561–1621)

Born Mary Sidney, this Renaissance woman was a writer and the patron of many other writers. She was the younger sister of the poet Philip Sidney and grew up at the Sidney home, Penshurst. As the wife of Henry Herbert, the earl of Pembroke, Mary associated with and encouraged many of the major poets of her time. She also worked on a verse translation of the biblical Book of Psalms and translated other works from Italian and French authors.

Hoby, Sir Thomas (1530–1566)

A diplomat, Sir Hoby translated *Il Cortegiano* into English. The book was the first translation of a secular work, and it became the text of instruction for the conduct, qualities, and functions of a courtier. The book was referred to as a courtesy book. His translation was completed about 1554 but was not published until 1561.

Southampton, Henry Wriothesley, third earl of (1573–1625)

A courtier and literary patron, the earl of Southampton was a favorite of Queen Elizabeth I until he became associated with a conspiracy against her that was headed by the earl of Essex. Shakespeare dedicated his two early narrative poems *Venus and Adonis* and *The Rape of Lucrece* to the earl of Southampton. Some critics believe that all Shakespeare's sonnets are addressed to Southampton.

EARLY SEVENTEENTH CENTURY 1603–1660

Condell, Henry (d. 1627)

An actor in the company of the Chamberlain's Men, Condell is known to have acted in Shakespeare's plays and to have played the role of the cardinal in Webster's *The Duchess of Malfi*. Along with John Heminges, Condell undertook the publication of Shakespeare's plays in the First Folio of 1623.

Heminges,
John (d. 1630)

An actor in the company of the Chamberlain's Men, Heminges acted in many of Shakespeare's plays, specializing in a fatherly role. Along with Henry Condell, Heminges undertook the publication of Shakespeare's plays in the First Folio of 1623.

Penshurst

The country estate of the aristocratic Sidney family, Penshurst is located in Kent, the rich country southeast of London. It is described as the ideal of English life in Ben Jonson's poem *To Penshurst*.

RESTORATION 1660–1700

Gwynn,
Eleanor
(1642–1687)

This actress, better known as Nell Gwyn or Guinn, was a comic star of the Restoration stage. She acted in the King's Company of players and eventually became mistress to King Charles II, who enabled her to retire from the stage.

Newgate

A central prison in London from the twelfth to the early twentieth century, Newgate was several times destroyed and rebuilt. It is the setting of many fictional and dramatic prison scenes, especially in Daniel Defoe's *Moll Flanders* and in John Gay's *The Beggar's Opera*.

Shaftesbury,
Anthony
Ashley
Cooper, first
earl of
(1621–1683)

A brilliant and energetic politician, the first earl of Shaftesbury had been a member of Oliver Cromwell's council of state during the Commonwealth government, but he later supported the restoration of King Charles II. About 1673, Shaftesbury became alienated from the king, whose pro-Catholic sympathies Shaftesbury opposed. Shaftesbury organized like-minded members of Parliament to form the Whig party and spearheaded an attempt to exclude the king's Catholic brother James from succeeding to the throne. This action was satirized by John Dryden in the poem *Absolom and Achitophel*, in which Shaftesbury is depicted as the villain. Shaftesbury was also a friend and patron of the philosopher John Locke, whose political theories were heavily influenced by Shaftesbury.

Tonson, Jacob
(c. 1656–1736)

A London literary publisher, Tonson made a fortunate early decision to purchase from John Milton the publication rights to *Paradise Lost*, which remained a source of great profit for many years. Tonson also published a series of miscellany volumes edited by John Dryden. In 1700 Tonson founded the Kit-Cat Club, a literary club that included as members Richard Steele and Joseph Addison. Tonson also published works by Alexander Pope.

EIGHTEENTH CENTURY 1700–1785

Arbuthnot, John (1667–1735)

Born in Scotland, Dr. Arbuthnot lived in London where he was both a practicing physician and a political writer. He originated the satirical character named John Bull to represent conservative England. Arbuthnot served as the personal physician to Queen Anne. He is especially known as a friend and associate of Pope, Swift, and John Gay; he was a member of the Scriblerus Club. Arbuthnot was immortalized as a personality in Pope's famous poem *Epistle to Dr. Arbuthnot*, where he represents the ideal friend.

Bickerstaffe, Isaac

Possibly borrowed from a street sign, this name was Jonathan Swift's pseudonym in a series of satirical pamphlets usually called *The Bickerstaffe Papers* (1708–1709). In these pamphlets Swift mocked a popular astrologer by predicting the man's death and later insisting, despite the astrologer's protests, that the death had taken place. In 1709 Richard Steele began using the same pseudonym for his persona as author of the periodical series of essays *The Tatler*. Later in the same century, there actually was an English playwright named Isaac Bickerstaffe (c. 1735–1812).

Bolingbroke, Henry St. John, Viscount (1678–1751)

An English politician and statesman, Bolingbroke served as secretary of state during the Tory administration during the reign of Queen Anne. In 1714, at the death of the queen, Bolingbroke was dismissed and impeached. He fled to France. His fall from power is loosely paralleled by Gulliver's fate in Book I of Swift's *Gulliver's Travels*. Pardoned in 1723, Bolingbroke returned to England to participate in the Tory opposition to the Whig administration of Sir Robert Walpole. After 1735 Bolingbroke retired from political life to write political/philosophical works that were greatly admired.

Garrick, David (1717–1779)

An actor, playwright, and theater manager, David Garrick was also one of Samuel Johnson's early pupils and later a member of Johnson's Club. Beginning as a Shakespearean actor, Garrick was popular because of his acting style, which was more straight-forward and natural and less formal and stilted than was customary at that time. He was manager of the Drury Lane Theatre in London from 1747 to 1776.

Grub Street

A London street in the neighborhood of the printing and bookselling establishments, this street housed many poor hack writers. The street name became associated with the kind of low-level writing produced there. Alexander Pope attacked the Grub Street writers in *The Dunciad* and other works.

Hogarth, William (1697–1764)

A painter of portraits and of satirical depictions of London life, the artist Hogarth became widely known through the publication of prints based on his paintings. He created series of paintings based on a unifying moral theme, showing the corruption of contemporary society. The most famous of these are "The Harlot's Progress," "The Rake's Progress," and "Marriage à la Mode." Hogarth was a friend and associate of the novelist Henry Fielding.

Montagu, Lady Mary Wortley (1689–1762)

A witty and unusually learned woman of London society, Lady Mary is known mainly as a letter writer. Her personal correspondence was so cultivated and polished that it was almost a literary creation. Lady Mary eloped with Edward Wortley Montagu in order to avoid the marriage her father had arranged for her. She traveled with her husband to Constantinople, where he served as the English ambassador to Turkey. On her return she introduced the Turkish method of inoculation against smallpox, starting with her own two children. Lady Mary was a cousin of Henry Fielding, whom she helped in his early career. She was also friendly with Joseph Addison and Richard Steele, the periodical writers, and with Alexander Pope until she and Pope had a political disagreement. Pope attacked her in his *Epistle to a Lady*.

Oxford, Robert Harley, earl of (1661–1724)

A statesman and politician, Harley was a member of the Tory administration that ruled during the reign of Queen Anne. As Lord treasurer he negotiated the Peace of Utrecht in 1710. The next year, with the fall of the Tories from power and the death of Queen Anne, Harley was imprisoned because of accusations of treason during the peace negotiations.

Harley was a friend and associate of Bolingbroke and the writer Jonathan Swift. When Bolingbroke and Harley quarreled near the end of their government administration, Swift tried unsuccessfully to heal the breach.

Rich, John (1692–1761)

An actor and pantomimist, John Rich was the manager of the Theatre Royal in Lincoln's Inn Fields. He first produced John Gay's ballad opera *The Beggar's Opera*, which had an unprecedented success, a run of sixty-two performances in its first season in 1728. This success enabled Rich to build a new theater in Covent Garden, which opened in 1732. It was said that *The Beggar's Opera* made Rich gay and made Gay rich.

Scriblerus Club

Scriblerus was a short-lived club formed by literary men who were opposed to some "modern" tendencies in public taste. Founded in 1713, the club disbanded the next year when the Tory government fell from power and the club members became somewhat dispersed. Members included Dr. John Arbuthnot, John Gay, Jonathan Swift, Alexander Pope, and Thomas Parnell. They created the persona of a dull modern scholar, Martinus

Scriblerus, to whom they attributed various dull and absurd works of literary scholarship and criticism. The club was important as the origin of satiric ideas that later were developed in Swift's *Gulliver's Travels*, in Gay's *The Beggar's Opera*, and in Pope's *Dunciad*.

Shaftesbury, Anthony Ashley Cooper, third earl of (1671–1713)

The grandson of the famous first earl, the third earl was educated by the philosopher John Locke. Shaftesbury wrote essays in aesthetics and moral philosophy, which were collected and published in 1711 under the title *Characteristics of Men, Manners, Opinions, Times*. Shaftesbury's philosophy assumes the essential goodness of human nature. Each person has a "moral sense," a natural instinct for goodness. These ideas underlie the literature of sensibility, which developed in the eighteenth century.

Twickenham

This is a suburb of London on the Thames River. Here the poet Alexander Pope established his home in 1718, remaining there for the rest of his life. At Twickenham he created a carefully planned informal garden and solved the problem of the road that passed between his house and his garden by creating an underground passage, his "grotto" where he could sit and write in privacy. Many of the leading public figures of the day visited Pope at Twickenham. The modern scholarly edition of Pope's *Works*, published by Yale University Press, is called "the Twickenham edition."

Walpole, Horace (1719–1797)

Son of the famous Whig politician Robert Walpole, Horace was an antiquarian and a great writer of letters. He was interested in influencing literary taste away from classical restraint and toward the Gothic or rustic medieval. His home, Strawberry Hill, was converted into a pseudo-medieval castle. Walpole was a schoolmate and friend of the poet Thomas Gray. He wrote the Gothic novel *The Castle of Otranto*.

Walpole, Sir Robert (1676–1745)

Prime minister of England and head of the Whig party from 1721 until 1742, Walpole developed the position of prime minister into the center of political power during an era of rather weak monarchs, the Hanoverian Kings George I and George II. Walpole's pride and corruption were satirized by many authors, including John Gay in *The Beggar's Opera*, Johnathan Swift in *Gulliver's Travels*, and Henry Fielding in *The Life of Jonathan Wild*.

Wild, Jonathan (1683–1725)

A notorious criminal figure of early eighteenth-century London, Wild organized the theft and resale of stolen property into a profitable business. He not only received stolen goods but sought out the original owners, in some cases, and returned the goods for a "reward." He also betrayed some of his thief-suppliers by turning them in to law officers in order to get a reward. In 1725 he was finally convicted as a receiver of stolen goods and was hanged. His career was described by John Gay in *The Beggar's Opera* and in biographies by Daniel Defoe and Henry Fielding. Fielding treats Wild satirically as a "great man."

Index

A

Absalom and Achitophel (Dryden), 155, 156–157, 268
Addison, Joseph, 194–196, 239, 242, 254, 268
   Spectator, 195–196, 239, 254
   Tatler, 195–196, 239, 254, 269
Advancement of Learning (Bacon), 144
Aglaura (Suckling), 110, 111
Alchemist (Jonson), 135
Alexander's Feast (Dryden), 157
Alfred the Great, 3, 263
Allegory, 225–226
Allegro, L' (Milton), 126
All for Love (Dryden), 158
Alliteration, 226
Allusion, 226–227
Altar (Herbert), 120
Amoretti (Spenser), 61, 65
Amphilanthus (Wrothe), 61–62
Anatomy, 143, 227
Anatomy of Melancholy (Burton), 145, 227, 233
Angles, 2–3
Anglo-Saxon Chronicle (Alfred), 3
Anglo-Saxon society, 5, 227
   image of heroism in, 13–14
   values in, 6–8
Anne, Queen, 178, 270
Arbuthnot, John, 269, 270
Areopagitica (Milton), 126, 127
Aristotle, 260
Art of Love (Capellanus), 235
Ascham, Roger, 92
   Schoolmaster, 92
   Taxophilus, 92
Aside, 227
Astell, Mary, 166–167
   Some Reflections upon Marriage, 167
Astrophel and Stella (Sidney), 61, 62
As You Like It (Shakespeare), 78
Aurenge-Zebe (Dryden), 158
Austen, Jane, 241
Autobiography, 228

B

Bacon, Francis, 143–144, 146, 236, 237
   Advancement of Learning, 144
   essays of, 144
Ballads, 44–45, 228
Batter My Heart, Three-personed God (Donne), 119
Battle of Maldon, 13–14
Battle of the Books (Swift), 186
Beast fable, 228
Becket, Thomas, 133, 265
Bede, 3, 264
Beggar's Opera (Gay), 180, 188–189, 211, 230, 268, 270, 272
Behn, Aphra, 164
   Love Letters between a Nobleman and His Sister, 164
   Oroonoko or *History of Royal Slave*, 164
   Rover, 164
Beowulf, 3, 4, 10, 227, 237–238, 240, 247, 265
   composition of, 10–11
   dragon episode in, 12–13
   form of, 11–13
   Grendel episode in, 11–12
Bermudas (Marvell), 108
Bible, 142–143
Bickerstaffe, Isaac, 269 *See also* Swift, Jonathan.
Bickerstaffe Papers, 269
Biography, 229

Birthnoth, Earl of, 263
Blank verse, 229
Bolingbroke, Henry St. John, 269
Book of Ayres (Campion), 67
Boswell, James, 199, 201, 229
   Life of Samuel Johnson, 202, 229
Browne, Thomas, 146
   Pseudoxia Epidemica or *Vulgar Errors*, 146
   Religio Medici, 146
Bunyan, John, 162–163
   Grace Abounding to Chief of Sinners, 163
   Pilgrim's Progress, 162–163
Burbage, Richard, 266
Burke, Sir Edmund, 200
Burlesque, 230
Burney, Fanny, 234
Burton, Robert, 144, 227, 233
   Anatomy of Melancholy, 145
Butler, Samuel, 162, 235
   Hudibras, 162

C

Caedmon, 7, 264
Caesura, 230
Campion, Thomas, 67
Canonization (Donne), 116
Canterbury Tales (Chaucer), 30, 228, 239, 241, 265
   form of, 29–30
Canto, 230
Careless Husband (Cibber), 211
Carew, Thomas, 110, 231
   Elegy upon the Death of Doctor Donne, Dean of Paul's, 110
   Rapture, 110
Carpe diem theme, 104, 106, 109, 156, 230

Castiglione, Baldassare, 91, 234, 266
Castle of Otranto (Walpole), 220, 271
Cavalier poets, 99, 231
   Carew, Thomas, 110
   Herrick, Robert, 106–107
   Jonson, Ben, 102–105
   Lovelace, Richard, 111
   Marvell, Andrew, 108–109
   Suckling, John, 110–111
Caxton, William, 265
Chanson de Roland, 263
*Characteristics of Men, Manners,
     Opinions, Times* (Cooper),
     257, 271
Charlemagne, 263
Charles I, 97, 106, 112, 120, 150
Charles II, 97, 106, 150, 151, 152, 156,
     165, 268
Chaucer, Geoffrey, 28–29, 228, 240,
     241, 244, 265
   Canterbury Tales, 29–40, 228, 240,
     241, 265
   minor poetry of, 39
Chivalry, 231
Christian epic, in seventeenth century,
     124–132
Christianity, 3
*Chronicles of England, Scotland
     and Ireland* (Holinshed), 78
Cibber, Colley, 211
Civil War, 97
Clarissa (Richardson), 218, 239, 256
Collar (Herbert), 120
Collier, Jeremy, 153
Collins, William, 206
   Ode to Evening, 206
Comedy, 231
Comedy of Humors, 231
Comedy of Manners, 231–232
Comedy of Errors (Shakespeare), 78
*Comparison between Laughing and
     Sentimental Comedy*
     (Goldsmith), 212
Complaint to His Purse (Chaucer), 39
Compleat Angler (Walton), 145
Conceit, 232
Condell, Henry, 78, 267, 268
Confessio Amantis (Gower), 266
Congreve, William, 173–175, 232
   Double Dealer, 173
   Old Bachelor, 173
   Way of the World, 173–174
Conquest of Granada (Dryden), 158,
     171–172
Conscious Lovers (Steele), 195, 211,
     258
Constable, Henry, 61
Convention, 232–233
Cooper, Anthony Ashley, 257–258

Cooper's Hill (Denham), 260
Copia, 143, 233
Coquette, 233
Corinna's Going A-Maying, 107
Corruption (Vaughan), 122
Cortegiano, Il (Castiglione), 91, 234,
     266, 267
Country Wife (Wycherley), 172–173,
     246, 256
Couplet, 233–234
Courtesy Book, 234
Courtier (Hoby), 91–92
Courtly love, 234
Cowley, Abraham, 121, 157, 201,
     252
   Ode: Of Wit, 122
Crashaw, Richard, 120–121
   Flaming Heart, 121
   On Our Crucified Lord, 121
   *On the Wounds of Our Crucified
     Lord*, 121
Cromwell, Oliver, 97, 150
Cynewulf, 264
Cynthia's Revels (Jonson), 104

D

Danegeld, 264
Danelagh, 264
Daniel, Samuel, 61
Dante, 59
Death Be Not Proud (Donne), 118
Defense of Poesy (Sidney), 62–63, 267
Defoe, Daniel, 216–217, 228, 272
   Essay Upon Projects, 216
   Moll Flanders, 217, 228, 268
   Robinson Crusoe, 216–217, 228
   Roxanne or *Fortunate Mistress*, 217
Dekker, Thomas, 56
Delia (Daniel), 61
Delight in Disorder (Herrick), 106
Denham, John, 260
Deor's Lament, 14
Descartes, Rene, 236, 237
Deserted Village (Goldsmith), 207
Devereux, Penelope, 62
Devotions upon Emergent Occasions
     (Donne), 119
Dialogue between the Soul and Body
     (Marvell), 108
Diary (Pepys), 166
Dictionary of English Language
     (Johnson), 199
Didactic, 235
Disabled Debauchee (Wilmot), 165
Discourse on Method (Descartes), 237
Doggerel, 235
Donne, John, 62, 99, 109, 110, 114–115,
     201, 241, 249

Donne, John (*cont'd*)
   *Batter My Heart, Three-personed
     God*, 119
   Canonization, 116
   Death Be Not Proud, 118
   Devotions upon Emergent Occasions,
     119
   Ecstasy, 117
   Elegy 19, 117
   Flea, 116–117
   Good-Morrow, 115
   Holy Sonnets, 115, 118, 249
   Hymn to God the Father, 118
   I Am a Little World Made Cunningly,
     118
   Meditation XVII, 119
   Song, 115
   Sun Rising, 116
   Valediction: Forbidding Mourning,
     117
Double Dealer (Congreve), 173
Drama
   in eighteenth century, 180. 209–214,
     221
   in Renaissance, 56, 68–74, 77–87
   in Restoration literature, 152–153,
     170–175
   in seventeenth century, 134–140
   speakers in, 224
   strategy in, 224
Drayton, Michael, 61
Dream of the Rood, 265
Dryden, John, 152, 155–159, 171, 229,
     252, 256, 257, 268
   Absalom and Achitophel, 155,
     156–157
   Alexander's Feast, 157
   Essay of Dramatic Poesy, 155–156
   Mac Flecknoe, 157
   plays of, 158
   Secular Masque, 155
   Song for Saint Cecilia's Day, 157
   Song from Marriage a la Mode, 156
   *To the Pious Memory of the Ac-
     complished Young Lady Mrs.
     Anne Killegrew*, 158
Duchess of Malfi (Webster), 138–140,
     267
Dunciad (Pope), 193–194, 249, 269,
     271
Dystopia (Swift), 235

E

Early Christian poetry, 7
Easter Wings (Herbert), 120
*Ecclesiastical History of the English
     People* (Bede), 3, 7
Eclogue, 235

Ecstasy (Donne), 117
Egerton, Sir Thomas, 114
Eighteenth-century English literature
  Addison, Joseph, 194–195
  ancients and moderns in, 179
  Boswell, James, 201–202
  chronology of, 176–178, 183–184,
      197–198, 203–204, 209–210,
      269–269
  Collins, William, 206
  Defoe, Daniel, 216–217
  drama in, 179, 180, 209–214, 221
  Fielding, Henry, 218–219
  Finch, Anne, 204–205
  Gay, John, 188–189
  Goldsmith, Oliver, 208, 212–213
  Gray, Thomas, 205–206
  Johnson, Samuel, 198–201
  literary forms in, 179–181
  lyric poetry, 203–208
  novels in, 180, 209–211, 214–221
  periodical essay in, 181
  poetry in, 180
  Pope, Alexander, 189–194
  Richardson, Samuel, 217–218
  satire in, 179
  of sensibility, 179
  Sheridan, Richard Brinsley, 214
  Smart, Christopher, 206–207
  Steele, Richard, 194–195
  Sterne, Laurence, 219–220
  Swift, Jonathan, 184–185
  Thomson, James, 205
  Walpole, Horace, 220
Elegy, 235–236
Elegy XIX, (Donne), 117
Elegy Written in a Country Churchyard
      (Gray), 206, 235, 256
Elegy upon the Death of Doctor Donne,
      Dean of Paul's (Carew), 110
Elizabethan, 236
Elizabeth I, 66, 96, 104, 135
Emblem, 236
Emblems (Quarles), 236
Empiricism, 144, 236
End-stopped line, 236
English
  middle, 21–23
  old, 4–5
Enjambement, 237
Enlightenment, 237
Envoy, 237
Epic, 237–238
Epic simile, 238
Epistle, 239
Epistle to a Lady (Pope), 270
Epistle to Dr. Arbuthnot (Pope), 194,
      238, 269
Epistolary novel, 239

Epithalamion (Spenser), 65–66, 252
Erasmus, Desiderius, 90, 244, 267
Essais, 239
Essay, 239
  in eighteenth century, 180–181
Essay Concerning Human Under-
      standing (Locke), 167–168, 236
Essay of Dramatic Poesy (Dryden),
      155–156, 171
Essay on Criticism (Pope), 190, 230,
      233–234
Essay on Man (Pope), 192–193
Essay on the Theatre (Goldsmith), 212
Essay upon Projects (Defoe), 216
Etherege, Sir George, 172
  Love in a Tub, 172
  Man of Mode, 172
  She Would if She Could, 172
Euphues: The Anatomy of Wit (Lyly),
      92–93
Evelina (Burney), 234
Everyman, 47, 226, 250
Every Man in His Humour (Jonson),
      231, 244
Exemplum, 240
Exeter Book, 264

F

Fabliau, 23, 240
Faerie Queene (Spenser), 63–65, 226,
      230, 234, 236, 238, 248, 259
Farce, 240
Fielding, Henry, 180, 211, 219, 238,
      244, 270, 271
  History of Tom Jones, a Foundling,
      219, 243
Figurative language
  Kenning, 5
  litotes, 5
Finch, Anne, 204
  Miscellany Poems on Several
      Occasions, Written by a
      Lady, 204
  Nocturnal Reverie, 205
Fit, 239
Flaming Heart (Crashaw), 121
Flea (Donne), 116–117
Flecknoe, Richard, 157
Foil, 240
Folio, 240
Foot, 241
Formal verse satire, 240–241
Formulaic poetry, 4–5

G

Garden (Marvell), 109

Garrick, David, 199, 200, 269
Gaunt, John of, 265
Gay, John, 179, 180, 188, 211, 230, 268,
      269, 270, 272
  Beggar's Opera, 180, 188–189, 211,
      229, 268, 270, 272
Geats, 264
Gentilesse (Chaucer), 39, 241
Gentleman Dancing Master
      (Wycherley), 172
George I, 178
Georgic, 241
Goldsmith, Oliver, 180, 200, 207, 211,
      212–213, 232
  Comparison between Laughing and
      Sentimental Comedy, 212
  Deserted Village, 207–208
  Essay on the Theatre, 212
  Good-Natured Man, 207
  She Stoops to Conquer, or *Mistakes*
      of a Night, 212–213
Good-Morrow (Donne), 115
Good-Natured Man (Goldsmith), 207
Gosson, Stephen, 62, 267
Gothic, 242
Gothic novel, 242
Gower, John, 265, 266
Grace Abounding to Chief of Sinners
      (Bunyan), 162–163
Gray, Thomas, 205, 220, 236, 256, 272
  Elegy Written in a Country
      Churchyard, 206, 236, 256
  Ode on a Distant Prospect of Eton
      College, 206, 220
Grub Street, 199, 269
Gulliver's Travels (Swift), 186–187,
      226, 235, 269, 271
Gwynn, Eleanor, 268
Gwynn, Nell, 153

H

Hack writer, 242
Hagiography, 242
Hamlet (Shakespeare), 78, 85–87, 240,
      256
Harley, Robert, 270
Heminges, John, 78, 267, 268
Henrietta Maria, 120
Henry IV (Shakespeare), 78–90, 244,
      253
Herbert, George, 119
  Altar, 120
  Collar, 120
  Easter Wings, 120
  Pulley, 120
  Temple, 120
  Virtue, 120
Herbert, Mary, 62, 66, 267

Hero, 243
Heroic couplet, 243
Herrick, Robert, 106, 231
Hesperides (Herrick), 106
Histoires Tragiques (Belleforest), 81
Historia Regum Britanniae (Geoffrey of
    Monmouth), 23–24
Historica Danica, 81
History, 243
History of George Barnwell (Lillo), 211
History of Tom Jones, a Foundling
    (Fielding), 219, 244
Hobbes, Thomas, 146–147
    Leviathan, 147
Hoby, Sir Thomas, 91, 234, 267
Hogarth, William, 270
Holinshed, Raphael, 78
Holy Sonnets (Donne), 115, 118, 119,
    248
Howard, Henry, 60–61, 229
Hudibras (Butler), 162, 235
Humanism, 244
Humors, 244–245
Husband's Message, 15
Hymn (Caedmon), 7
Hymn to God the Father (Donne), 118

I

I Am a Little World Made Cunningly
    (Donne), 118
Iambic pentameter, 245
Idea (Drayton), 61
Idler (Johnson), 199
Indian Queen (Dryden), 158
In Praise of Folly (Erasmus), 267
Inviting a Friend to Supper (Jonson),
    103
Italian sonnet, 60

J

James I, 96, 103, 104, 105, 114, 135,
    178
James II, 151, 156
Johnson, Samuel, 99, 198–199, 207,
    241, 257, 269
    club of, 200
    Dictionary of English Language, 199
    Idler, 199
    *Journey to the Western Islands of
        Scotland*, 199
    Lives of the Poets, 199, 201
    London, 200
    On the Death of Dr. Robert Levet,
        200
    poetry of, 200
    prose of, 200–201

Johnson, Samuel (*cont'd*)
    Rambler, 199
    Rasselas, 199, 200–201
    Short Song of Congratulation, 200
    Vanity of Human Wishes, 200, 241
Jonson, Ben, 99, 102–103, 106, 112,
    135, 225, 231, 245, 257, 260,
    268
    Alchemist, 135
    Inviting a Friend to Supper, 103
    Ode to Himself, 105
    On My First Son, 103
    Pleasure Reconciled to Virtue, 105
    songs from plays of, 104
    To Penshurst, 104, 136, 260, 268
    *To the Memory of My Beloved, the
        Author Mr. William
        Shakespeare, and What He
        Hath Left Us*, 104–105
    Volpone, 104, 135–138, 226, 231,
        245
Jonson, Henry, 229
Joseph Andrews (Fielding), 238
*Journey to the Western Islands of Scot-
    land* (Johnson), 199
Jutes, 2–3

K

Kemp, Margery, 43
Kenning, 5, 245
Killegrew, Anne, 155–158
King, Edward, 126–127, 236
King Lear (Shakespeare), 78
Kit-Cat Club, 268

L

Lais, 22
Langland, William, 25, 266
Lay, 245
*Letter Containing His Theory about
    Light and
    Colors* (Newton), 168
Leviathan (Hobbes), 147
Libertine, 245–246
*Life and Opinions of Tristram Shandy,
    Gent.* (Sterne), 219–220
Life of Dr. John Donne (Walton),
    145–146
Life of Jonathan Wild (Fielding), 271
Life of Samuel Johnson (Boswell), 202,
    229
Lillo, George, 211
Lindisfarne Gospels, 264
Litotes, 5, 247
Lives of the Poets (Johnson), 199, 201
Locke, John, 167–168, 236, 268

Locke, John (*cont'd*)
    *Essay Concerning Human Under-
        standing*, 167–168, 236
    Two Treatises of Government, 167
Lodge, Thomas, 61
London (Johnson), 200
London Merchant (Lillo), 211
Love in a Tub (Etherege), 172
Love in a Wood (Wycherley), 172
Lovelace, Richard, 111, 231
    To Althea from Prison, 111
    To Lucasta, Going to the Wars, 111
*Love Letters between a Nobleman and
    His Sister* (Behn), 164
Lycidas (Milton), 126–127, 201, 235,
    253
Lyly, John, 92
    Euphues: The Anatomy of Wit, 92–93
Lyric forms
    speaker in, 223
    strategy in, 224
Lyric poetry, 247
    in eighteenth century, 203–208
    in Old English, 7, 14–15
    in Renaissance, 55–56
    in seventeenth century, 99–100

M

Macbeth (Shakespeare), 78
Mac Flecknoe (Dryden), 157
Machinery, 247
Magna Carta, 266
Malapropism, 247–247
Malory, Sir Thomas, 48–49, 231, 265
Man of Mode (Etherege), 172
Marlowe, Christopher, 67, 71–72, 253
Marriage, a la Mode (Dryden), 158
Marvell, Andrew, 108
    Bermudas, 108
    Dialogue between the Soul and Body,
        108
    Garden, 109
    Mower against Gardens, 109
    To His Coy Mistress, 109
Mary, 151, 153
Masques, 71, 247
Materialism, 147
Mead hall, 264
Measure for Measure (Shakespeare), 78
Medieval English literature, 43,
    265–264
    Castiglione, Baldassare, 91, 234, 266
    Caxton, William, 265
    Chaucer, 27–39, 228, 239, 241, 244,
        265
    chronicles in, 20
    chronology in, 16–19, 27–28,
        41–42

Medieval English literature (*cont'd*)
  drama in, 45–47
  English story telling, 20–21
  Erasmus, Desiderius, 90, 243, 267
  Gosson, Stephen, 267
  Gower, John, 266
  Kemp, Margery, 43
  language and forms in, 21–23
  lyrics and ballads in, 43–45
  Malory, Sir Thomas, 48–49
  narrative forms in, 23–26
  Peasants' Revolt of 1381, 21
  prose in, 41–49
  religious liturgy, 19
  Tale of Sir Thopas, 37–38
Meditation XVII (Donne), 119
Merchant of Venice (Shakespeare), 78
Metaphor, 247
Metaphysical school, 99–100, 114, 247–247
  Cowley, Abraham, 121–122
  Crashaw, Richard, 120–121
  Donne, John, 114–119
  Herbert, George, 119–120
  Vaughan, Henry, 122–123
Meter, 247
Microcosm, 248–249
Middle English, 249
  lyrics and ballads, 43–45
  poetry, 22
Midsummer Night's Dream
    (Shakespeare), 78
Milton, John, 62, 98, 108, 125–132, 227, 233, 235, 238, 253, 268
  Allegro, L', 126
  Areopagitica, 126, 127
  Lycidas, 127, 201, 235, 253
  On the Late Massacre in Piedmont, 128
  On the Morning of Christ's Nativity, 126
  Paradise Lost, 128–131, 151, 227, 229, 233, 238, 268
  Paradise Regained, 131
  Il Penseroso, 126
  Samson Agonistes, 130, 131–132
  When I Consider How My Light Is Spent, 128
Miracle Play, 249
Miscellaneous Poems (Marvell), 108
*Miscellany Poems on Several
    Occasions, Written by a Lady*
    (Finch), 204
Mock-epic, 249
Modest Proposal (Swift), 188, 255
Moll Flanders (Defoe), 217, 228, 268
Montagu, Edward Wortley, 270
Montaigne, 239
Morality play, 47, 249–250

More, Ann, 114
More, Sir Thomas, 90, 244, 261
  Utopia, 90–91, 243
Morte Darthur (Malory), 23, 48, 231, 265
Mower against Gardens (Marvell), 109
Mysteries of Udolpho (Radcliffe), 220, 241
Mystery play, 45–47, 250

N

Narrative forms
  source of, 23–26
  speaker in, 223
  strategy in, 223
Narrator, 250
Nature, 250–251
Newgate, 268
New Inn (Jonson), 105
Newton, Sir Isaac, 168
  *Letter Containing His Theory about
      Light and Colors*, 168
Noble Numbers (Herrick), 106
Nocturnal Reverie (Finch), 205
Northanger Abby (Austen), 241
Northumbria
  Northumbrian Psalter, 19
  Northumbrian Renaissance, 264
Novels, 251–252
  in eighteenth-century literature, 180, 209–211, 214–221
Novum Organum (Bacon), 237
Numbers, 252
Nymph's Reply to the Shepherd
    (Raleigh), 253

O

Occasional poetry, 252
Ode, 252
Ode: Of Wit (Cowley), 122
*Ode on a Distant Prospect of Eton
    College* (Gray), 206, 220
Ode to Evening (Collins), 206
Ode to Himself (Jonson), 105
Of Marriage and Single Life (Bacon), 144
Old Bachelor (Congreve), 173
Old English literature, 4–5, 9–15, 252, 263–265
  Beowulf, 3, 4, 10, 227, 237–238, 239, 247, 264, 265
  Chaucer, 27–39
  chronicles, 20
  chronology in, 1–2, 9–10
  Cynewulf, 264
  English story telling in, 20–21

Old English literature (*cont'd*)
  Exeter Book, 264
  general prologue, 30–34
  language and forms, 21–23
  narrative forms in, 23–26
  Peasants' Revolt of 1381, 21
  poetic forms in, 4–5, 10–13
  religious liturgy in, 19
Omniscient narrator, 252
On My First Son (Jonson), 103
On Our Crucified Lord (Crashaw), 121
On the Death of Dr. Robert Levet
    (Johnson), 200
On the Late Massacre in Piedmont
    (Milton), 128
On the Morning of Christ's Nativity
    (Milton), 126
On the Wounds of Our Crucified Lord
    (Crashaw), 121
Oral-formulaic, 252–253
Ormulum (Ormin), 19
Oroonoko or *History of Royal Slave*
    (Behn), 164
Osborne, Dorothy, 147
  letters of, 147–148
Othello (Shakespeare), 78
Ottava rima, 253
Out upon It! (Suckling), 111

P

Pamela or *Virtue Rewarded*
    (Richardson), 218
Pamphilia (Wrothe), 61–62
Paradise Lost (Milton), 128–130, 151, 227, 229, 233, 238, 268
Paradise Regained (Milton), 131
Paradox, 253
Parnell, Thomas, 270
Parody, 253
Passionate Shepherd to His Love
    (Marlowe), 67, 253
Pastoral, 253–254
Pastoral poems, in Renaissance, 55–56
Patience, 23
Patronage, 254
Pearl, 23
Peasants' Revolt of, 1381, 21, 266
Penseroso, Il (Milton), 126
Penshurst, 268
Pentameter, 254
Pepys, Samuel, 165–166
  Diary, 166
Pericles (Shakespeare), 78
Periodical essay, 254
Persona, 255
Personification, 256
Petrarch, 59

Philips, Katherine, 163
    To My Antenor, March 16, 1661, 163
    *To My Excellent Lucasia, on Our
        Friendship*, 163
Pilgrim's Progress (Bunyan), 162–163
Plain Dealer (Wycherley), 172
Plautus, 69
Play of the Crucifixion, 47
Pleasure Reconciled to Virtue (Jonson),
    105
Poetic justice, 256
Poetics (Aristotle), 260
Poetry. *See also* Lyric poetry.
    in eighteenth-century literature, 180
    early Christian, 7–8
    formulaic, 4–5
    Middle English, 22
    occasional, 252
    Old English, 4–5, 10–13
    in Renaissance, 58–67
    in Restoration literature, 152,
        162–166
    in seventeenth century, 99–123
Pope, Alexander, 179, 189, 230, 233,
        238, 242, 243, 247, 249, 256,
        257, 260, 268, 269, 270, 271
    Dunciad, 193–194, 249, 269, 271
    Epistle to Dr. Arbuthnot, 194, 238,
        269
    Essay on Criticism, 190, 230, 234
    Essay on Man, 192–193
    Rape of the Lock, 190–191, 233, 243,
        247, 249, 256, 259
Pricke of Conscience, 20
Prose
    in Medieval literature, 41–49
    in Renaissance literature, 89–93
    in Restoration literature, 151–152,
        166–168
    in seventeenth century, 141–148
Prosody, 256
Prude, 256
Pseudodoxia Epidemica or *Vulgar
        Errors* (Browne), 146
Pulley (Herbert), 120
Purity, 23

Q

Quarles, Frances, 236
Quatrain, 256
Queen and Huntress (Jonson), 104

R

Radcliffe, Anne, 220, 242
    Mysteries of Udolpho, 220
Rake, 256

Raleigh, Sir Walter, 67, 253
Rambler (Johnson), 199
Rape of Lucrece (Shakespeare), 77, 267
Rape of the Lock (Pope), 190–191, 233,
        242, 247, 249, 256, 259
Rapture (Carew), 110
Rasselas (Johnson), 199
Recuyell of the Historyes of Troye
        (Caxton), 265
Rehearsal (Buckingham, duke of), 158
Religio Medici (Browne), 146
Religious liturgy, 19
Religious lyrics, 44
Remorse of Conscience, 19
Renaissance literature
    acting companies in, 71
    actors in, 69–70
    Ascham, Roger, 92
    classical influence on, 69
    chronology in, 50–52, 68, 75–76,
        88–89
    drama, 58, 68–74, 77–87
    education and the Renaissance man,
        53
    forms, 55–57
    Hoby, Sir Thomas, 91–92
    humanism in, 54
    Lyly, John, 92–93
    lyric poetry in, 66–67
    masque in, 71
    More, Sir Thomas, 90–91
    patronage in, 54
    playwrights in, 71–74
    poetry in, 58–67
    prose in, 89–93
    religion and nationalism in, 53
    Shakespeare in, 61, 77–87, 104–105,
        135, 239, 243, 256
    sonnet form in, 58–66
    theater in, 70
    theater audience in, 54–55
Restoration literature, 268
    Astell, Mary, 166
    Behn, Aphra, 164
    Bunyan, John, 162–163
    Butler, Samuel, 162
    chronology in, 149–151, 154–155,
        160–161, 170–171
    drama in, 152–153, 170–175
    Dryden, John, 155–159
    literary forms of, 151–153
    Locke, John, 167–168
    Newton, Sir Isaac, 168
    Pepys, Samuel, 165–166
    Philips, Katherine, 163
    poetry in, 58–67, 152, 162–166
    prose in, 151–152, 166–168
    Wilmot, John, 165
Retreat (Vaughan), 122

Reynolds, Sir Joshua, 200
Rich, John, 270
Rich, Robert, 62
Richard II, 266
Richardson, Samuel, 217–218, 239, 256
    Clarissa, 218, 239, 256
    Pamela or *Virtue Rewarded*, 218
Rivals (Sheridan), 214, 247
Robinson Crusoe (Defoe), 216–217, 228
Romance, 256
    Arthurian, 23–25
    narrative, 22
Romance of Sir Tristram, 20
Roman de la Rose, 29
Romeo and Juliet (Shakespeare), 78
Rover (Behn), 164
Roxanne or *The Fortunate Mistress*
        (Defoe), 217
Rule Britannia (Thomson), 205
Ruthwell Cross, 265
Rymer, Thomas, 256

S

Samson Agonistes, 130, 131–132
Satire, 257
Satyre against Mankind (Wilmot), 165
Saxons, 2–3
Sayings of Alfred, 20
School for Scandal (Sheridan), 214
Schoolmaster (Ascham), 92
School of Abuse (Gosson), 267
Scop, 265
Scriblerus Club, 179, 270–271
Scriblerus, Martinus, 270–271
Seasons (Thomson), 205
Second Shepherd's Play, 46, 250
Secular lyrics, 43–44
Secular Masque (Dryden), 155
Sensibility, 257
Sentimental comedy, 258
Seventeenth-century literature
    Bacon, Francis, 143–144
    Browne, Thomas, 146
    Burton, Robert, 144–145
    Cavalier poets in, 99, 101–111
    Christian epic in, 124–132
    chronology in, 94–96, 101–102, 113–
        114, 124–125, 134, 141–142
    Condell, Henry, 267
    Cowley, Abraham, 121–122
    Crashaw, Richard, 120–121
    Donne, John, 114–119
    drama in, 134–140
    Heminges, John, 268
    Herbert, George, 119–120
    Hobbes, Thomas, 146–147
    Jonson, Ben, 135–138
    literary forms in, 98–99

Seventeenth-century literature (*cont'd*)
lyric poetry in, 99–100
metaphysical poets, 99–100, 113–123
Milton, John, 125–132
Osborne, Dorothy, 147–148
Penshurst, 268
prose in, 141–148
translation of Bible in, 142–143
Vaughan, Henry, 122–123
Walton, Izaak, 145–146
Webster, John, 138–140
Shadwell, Thomas, 157
Shaftesbury, Anthony Ashley Cooper, first earl of, 268
Shaftesbury, Anthony Ashley Cooper, third earl of, 271
Shakespeare, William, 61, 77, 104–105, 135, 240, 244, 256
Hamlet, 78, 81–85, 240, 256
Henry IV, 78–80, 244, 253
myths about, 77–78
plays of, 78–87
sonnets of, 66
Tempest, 70, 77, 85–87, 240
Shepheardes Calender (Spenser), 63, 235, 253–254
Sheridan, Richard Brinsley, 214, 232, 247
Rivals, 214
School for Scandal, 214
She Stoops to Conquer, or *The Mistakes of a Night* (Goldsmith), 207, 211–213
She Would if She Could (Etherege), 172
Shoemaker's Holiday (Dekker), 56
Short Song of Congratulation (Johnson), 200
Short View of Immorality and Profaneness of the English Stage (Collier), 153
Sidney, Sir Philip, 61, 62, 66, 104, 267
Astrophel and Stella, 61, 62
Defense of Poesy, 62–63, 267
Silex Scintillans (Vaughan), 122
Simile, 258
Sir Gawain and the Green Knight, 23–25, 256
Sir Martin Mar-All (Dryden), 158
Slow, Slow, Fresh Fount (Jonson), 104
Smart, Christopher, 206–207
Song to David, 207
Soliloquy, 258–159
Some Reflections upon Marriage (Astell), 167
Song (Donne), 115
Song for Saint Cecilia's Day (Dryden), 157, 252
Song from Marriage a la Mode (Dryden), 156

Songs and Sonnets Written by the Right Honorable Lord Henry Howard Late Earl of Surrey and Others, 56
Song to David (Collins), 207
Sonnet, 259
in English Renaissance, 55–56, 59–66
Sonnet cycles, 61
Sons of Ben, 103, 106, 230
Southampton, Henry Wriothesley, 267
Spectator (Addison and Steele), 195–196, 239, 254
Spenser, Edmund, 61, 63, 230, 234, 235, 236, 247, 252, 253, 259
Amoretti, 65
Epithalamion, 65–66
Faerie Queene, 63–65, 226, 230, 234, 236, 238, 247, 259
Shepheardes Calender, 63
Steele, Richard, 194–196, 211, 239, 254, 258, 268, 269, 270
Spectator, 195–196, 239, 254
Tatler, 195–196, 239, 254, 269
Sterne, Laurence, 219
Life and Opinions of Tristram Shandy, Gent., 220
Still to Be Neat (Jonson), 106
Suckling, John, 111, 231
Out upon It!, 111
song from *Aglaura*, 111
Sun Rising (Donne), 116
Swift, Jonathan, 173, 179, 184–185, 235, 255, 257, 269, 270, 271
Battle of the Books, 186
Gulliver's Travels, 186–187, 226, 235, 269, 271
Modest Proposal, 188
Tale of a Tub, 185, 186
Verses on the Death of Dr. Swift, 185–186
Symbols, 259

T

Tale of a Tub (Swift), 185, 186
Tamburlaine (Marlowe), 72
Taming of the Shrew (Shakespeare), 78
Tatler (Addison and Steele), 195–196, 239, 254, 269
Tempest (Shakespeare), 70, 77, 87–87, 240
Temple (Herbert), 120
Temple, William, 147
Terence, 69
There Is a Garden in Her Face (Campion), 67
They Are All Gone into the World of Light (Vaughan), 123

Thomson, James
Rule, Britannia, 205
Seasons, 205
To Althea from Prison (Lovelace), 111
To Celia (Jonson), 104
To His Coy Mistress (Marvell), 108–109
To Lucasta, Going to the Wars (Lovelace), 111
To My Antenor, March 16, 1661 (Philips), 163
To My Excellent Lucasia, on Our Friendship (Philips), 163
Tonson, Jacob, 268
To Penshurst (Jonson), 104, 136, 260, 268
Topographical poem, 104, 260
To the Memory of My Beloved, the Author Mr. William Shakespeare, and What He Hath Left Us (Jonson), 104–105
To the Pious Memory of the Accomplished Young Lady Mrs. Anne Killegrew (Dryden), 158
Tottel, Richard, 56
Tottel's Miscellany, 56, 61
To Virgins to Make Much of Time (Herrick), 107, 230
Toxophilus (Ascham), 92
Tragedy, 260–259
Tragedy of Tom Thumb (Fielding), 211
Tragical History of the Life and Death of Doctor Faustus (Marlowe), 72–73
Tragicomedy, 260–261
Tribal scop, poetry of, 6–7
Troilus and Criseyde (Petrarch), 266
Truth (Chaucer), 39
Twelfth Night (Shakespeare), 78
Twickenham, 271
Two Treatises of Government (Locke), 167

U

Unities, dramatic, 261
Upon Julia's Clothes (Jonson), 106
Utopia, 261
Utopia (More), 90–91, 244

V

Valediction: Forbidding Mourning (Donne), 117
Vanity of Human Wishes (Johnson), 200, 241
Vaughan, Henry, 122
Corruption, 122
Retreat, 122

Vaughan, Henry (*cont'd*)
  Silex Scintillans, 122
  *They Are All Gone into the World of
    Light*, 123
  World, 123
Venus and Adonis (Shakespeare), 77,
  267
Verses on the Death of Dr. Swift (Swift),
  185–186
Vicar of Wakefield (Goldsmith), 207
Virtue (Herbert), 120
Vision of Piers Plowman (Langland),
  20, 25–26, 226, 266
Volpone (Jonson), 104, 135–138, 225,
  226, 231, 244
Vox Clamantis (Gower), 266

W

Walpole, Horace, 179, 220, 271
  Castle of Otranto, 220
Walpole, Robert, 178, 188, 269, 271

Walton, Izaak, 145
  Compleat Angler, 145
  Life of Dr. John Donne, 145–146
Wanderer, 14
Way of the World (Congreve), 173–174,
  232
Webster, John, 138, 267
  Duchess of Malfi, 138–140
  White Devil, 138
Weird, 261
Weland, 265
Wergild, 264
When I Consider How My Light Is Spent
  (Milton), 128
White Devil (Webster), 138
Wife of Usher's Well, 226
Wife's Lament, 15
Wild, Jonathon, 271–272
Wilde, Oscar, 232
Wild Gallant (Dryden), 158
William, 153
William of Orange, 151
William of Shoreham, 19

Wilmot, John, 165, 241
  Disabled Debauchee, 165
  Satyre against Mankind, 165
Windsor Forest (Pope), 260
Wit, 264
Wordsworth, William, 62
Works (Jonson), 103
Works (Pope), 271
World (Vaughan), 123
World Well Lost (Dryden), 158
Wortley, Mary, 270
Wrothe, Lady Mary, 61–62
Wulf and Eadwacer, 15
Wyatt, Sir Thomas, the Elder, 60
Wycherley, William, 172–173, 246, 256
  Country Wife, 172–173, 245
Wycliff, John, 266

Y

York Play of the Crucifixion, 47